From Marx and Mao to the Market

From Marx and Mao to the Market

The Economics and Politics of Agricultural Transition

Johan F. M. Swinnen
Scott Rozelle

OXFORD
UNIVERSITY PRESS

Great Clarendon Street, Oxford OX2 6DP

Oxford University Press is a department of the University of Oxford.
It furthers the University's objective of excellence in research, scholarship,
and education by publishing worldwide in

Oxford New York

Auckland Cape Town Dar es Salaam Hong Kong Karachi
Kuala Lumpur Madrid Melbourne Mexico City Nairobi
New Delhi Shanghai Taipei Toronto

With offices in

Argentina Austria Brazil Chile Czech Republic France Greece
Guatemala Hungary Italy Japan Poland Portugal Singapore
South Korea Switzerland Thailand Turkey Ukraine Vietnam

Oxford is a registered trade mark of Oxford University Press
in the UK and in certain other countries

Published in the United States
by Oxford University Press Inc., New York

© J. F. M. Swinnen and S. Rozelle, 2006

British Library Cataloguing in Publication Data

Data available

Library of Congress Cataloging in Publication Data

Data available

Typeset by Newgen Imaging Systems (P) Ltd., Chennai, India
Printed in Great Britain
on acid-free paper by
Biddles Ltd., King's Lynn, Norfolk

ISBN 0-19-928891-7   978-0-19-928891-5

10 9 8 7 6 5 4 3 2 1

Preface

This book is global in its coverage and its creation.

The study covers more than twenty-five countries, more than 300 million hectares of land—a vast share of the world's surface—and more than 1.5 billion people; including hundreds of millions of people who are living or once lived in dire poverty. The book analyses, on one hand, arguably, the most successful sets of policies in history that have lifted people out of poverty, raising productivity and, in places, output by staggering amounts. At the same time our research documents and measures dramatic failures in policy processes and reforms that caused hunger and led to new poverty where before there had not been any. In many cases, government measures simply had a devastating effect on economic growth and development for millions of other people.

The book has its roots in Ithaca, NY, where, as graduate students, we shared adjacent offices in Cornell University's Warren Hall. At the time, neither of us could have imagined this would happen.

While Scott's office was already stacked with thousands of survey forms from China and a continuous flow of Chinese students and scholars, the Berlin Wall was just coming down and Jo was still happily studying the political economy of trade and agricultural policy. The most intense interaction between the co-authors at the time were the jokes, stories, and laughter coming through the wall; unfortunately for Jo, it was all in incomprehensible Mandarin.

Only after returning to Europe, did Jo turn his attention to study the transition process which had started in Central Europe and which was spreading rapidly east—from Prague to Vladivostok. During his first years back in Europe he was still writing on more traditional agricultural and trade policies; but, soon, the study of transition in Central and Eastern Europe irresistibly drew him to the East, into the field of comparative economics and transition economies. Then he was captured by Brussels where the issue of eastern enlargement of the European Union was increasingly occupying the minds of policy makers in the European institutions.

During this time, Scott was building a parallel career with his research in China, splitting his time between teaching and working with students in Stanford and Davis, working with policy makers in Beijing, and travelling through rural China. A large part of his time was spent in the field, collecting data and observing first hand the reform miracle that was being played out in East Asia.

As we realized later, both of us, with our respective research groups, had spent a great deal of time and effort trying to understand the process of transition in Asia and Europe by collecting original data and trying to construct innovative indicators to measure the process of reform and its effects. When possible, we tapped into existing sources of information. Many times, however, the only option was to collect, enter, and analyse our own survey data.

It was not until ten years later, in 1999, that we met up again, at an annual meeting of the American Agricultural Economics Association (AAEA) in Salt Lake City. On a mountain bike in the Rocky Mountains, and later over a beer, we discovered that in fact our research interests and discoveries were in many ways mirror images of one another. Slowly, it dawned upon us that there were a tremendous number of synergies in our work. By just exchanging 'war stories', we realized that there was so much we could learn from comparing the transition processes in Europe and Asia.

The first step was to swap papers. This led to an intensive exchange of emails and phone calls. It was not long after that we were convinced that a comparative study of the reform processes across the transition world with such vastly different experiences as the so-called 'Chinese miracle' and 'Russian disaster' was both needed and could yield truly important insights. One of the most remarkable findings that became clear to us during those first years was that such comparative analysis and its lessons would be important not just for transition policies but also for reforms and development strategies that went beyond former Communist countries. This realization was followed by several small steps that put us in public forums and let us begin to flesh out our ideas. It led to a joint principal session at the following AAEA annual conference, and to a plenary session at the International Association of Agricultural Economists conference in Berlin in 2000. The process of integrating our findings and insights had begun.

At some point during this process the idea of this book emerged. We started jotting down our ideas on scraps of paper. The shreds of papers begat printed outlines and the outlines begat a proposal. At first we thought it would be a simple compilation of our past work. But soon we discovered that this would be unsatisfactory. The only effective way to do it was to truly compare the processes—phase by phase; policy by policy; from determinants to outcomes to political economy. We ended up going far back into pre-reform history and pushing forward through the second decade of reform and beyond. We went back to the drawing board more times than we would like to remember. At times our project seemed lost or stalled amidst that quagmire of other demands. But many of our colleagues kept reminding us that we were on to something important. This kept our spirits up through the numerous revisions.

The prospect of progress and fellowship—at venues spread all over the globe—perhaps more than anything kept the work alive. Various ideas and versions of the chapters were discussed and written in Davis, Leuven, Beijing, Takoma Park, at the European Commission in Brussels and the World Bank in Washington, DC. We met in hotel suites and coffee shops in places like Berlin, Tampa, Denver, Durban, and between working sessions we reflected on our progress on skis in the Sierra Nevada mountains and on bike trails through the meadows of Whistler, and at the birthday party of our friend Cis in Lubbeek. The final revisions were made—where more appropriate?—in an establishment in Brussels where Karl Marx worked on his Communist Manifesto.

Although our names appear as authors on this book, the insights in it are based on more than a decade of research and collaborations with many co-authors and students throughout the world. We owe thanks to many people. Both of us have taken pleasure in collaborating and discussing with many people in our studies on the issues covered in this work, in many cases people from the countries which we studied. Our gratitude goes to all of them. Unfortunately they are too numerous to name completely.

A couple of people, however, deserve mention in particular. Above all, we would like to thank Jikun Huang and Karen Macours for many discussions and collaborations on related projects. Much of this work contains their blood, sweat, and tears. Other colleagues we should thank include Gejza Blaas, Richard Boisvert, Stefan Bojnec, Loren Brandt, Karen Brooks, Allan Buckwell, Colin Carter, Pavel Ciaian, Csaba Csaki, Azeta Cungu, Sophia Davidova, Alan deBrauw, Harry de Gorter, Klaus Deininger, Tomas Doucha, Liesbeth Dries, Wally Falcon, Gershon Feder, Tibor Ferenczi, Klaus Frohberg, Dinu Gavrilescu, Eva Germenji, Matthew Gorton, Hamish Gow, Konrad Hagedorn, Jason Hartell, Ruifa Hu, Marvin Jackson, Songqing Jin, Joep Konings, Andrzej Kwiecinski, Zvi Lerman, Guo Li, Bill

Liefert, Bryan Lohmar, John McMillan, Olga Melyukhina, Gilles Mettetal, Wolfgang Münch, Nivelin Noev, Albert Park, Scott Pearson, Jan Pokrivcak, Ewa Rabinowicz, Marian Rizov, Gérard Roland, Mike Ryan, Alexander Sarris, Andrea Segre, Eugenia Serova, Daniel Sumner, Stefan Tangermann, J. Edward Taylor, Alexandra Trzeciak-Duval, Laura Tuck, Liesbet Vranken, Jerzy Wilkin, Linxiu Zhang, and members of the OECD ad hoc expert group on agricultural policies in non-member countries.

Members of the Centre for Chinese Agricultural Policy in Beijing, affiliates of the LICOS Centre for Transition Economics, and the Research Group on Food Policy, Transition, and Development in Leuven have given tremendous and invaluable help in assisting us with the data work in this book. Anneleen Vandeplas did excellent editing work for the final version of the manuscript.

Finally, we should thank Oxford University Press for being so patient and persistent. And, of course, our families for supporting our work on this book and our careers in so many different ways.

J. S.

S. R.

Contents

List of Tables

List of Figures

List of Figures

Abbreviations

ACC	agricultural collective contract
AIC	Agricultural Inputs Corporation
ALP	agricultural labour productivity
APK	agro-industrial complexes
CEE	Central and Eastern Europe
CEECs	Central and Eastern European countries
CIS	Commonwealth of Independent States
CP	Communist Party
EU	European Union
FSU	former Soviet Union
GAO	gross agricultural output
HRS	household responsibility system
TFP	total factor productivity
TVE	township and village enterprises
WTO	World Trade Organization

1

Introduction

The emergence of China as a global economic powerhouse, the integration of ten Central and Eastern European countries into the European Union (EU), and the uncertain path of Russia towards a market economy have occupied the minds and agendas of policy makers, business leaders, and scholars throughout the world since the last part of the twentieth century. Twenty years ago these developments were unimaginable. The extent and the speed of the changes have taken everybody by surprise. The developments occurred so fast and the impact of the changes has been so vast that the importance of understanding the forces that unleashed this process, the importance of understanding how these changes became possible, and the importance of understanding the lessons for other developing countries cannot be overestimated. This is the overall goal of this book.

It all started in the Chinese countryside in the late 1970s. Until then, a large share of the globe—from the centre of Europe to the south-east reaches of Asia—was under Communist rule. The lives of more than 1.5 billion people were directly controlled by Communist leaders. The lives of many more were being affected by what was happening in the Communist bloc.

Changes emerged in the late 1970s and things have not been the same since. In 1978 China embarked on its economic reform path by introducing the household responsibility system (HRS) in agriculture. A few years later, Vietnam followed. Both countries reduced price distortions and reallocated key land rights from collective farms to rural households. The impact was dramatic. Productivity and incomes in both countries soared (Lin 1992; McMillan, Whalley, and Zhu 1989; Pingali and Xuan 1992). The reforms lifted hundreds of millions of rural households out of dire poverty (World Bank 2000). Economists praise the Chinese reforms as the 'biggest anti-poverty program the world has ever seen' (McMillan 2002: 94) and have claimed that the reform policies have led to 'the greatest increase in economic well-being within a 15-year period in all of history' (Fischer 1994: 131).

1

As a consequence, expectations were high ten years later when leaders in many nations of Central and Eastern Europe (CEE) and the former Soviet Union (FSU) began to dismantle Socialism and liberalize their agricultural economies. Reformers implemented a bold series of policies, increasing incentives and modifying the institutions within which rural residents lived and worked. The reforms, however, disappointed many nations. Farm output fell and rural poverty increased (Brooks and Nash 2002).

The sharp differences among nations in the early impacts of agricultural reform and transition in the rest of the economy triggered an intense debate on the sources of growth (Dewatripont and Roland 1992, 1995; Murphy, Shleifer, and Vishny 1992; McMillan and Naughton 1992; Sachs and Woo 1994; Roland 2000). Some researchers, especially those studying East Asia, credit the gradual sequencing of reforms that initially focused mainly on reforming property rights and delayed any major changes to the marketing system (Perkins 1988). For example, Lin (1992), McMillan, Whalley, and Zhu (1989), and Pingali and Xuan (1992) attribute most of the success of the agricultural reforms in China and Vietnam to the rise in the incentives provided by decollectivization. The case of China demonstrated that transition in agriculture could succeed, at least in the early years, without the disruption caused by the dismantling of government-run marketing channels and in the absence of well-functioning markets (McMillan and Naughton 1992; deBrauw, Huang, and Rozelle 2000, 2004).

In reaction to the claims about East Asia, sceptics responded that rural development in China and Vietnam occurred primarily as a result of low initial levels of development (Sachs and Woo 1994). Post-reform growth was nothing more than the rise in economic activity that was experienced elsewhere in East Asia during the post-Second World War era. Others have been even more negative. Balcerowicz (1994: 34) writes that the use of the 'Chinese Way' as an argument in favour of gradual reforms in CEE and the Commonwealth of Independent States (CIS) is 'a patent misuse of the facts'. Hughes (1994: 135–6) states that 'China's path is in no way relevant to the structural problems faced in Eastern Europe and the FSU' and should be 'no guide to what can or should happen'.

As the reforms in CEE and the CIS have unfolded, differences in economic performance among transition nations outside East Asia complicate the puzzle. As we show in detail later in this book, although agricultural output fell uniformly across Europe in the wake of the reforms, based on other measures, within a short period of time the farming sectors in Hungary, the Czech Republic, Slovakia, and other nations responded positively. Output per unit of labour rose sharply. Total factor productivity (TFP) in agriculture grew as strongly in CEE within a few years after the fall of the Berlin Wall as it did at a similar point in the reform process of China and Vietnam (Jin et al. 2002; Benjamin and Brandt 2001; Macours and Swinnen 2000*a*).

Agriculture, however, did not fare as well in most CIS countries. Although many policies—especially price adjustments and subsidy removals—were common across CEE and the CIS nations, others, such as farm restructuring and the liberalization of marketing institutions, proceeded more gradually in most CIS nations. A careful examination of the subsequent outcomes suggests that the nature of reform matters. While the magnitude of the collapse *in terms of output* was no worse in the CIS nations than in CEE, when measured *in terms of productivity*, the go-slow strategy in the CIS nations faltered. Productivity in Russia, Ukraine, and Kazakhstan not only fell sharply during the immediate post-reform period, it continued falling or remained stagnant during most of the first decade of transition. Examined through the lens of productivity, the patterns of performance are more similar between East Asia and CEE than they are between CEE and the CIS nations.

1.1. Measuring success and identifying its determinants

Given these intriguing combinations of policies and performances that have unfolded during the first decade of transition in the agricultural sectors of the world's transition nations, we believe a renewed enquiry into the debate about the choice of the reforms and their impact on economic performance is due. The commonalities and differences of the nature of reform among East Asian, CEE, and the CIS nations and the subsequent productivity contours call for a careful comparative analysis. To do so, we turn to the literature, draw on our own work from over the years, and build an empirical picture of the policies and institutional shifts that triggered agricultural growth in some of the world's twenty-eight transition nations and led to stagnation in others. The lessons learned from the process of transition in the agrarian development of most of the formerly Socialist countries can inform policy makers and scholars about the choice of reform strategy, the constraints in making these choices, and the relationship between reform and economic growth.

Focusing on agriculture to analyse which policies contribute to success and failure of economic reform has several benefits. The sharpness of the policy changes in agriculture and the fundamental differences among countries provide as clean a test as we can get. The relative simplicity of agricultural relationships—a farm is an easier production entity to analyse than an industrial firm—also adds clarity to the analysis. Hence, far from being a limitation of the study, our analysis of the reforms of price policy, property rights, and market liberalization in agriculture will yield important general lessons for those interested in the more fundamental relationships between reform, institutional change, and growth.

A book centring on agriculture also is inherently interesting, especially to those studying economic development. For example, in most East and Central Asian nations agriculture dominated the economy during transition and the changes in the sector have had an important impact on overall economic performance (Perkins 1994; Chan, Kerkvliet, and Unger 1999; Green and Vokes 1998). When more than 50 per cent of a nation's labour force is employed in agriculture, and when the major share of consumer income is spent on food, successful agricultural reform can have a major impact on poverty reduction and the welfare of the population. In fact, in studying the link between policy and performance, we believe that there are lessons for those studying economic performance outside the transition world.

Although we will provide a lot of data, include a lot of analysis, and review many studies, our work in this book is still best classified as a mega-analysis. Despite some variation from study to study, we believe that one of the most remarkable conclusions of our work in this book is that there is a fairly clear and consistent set of findings.

To meet this goal, in the first part of our book we pursue several specific objectives in analysing the economics of agricultural transition. In Chapter 2, we systematically document the post-reform trends in the agricultural performance in all transition countries of Asia and Europe. A list of the twenty-eight transition countries that we examine (some in more depth than others) by their geographical categorizations is in Table 1.1. In Chapter 3, we present a conceptual model to help clarify some of the essential characteristics of agricultural transition. In Chapter 4, we discuss in detail several key reforms, such as price and subsidy changes, property rights reform, and market liberalization. In Chapter 5, we review the evidence linking these reforms to the observed rises and falls in output and productivity and present quantitative assessments of the reforms' effects. In Chapters 10 and 11 of the book, we review our general findings and draw a series of lessons.

While the transition literature is rich and we document, analyse, and discuss many issues, we believe studying agriculture reform and performance leads to several new sets of insights. First, unlike the view of sceptics who find little in common among reform experiences across the transition world, the literature and data from East Asia, Central Europe, and the CIS nations provide a consistent picture linking reforms in agriculture to the performance of the sector. In particular, the miraculous growth of output in East Asia and the crash in output in CEE and the CIS nations can almost fully be explained by the shifts in the relative terms of trade. Second, while the performances during the initial reform years differ dramatically in terms of output contours between East Asia and CEE, when measured in productivity, however, the paths are remarkably similar. Property rights

Table 1.1 List and classification of transition countries

Regions	Transition countries	Central and Eastern Europe (CEE)	Commonwealth of Independent States (CIS)	Former Soviet Union (FSU)
East Asia	China			
	Vietnam			
	Laos			
	Myanmar			
Central Asia	Mongolia			
	Kazakhstan		x	x
	Kyrgyzstan		x	x
	Tajikistan		x	x
	Turkmenistan		x	x
	Uzbekistan		x	x
Transcaucasus	Armenia		x	x
	Azerbaijan		x	x
	Georgia		x	x
European CIS	Belarus		x	x
	Moldova		x	x
	Russia[a]		x	x
	Ukraine		x	x
Baltics	Estonia	x		x
	Latvia	x		x
	Lithuania	x		x
Central Europe	Czech Republic	x		
	Hungary	x		
	Poland	x		
	Slovakia	x		
Balkans	Albania	x		
	Bulgaria	x		
	Romania	x		
	Slovenia	x		

[a] Geographically, only part of Russia, including Moscow, is in Europe.

reform—decollectivization in East Asia and land restitution and farm restructuring in some CEE nations—gave strong income and control rights to producers which in turn resulted in strong productivity growth. The emergence of institutions of exchange also played an important role in explaining East Asian and CEE productivity growth. Finally, our analysis demonstrates that the real outliers in the reform process are the CIS nations. The absence of markets and poor property rights exacerbated the deteriorating performance caused by falling output-to-input price ratios and mired many CIS countries in a decade of productivity stagnation.

Based on these insights, several general lessons emerge. When measuring success, it is important to carefully compare the performance of transition nations on the basis of productivity, not output. Definition of success changes fundamentally when comparisons are based on productivity. In addition, while we find that initial conditions and the sequencing of policies do make a difference in making reform policies successful, our analysis suggests that above all success requires two key elements: good rights and an institutional environment within which agents can exchange goods and services and access inputs. However, despite the need for rights and markets or market substitutes, we also find that there clearly is much room for experimentation and heterogeneity. In the final analysis, on the basis of our study of the first decade of agricultural transition we find that growth and rising efficiency occurred in almost all nations in which reformers created property rights and improved the marketing environment.

1.2. Choosing the reform path: a political economy analysis

While the findings in the first part of the book are important, the analysis purposely ignores several fundamental questions: if price reform, property rights reform and farm restructuring, and market liberalization raise output and increase productivity, why is it that some nations still had not implemented these policies even by the end of the first decade of transition? If the policies as a set are most effective, why is it that some nations implemented the policies gradually while others implemented them all at once? And even more fundamentally, why is it that the policies were implemented by the leaders of some Communist regimes while in others it took a major regime shift for policies to gain momentum? In other words, in the first part of the book, we implicitly assume that reform policies are exogenous, determined by leaders by some unknown process which was beyond the scope of the impact analysis. But, according to the political economy literature, the choices of policies are decisions that are made by leaders who are seeking to optimize some complex objective function. In making their decisions, leaders take action in an environment constrained by economic, institutional, and social factors including the behaviour of the agents whom they are trying to influence. Looked at in this way, reform choices are choices endogenously made by leaders, functions of series of material and behavioural constraints, not the least of which is the enthusiasm of those at the grassroots, which in the case of the agricultural reforms means the farmers and the local officials and farm managers.

In the second part of the book, we explore the political economy of agricultural reform policies in transition countries. There is a vast political economy literature, both normative and positive.[1] Our approach in this book is strongly empirical and positive. In other words, we try to explain why certain policies have been chosen. We try to understand the objectives, incentives, and constraints that have induced leaders in different transition countries to choose the policy paths that they took. Such an empirical approach distinguishes the analysis from many of the earlier political economy papers on transition which have a strong normative emphasis (for example Dewatripont and Roland 1992, 1995).

Second, we also base our analysis, as we do in the first part of the book, on broad regional comparisons. We also focus the analysis on the reforms to the agricultural sector. Our choice to study comparatively the agricultural reforms is one of the primary ways in which the research in this book is distinguished from other empirically based political economy studies of reform (for example Fidrmuc 2000; Hellman 1998), or those limited to a smaller region (for example Yang 1996; Wegren 1998).

Third, we take a longer time horizon than most political economy studies. A large fraction of the book, as is common in much of the rest of the literature, does centre its attention on the post-1989 transition world. Our analysis, however, goes further. We believe it is also important and instructive to study why the reforms did not occur earlier in either China or the former Soviet Union, even though there were certain conditions that made it appear the time was right for reform.

In putting together the political economy story of agricultural reform, our analysis is conducted at two levels. First, we examine how the differences in the political process of the agricultural reforms affected the outcomes. To do so, we examine who supported the process of reform and who resisted and show that it was in those nations where there was a congruence of interests between the grassroots and the top leadership that agricultural reform could occur. In some sense, however, in linking politics of the reform to the choice of reform strategy we are looking only at the proximate causes. In much of the analysis, we go further, seeking to uncover the fundamental determinants of not only the reform choices, but also the reasons why the support of those at the grassroots differed among nations.

Because the number of nations, the complexities of the policies, and the timing of reforms differ so substantially, we must necessarily limit the scope of our enquiry in this part of the book, too. As before we primarily restrict our attention to a subset of policies: property rights reform and farm restructuring and market liberalization.[2] In examining the determinants of these reform policies we also limit ourselves to three broad questions. Why was the Communist government in China able to guide the reform process while it took a regime change in Russia (and in most of CEE and the other CIS nations) to start the reforms? Why did the market liberalization and other reforms happen so fast in some nations and happen only gradually in others? Why did the nature of property rights reform in land and farm restructuring differ so dramatically from nation to nation?

Even restricting the analysis in the second part of the book to addressing these three questions, however, is an ambitious task and needs to be narrowed further. While there certainly are many reasons for the observed differences among the choices that different leaders make, we focus on four general categories of determinants: initial technology differences in farming practices and the environment within which farming occurs; differences in wealth and the structures of the economies; the ways the different governments are organized—especially focusing on the degree of decentralization; and the historical legacy of Socialism and the dependency of certain reform measures on decisions that had been made during the Communist era.

The second part of the book is organized as follows. Chapter 6 presents several factors that we believe have had an important impact on leaders and their choices of reform strategies. The chapter establishes a vocabulary, defining what we mean by initial technology, the level of wealth, the degree of decentralization, and other factors that may be affecting the political economy of reform. The rest of the second part consists of four sections that attempt to answer our four main questions. Chapter 7 analyses what caused the introduction of radical reforms of rights and farm organization under the Communist regime in China, and why the Communist leaders in the former Soviet Union did not introduce similar reforms. Chapter 8 focuses on why China gradually implemented its market liberalization policies while, after the political changes in the early 1990s, nations in CEE and the CIS nations more or less simultaneously introduced property rights reforms and farm restructuring and market liberalization. Chapter 9 provides an explanation of the differences among nations in their choice of land reform and farm restructuring strategies. In this discussion we will examine several questions. Why did some countries privatize land while others did not? What led some countries to practise restitution? Why is it that some nations distributed land in kind to the tiller, while others distributed land to groups of farmers as shares? Why have some nations moved to individual family farming while others have not? And, finally, what role have hard budget constraints played in making countries such as Russia, Ukraine, and many of the Central Asian countries so much slower in restructuring their farms than countries in Central Europe?

The final part of the book presents the conclusions of the analyses in both parts of the book, draws a series of lessons, and looks at more recent and future developments. Chapter 10 presents the conclusions of Parts I and II of the book and Chapter 11 discusses general lessons from our analysis. In the final Chapter 12 we analyse recent developments in the transition world—the second decade of transition—and how our analysis is relevant for understanding the changes that took place during this period.

Notes

1. Surveys of political economy studies applied to general economic issues are e.g. Mueller (2003) and Persson and Tabellini (2000); surveys specific to agriculture are e.g. de Gorter and Swinnen (2002), and specific to transition reforms e.g. Roland (2002).
2. Since virtually all nations opted for price reform, there are few differences among nations to study.

Part I

The Economics of Agricultural Transition

2

Patterns of Transition

2.1. Measuring performance

Before trying to reconstruct the record of the agricultural sectors in transition economies, we must agree on what constitutes success. As noted by early development economists, agriculture performs several important tasks for a developing nation—especially in the early stages of development (Johnston 1970). Agriculture is a source of plentiful and inexpensive food. It also provides labour for the industrial and service sectors of developing nations. In addition, agriculture supplies non-food commodities (for example fibre products, coffee and cacao, and tobacco) for the domestic consumers and traders. Finally, the sector also creates linkages with other domestic industries and generates consumer demand.

Within the context of such a conceptual framework it is easy to see why so many nations—especially those that are fairly poor—attach great importance to the production of agricultural output. Higher food production increases the supply in domestic food markets and can lead to lower prices. Increased output also provides higher incomes. For these and other reasons, many nations assess the success of their agricultural economy largely on the basis of output growth.

In some cases, however, output may not be an ideal measure. Specifically, using rising output as a metric of success could be deceiving for transition nations since prior to reform most economies were characterized by high levels of distortion.[1] In fact, it is possible that, if the prices at the beginning of transition were distorted enough, output would fall or rise sharply merely in response to policies that allow prices to shift back to those that better reflect the long-run scarcity value of the resources. Following this logic, if a country had heavily subsidized inputs and output prices prior to reform, successful price reform should reduce domestic production.

In contrast, in all countries (both those in which rising output is a sign of success and those in which it is not), rising productivity is necessary for a successful agricultural sector. In assessing ways that agriculture can play a positive role in an economy, rising productivity can help policy makers meet many of their economic goals. Rising productivity through policies that provide better incentives and reduce resource waste (as a result of both better incentives and more complete control rights) will (*a*) lead to rising food and non-food agricultural production; (*b*) contribute to higher income; and (*c*) make the sector more modern. Getting more output out of fewer inputs can leave scarce resources free to either expand output, or allow resources to shift to higher productive activities.

In fact, as will become clear in this chapter, productivity trends sometimes tell a somewhat different story from output trends of how transition affects agricultural performance. While productivity trends evolve similarly to output in certain countries, strongly diverging patterns emerge in others. Because of the above arguments, in this book we track both output and productivity. Productivity, however, will be our primary metric of success. We recognize that it is not complete and does not capture all dimensions of the short- and long-run effects of reforms on those inside the sector or on the sector's ultimate impact on the economy as a whole. However, rises in productivity of the sector do have many benefits and are an important indicator of the sector's health.

To get a comprehensive picture of productivity developments and to accommodate important data constraints, we analyse three sets of productivity indicators: labour productivity (output per unit of labour use), yields (output per unit of land), and total factor productivity (TFP). While the most comprehensive indicator of productivity is TFP, comparative and reliable estimates of TFP are scarce because of data and methodological problems. For some transition countries TFP measures and the data needed to calculate TFP measures are simply not available. For those countries in which TFP series are available, comparisons have to be done carefully because of differences in methodologies, time frames, sampling, and commodity coverage. Information for the partial productivity measures is more readily available, and so we start by examining indicators of partial productivity and complement the analysis with a review of estimates of TFPs from the literature.

2.2. Changes in agricultural output

Remarkable differences can be observed when examining the performance of agriculture in transition countries during the first decade of reform. From the start of the reforms, output increases rapidly in East Asian transition countries (see Table 2.1). In China output increases by 60 per cent; in Vietnam output also rises sharply, increasing by nearly 40 per cent (see Figure 2.1).

Outside East Asia agricultural output trends follow a different set of contours (see Figure 2.1). Production falls steeply in the first years of transition in almost all CEE and CIS countries. Importantly, however, the length of time between the beginning of reform and the bottom of the trend line

Table 2.1 Growth of gross agricultural output (GAO) index in transition countries (index equals 100 in first year of reform)

	Year after start reform lowest GAO	GAO in year of lowest GAO	GAO after 5 years of reform	GAO after 10 years of reform	Avg growth rate GAO yr 0–5 (%)	Avg growth rate GAO yr 5–10 (%)
East Asia						
China	0	100	132	166	5.7	4.7
Vietnam	0	100	128	152	5.0	3.5
Laos	2	90	109	127	1.7	3.2
Myanmar	2	100	127	155	4.9	4.0
Central Asia						
Mongolia	4	81	84	86	−3.4	0.4
Kazakhstan	8	41	53	52	−11.9	−0.4
Kyrgyzstan	5	79	79	110	−4.7	6.9
Tajikistan	9	48	61	53	−9.4	−2.9
Turkmenistan	6	69	106	99	1.2	−1.3
Uzbekistan	6	90	98	97	−0.4	−0.3
Transcaucasus						
Armenia	3	72	82	80	−3.9	−0.5
Azerbaijan	5	55	55	72	−11.3	5.5
Georgia	10	51	62	51	−9.1	−4.0
European CIS						
Belarus	9	57	61	58	−9.3	−1.3
Moldova	9	42	66	46	−8.0	−7.0
Russia	8	58	64	62	−8.7	−0.5
Ukraine	9	51	69	55	−7.3	−4.4
Baltics						
Estonia	8	41	55	42	−11.3	−5.2
Latvia	9	37	50	38	−12.9	−5.2
Lithuania	9	64	69	65	−7.3	−1.1
Central Europe						
Czech Republic	8	75	75	77	−5.6	0.5
Hungary	6	69	70	73	−6.9	0.8
Poland	5	77	77	85	−5.2	2.1
Slovakia	10	68	77	68	−5.0	−2.5
Balkans						
Albania	2	77	100	113	−0.1	2.6
Bulgaria	7	57	63	62	−8.7	−0.6
Romania	3	75	93	93	−1.4	−0.1
Slovenia	3	65	81	79	−4.1	−0.5

Source: Based on FAO statistics.

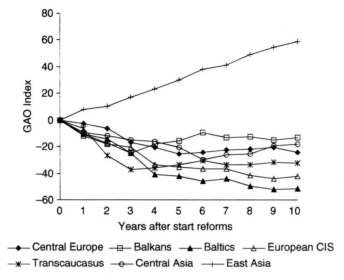

Figure 2.1 Changes in gross agricultural output (GAO) index during first 10 years of reform in transition countries.

Note: European CIS excludes Moldova; East Asia includes China and Vietnam only.

Source: see Table 2.1.

varies among nations (see Table 2.1, column 1). For example, the decline in agricultural output stops soonest in Balkan countries as Albania, Romania, and Slovenia (after two to three years). In most Central European countries, such as Poland, Hungary, and the Czech Republic, and in some Central Asian countries, such as Kyrgyzstan, Turkmenistan, and Uzbekistan, the decline lasts somewhat longer (five to six years). Finally, in a group of other countries, including the Baltic nations and several of the CIS nations, such as Russia, Belarus, Ukraine, Kazakhstan, output declines for most of the decade after reform, falling to around 50 per cent of pre-reform output.

2.3. Changes in labour productivity

For the entire reform period, trends in agricultural labour productivity (ALP), measured as output per farm worker, parallel those of output for some countries, but differ for others (see Figure 2.2). Like output, ALP of farm households in China and Vietnam rises steadily albeit much more strongly in China than Vietnam (see Table 2.2). In both countries labour productivity increases especially several years after the initiation of the

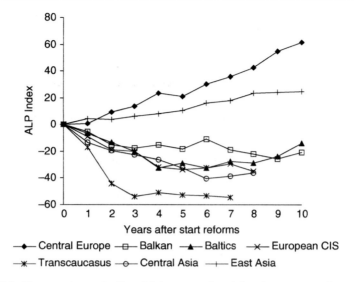

Figure 2.2 Changes in agricultural labour productivity (output per farm worker, ALP) index during first 10 years of reform in transition countries.

Note: European CIS excludes Moldova; Transcaucasus excludes Georgia; East Asia includes China and Vietnam only.

Source: see Table 2.2.

reforms. The path of ALP for Russia, Ukraine, and Central Asia also mirrors that of the nation's output, falling between 35 and 50 per cent between 1990 and 1999. Agricultural labour productivity trends for several CEE countries, however, differ from those of output, actually outperforming East Asia (see Figure 2.2 and Table 2.2). For example, despite falls in aggregate output, output per worker more than doubles over the first decade after transition in Hungary. ALP also rises strongly in the Czech Republic, Slovakia, and Estonia. In Poland, Latvia, and Lithuania, although ALP falls immediately after reform, the indicator recovers and rises after the first four years. In Albania, ALP increased rapidly between 1992 and 1995 but levelled off afterwards.

Despite the difficulties of working with official data on labour use in agriculture in transition economies, labour use patterns help explain part of the divergence of output and ALP patterns for some countries (see Figure 2.3).[2] The dramatic reduction in the use of agricultural labour drives the rise of ALP in the Central European countries. Official employment data from Central Europe show an average reduction of labour use of 35 per cent during the first five years of transition. The strongest reductions occur

17

in Hungary (57 per cent) and the Czech Republic (46 per cent). The same process occurs in Estonia, a country in which labour use declines by 58 per cent within the first five years of reform.

In contrast, agricultural labour use rises in East Asia and part of the CIS nations, affecting ALP in either a neutral or negative way (see Figure 2.3). For example, although ALP rises in East Asia, as it does in Central Europe, labour use does not fall. Labour use in agriculture (as a whole—that is cropping,

Table 2.2 Growth of agricultural labour productivity (output per farm worker, ALP) in transition countries (index equals 100 in first year of reform)

	Year after start reform lowest ALP	ALP in year of lowest ALP	ALP after 5 years of reform	ALP after 10 years of reform	Avg growth rate ALP yr 0–5 (%)	Avg growth rate GAO yr 5–10 (%)
East Asia						
China	0	100	120	146	3.7	4.0
Vietnam	0	100	102	107	0.4	1.0
Myanmar	2	96	115	132	2.9	2.7
Central Asia						
Mongolia	10	57	61	57	−9.3	−1.6
Kazakhstan	6	58	60	n.a.	−9.7	n.a.
Kyrgyzstan	5	58	58	67	−10.2	2.8
Tajikistan	9	36	46	39	−14.2	−3.3
Turkmenistan	6	55	88	71	−2.6	−4.2
Uzbekistan	6	80	88	98	−2.5	2.1
Transcaucasus						
Armenia	7	38	42	45	−15.8	1.0
Azerbaijan	9	48	57	53	−10.8	−1.5
Georgia	2	69	84	79	−3.5	−1.3
European CIS						
Belarus	4	69	72	86	−6.4	3.6
Moldova	9	39	58	41	−10.3	−6.9
Russia	10	62	63	62	−8.7	−0.5
Ukraine	9	52	65	55	−8.4	−3.1
Baltics						
Estonia	1	76	139	163	6.8	3.2
Latvia	6	46	54	65	−11.5	3.7
Lithuania	5	62	62	77	−9.2	4.6
Central Europe						
Czech Republic	0	100	126	177	4.7	7.0
Hungary	0	100	175	220	11.8	4.7
Poland	3	96	99	144	−0.2	7.8
Slovakia	0	100	110	132	1.9	3.8
Balkans						
Albania	2	77	108	104	1.5	−0.8
Bulgaria	7	58	69	63	−7.3	−1.7
Romania	9	59	67	63	−7.7	−1.2
Slovenia	3	61	85	83	−3.2	−0.4

Sources: Based on national statistics, ILO, World Bank, Asian Development Bank.

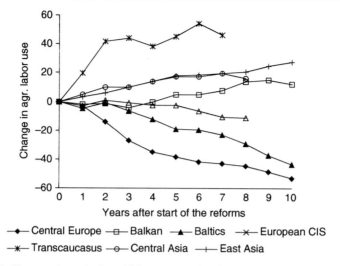

Figure 2.3 Changes in agricultural labour use index during first 10 years in transition countries.

Note: European CIS excludes Moldova; Transcaucasus excludes Georgia; East Asia includes China and Vietnam only.

Source: see Table 2.4, columns 7 and 8.

livestock, and other subsectors) actually increases in both China (10 per cent) and Vietnam (25 per cent). In both countries the increase in ALP evidently comes from the strong increase in output. Agricultural labour use also increases in some CIS countries, in particular in Central Asia.[3] For example, in Kyrgyzstan agricultural employment surged between 1990 and 2000, rising by 64 per cent (ILO 2001). There, as in other countries in the region, a rising number of people in agriculture coupled with stagnant output led to the fall in ALP.

2.4. Changes in yields

The performance of yields parallels that of ALP (see Table 2.3 and Figure 2.4). In China yields increase rapidly from the beginning of transition, rising by 9 per cent annually during the first five years after reform (see Table 2.3, row 1). Between five and ten years after reform, yields continue to rise, although the rate of rise slows. Pingali and Xuan (1992) also document the rise in yields during the early years of Vietnam's transition. In contrast, average yields fall during the first few years after reform for all CEE and CIS countries.[4]

But, as in the case of labour productivity, after the initial post-transition years, the paths of yields differ strongly between the two regions. Figure 2.4 summarizes yield evolutions for selected crops (grains, sugar beet, and cotton) and milk. In the European CIS states, including Russia and Ukraine, yields fall rapidly during the first five years to levels about 25 per cent lower than pre-reform yields. In the second part of the 1990s yields stay at this low level and in some cases continue to decline. In Central Asia, yields also

Table 2.3 Growth of index of agricultural yields in transition countries (index equals 100 in first year of reform)

	Grains[a]		Sugar beet/ Cotton		Milk		Avg. agric.[c]		Avg. agric. per year	
	5	10	5	10	5	10	5	10	0–5	5–10
East Asia										
China	133	142	207	211	96	113	145.3	155.3	9.1	2.0
Central Asia										
Kazakhstan[b]	41	59	79	55	n.a.	n.a.	60.1	57.4	−8.0	−0.6
Kyrgyzstan[b]	57	93	79	96	n.a.	n.a.	68.0	94.9	−6.4	5.4
Tajikistan[b]	66	85	52	51	n.a.	n.a.	59.4	68.3	−8.1	1.8
Turkmenistan[b]	82	108	79	62	n.a.	n.a.	80.7	85.0	−3.9	0.9
Uzbekistan[b]	100	148	95	80	n.a.	n.a.	97.8	114.0	−0.4	3.2
European CIS										
Belarus	74	64	66	92	77	70	72.3	75.3	−5.5	0.6
Moldova	82	90	n.a.	n.a.	51	54	n.a.	n.a.	n.a.	n.a.
Russia	63	61	80	79	74	84	72.3	74.7	−5.5	0.5
Ukraine	70	56	88	76	77	81	78.3	71.0	−4.3	−1.5
Baltics										
Estonia	69	80	103	109	86	112	86.0	100.3	−2.8	2.9
Latvia	71	98	88	97	89	116	82.7	103.7	−3.5	4.2
Lithuania	61	81	100	100	81	93	80.7	91.3	−3.9	2.1
Central Europe										
Czech Republic	87	89	102	131	100	126	96.3	115.3	−0.7	3.8
Hungary	72	83	72	101	95	110	79.7	98.0	−4.1	3.7
Poland	80	93	86	99	96	108	87.3	100.0	−2.5	2.5
Slovakia	89	89	99	117	89	116	92.3	107.3	−1.5	3.0
Balkans										
Albania	85	86	72	76	125	138	94.0	100.0	−1.2	1.2
Bulgaria	63	65	57	72	86	90	68.7	75.7	−6.3	1.4
Romania	85	93	80	81	137	134	100.7	102.7	0.1	0.4
Slovenia	n.a.	n.a.	97	95	99	112	n.a.	n.a.	n.a.	n.a.

[a] Grains include wheat, rice (milled weight) and coarse grains.

[b] Central Asia: cotton instead of sugar beet; average agriculture (cols. 7 and 8) is average of grains and cotton only.

[c] Average agricultural yields is simple average of the yields of grains, sugar beet/cotton, and milk.

Sources: USDA for grains; sugar beet yields are from FAO for Central Europe, Balkans, and China, and from Zentrale Markt- und Preisberichtstelle für Erzeugnisse der Land-, Forst-, und Ernährungswirtschaft (ZMP) and FAO for Central Asia, Transcaucasus, and European CIS; milk yields are from ZMP for Central Europe, Balkans, Central Asia, Transcaucasus, and European CIS, and from State Statistical Bureau (SSB) for China.

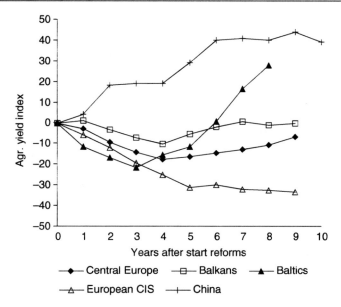

Figure 2.4 Changes in agricultural yield index during first 10 years of reform in transition countries.

Note: Agricultural yield index is calculated as the average yield index of grains, sugar beet/cotton and milk.

Source: See Table 2.3, columns 7 and 8.

fall by more than 25 per cent during the first years of transition. In the final years of the first decade of reform, the yields of some crops, such as grains, begin to recover; however, those of cotton, the most important commodity in several Central Asian countries, continue to fall.

In contrast, in Central Europe yields not only decline less than those in the CIS states, by 10 to 15 per cent on average during the first few years of transition, they also begin recovering faster (generally from the third year of transition onward). Between 1992 and 1999 agricultural yields increase, on average, by 2.5 per cent annually. A similar, but more pronounced, yield pattern can be observed in the Baltics. Average yields in the Baltics dropped initially to almost 25 per cent below their pre-reform levels. In the second half of the 1990s, however, they recovered, rising by an average of 3 per cent annually. As in Central Europe, yields decline less in the Balkan countries, only 10 to 15 per cent (in total), on average, although their yield recovery is slower, an average of 0.9 per cent annually during the second half of the 1990s.

In the same way that changes in labour use affect ALP, changes in the use of inputs (including labour and other inputs, such as land and fertilizer) affect

21

yields, although different inputs exhibit different rates of change (see Table 2.4). Tractor use, for example, declines sharply in most countries to around 70 per cent of the pre-reform rate (see Table 2.4, columns 3 and 4).

Table 2.4 Growth of input use indices for agriculture in transition countries (index equals 100 in first year of reform)

	Fertilizers		Tractors		Land		Labour		Animal stock[a]	
	5	10	5	10	5	10	5	8[b]	5	10
East Asia										
China	168	233	152	157	111	125	110	110	108	140
Vietnam	239	343	92	139	98	98	125	131	157	177
Laos	510	760	114	131	101	104	n.a.	n.a.	139	183
Myanmar	174	189	92	79	100	101	n.a.	n.a.	95	104
Central Asia										
Mongolia	14	19	67	64	94	94	137	152	112	124
Kazakhstan	16	5	78	29	96	96	89	58	77	38
Kyrgyzstan	n.a.	n.a.	99	104	99	102	135	146	61	61
Tajikistan	30	17	84	84	97	96	131	130	86	75
Turkmenistan	40	21	80	80	73	73	121	137	124	89
Uzbekistan	34	60	94	94	89	89	112	111	116	112
Transcaucasus										
Armenia	11	9	119	120	102	108	194	200	57	54
Azerbaijan	n.a.	n.a.	90	99	96	100	97	100	82	101
Georgia	22	29	71	43	86	86	76	n.a.	49	57
European CIS										
Belarus	25	40	92	62	98	97	86	73	79	64
Moldova	42	2	93	78	102	102	114	111	64	32
Russia	11	9	82	61	98	98	100	92	74	47
Ukraine	24	11	92	68	100	99	106	102	75	41
Baltics										
Estonia	17	20	106	109	107	106	40	35	50	32
Latvia	21	53	82	89	99	97	79	77	38	26
Lithuania	10	16	118	137	100	100	113	103	52	41
Central Europe										
Czech Rep.	29	24	58	82	103	103	54	44	69	53
Hungary	15	18	72	61	94	95	43	37	59	51
Poland	35	38	114	113	99	98	89	97	81	69
Slovakia	17	15	89	77	100	100	71	60	65	46
Balkans										
Albania	19	14	74	68	101	102	92	107	121	107
Bulgaria	25	14	69	51	98	98	92	99	47	42
Romania	27	17	106	110	100	100	118	110	63	50
Slovenia	56	52	56	118	91	83	95	87	86	82

[a] Since 1995 animal stock refers only to the change in cattle stock, the index for previous years measures an aggregate of 'animal units'.
[b] For Slovenia and Armenia, data are for seven years after the start of reforms.

Sources: Data on fertilizer, tractor, land use, and animal stock are from FAO; labour data from Asian Development Bank, ILO, national statistics, World Bank.

The input that best reflects the differences in how input use has responded is fertilizer (see Table 2.4, columns 1 and 2). In cases such as China, fertilizer application rates soar during the reform period, rising by more than 300 per cent (Stone 1988). While part of the reason that fertilizer rises so much in China and Vietnam is the release of supply-side constraints, reform policies also are important (Ye and Rozelle 1994; Pingali and Xuan 1992). In contrast, fertilizer use plummets in most CEE and CIS countries to around one-quarter of the pre-reform level of fertilizer use. On average, in the late 1990s fertilizer use outside East Asia is only 25 to 30 per cent of its level in the late 1980s.

2.5. Changes in total factor productivity

Although it is possible that partial and more complete measures of productivity could move in opposite directions, most of the evidence from the transition literature shows that, in fact, total factor productivity (TFP) trends move largely in the same direction as the partial measures (see Table 2.5). Several series of TFP estimates have been produced for China's agriculture (McMillan, Whalley, and Zhu 1989; Fan 1991, 1997; Lin 1992; Wen 1993; Huang and Rozelle 1996; Jin et al. 2002—see Table 2.5, rows 1 to 5, for Jin et al.'s estimates). The studies uniformly demonstrate that in the first years after reform (1978 to 1984), comprehensive measures of productivity (either constructed TFP indices or their regression-based equivalents) rose by 5 to 10 per cent per year. Although Wen (1993) worries that TFP quit growing in the post-reform period (1985 to 1989), Fan (1997) and Jin et al. (2002) demonstrate that during the 1990s, TFP continued to rise at a rate of around 2 per cent per year. During the early reform period in Vietnam between 1980 and 1985, Pingali and Xuan (1992) demonstrate that the productivity of agriculture (in this case rice, which makes up a large part of the nation's agricultural output) rises by 2 to 3 per cent annually. Although no one has analysed the rise in productivity between years 5 and 10 after the reforms, Benjamin and Brandt (2001) estimate that between 1992 and 1997, TFP for rice and total crop output generally continues to rise in Vietnam (though in the case of total crop output, TFP growth differs between the south—positive, and the north—negative).

Estimates of TFP changes in CEE and the CIS countries also show that measures of TFP generally move in a manner consistent with the partial ones (see Table 2.5). Macours and Swinnen (2000a) estimate that TFP indices in Central European agriculture decline during the first three years of

23

Table 2.5 Annual growth rates of total factor productivity for agriculture in various transition countries for selected years (%)

			1979–94	1979–84	1984–89	1989–94
East Asia	China	Rice	3.8	9.1	0.4	2.0
		Wheat	5.6	12.8	1.2	2.6
		Maize	6.1	13.5	−1.0	5.6
		Soybean	4.8	7.7	−1.6	8.1
		Crops (Av)	5.1	10.8	−0.2	4.6
			1976–80	1980–85	1993–98	
	Vietnam	Rice			3.0	
	North	Rice	−3.3	5.0	2.1	
	South	Rice	0.0	3.3	4.3	
	Vietnam	Crops			1.0	
	North	Crops			−0.7	
	South	Crops			3.0	
			1992–97			
Central Asia	Kazakhstan	GAO	−1.0			
	Kyrgyzstan	GAO	−0.4			
	Tajikistan	GAO	−2.4			
	Turkmenistan	GAO	−5.8			
	Uzbekistan	GAO	−2.2			
Transcaucasus	Armenia	GAO	4.6			
	Azerbaijan	GAO	−0.8			
	Georgia	GAO	6.6			
European CIS	Belarus	GAO	0.6			
	Moldova	GAO	0.4			
	Russia	GAO	1.4			
	Ukraine	GAO	0.4			
Baltics	Estonia	GAO	2.8			
	Latvia	GAO	−1.2			
	Lithuania	GAO	3.6			
			1989–95		1989–92	1992–95
Central Europe	Czech R.	Crops	2.7		1.1	4.3
	Hungary	Crops	1.1		−4.5	6.7
	Poland	Crops	−0.4		−5.1	4.3
	Slovakia	Crops	1.2		−0.6	3.1
Balkans	Albania	Crops	0.0		−9.3	9.2
	Bulgaria	Crops	−1.8		−7.5	3.8
	Romania	Crops	0.5		−7.8	8.7
	Slovenia	Crops	n.a.		−3.4	n.a.

Sources: China from Jin et al. (2002); Vietnam from Pingali and Xuan (1992) and Benjamin and Brandt (2001); FSU from Lerman et al. (2003); Central Europe and Balkans from Macours and Swinnen (2000*a*).

transition (between 1989 and 1991) by 2.3 per cent annually. The indices, however, rebound strongly after three years of reforms, rising by 4.5 per cent annually between 1992 and 1995. The Balkan countries demonstrate a similar, but more pronounced pattern, falling by around 7 per cent annually over the first three years before increasing by more than 7 per cent annually during the subsequent three years. TFP estimates by Lerman et al. (2003) show that productivity increases between 1992 and 1997 in two Baltic countries (Estonia and Lithuania) and, quite strongly, in two Transcaucasian countries, Armenia and Georgia. Similar to the movements of labour productivity and yields, TFP declines significantly in the Central Asian countries.

Perhaps because of the size and strategic importance of Russia and Ukraine, relatively more work on TFP has been done on these countries, although the results are less consistent than those for other parts of the reforming world. For example, Kurkalova and Jensen (2003) find that technical efficiency on Ukrainian collective and state farms declined during early transition (1989–92). Likewise, several studies find that the efficiency of Russian farms also declined significantly during transition, results that are consistent with the trends in ALP and yields (Sotnikov 1998; Sedik, Trueblood, and Arnade 1999; Trueblood and Osborne 2002). Trueblood and Osborne (2002: 10), for example, conclude that their results 'support the conventional wisdom that overall productivity [in Russian agriculture] has declined in the reform period' and that productivity declines by 2.1 per cent annually between 1993 and 1998 and they find 'no evidence of a productivity rebound'.

The case of Russia and Ukraine, however, is perhaps the only one in which the partial measures differ from the TFP measures from *some* of the studies. Lerman et al. (2003) estimate that TFP increases in Russia and Ukraine between 1992 and 1997, a time when its partial measures are falling. Likewise, Murova, Trueblood, and Coble (2004) find a slight increase in technical efficiency of Ukrainian crop farming over the 1991 to 1996 period.[5]

2.6. Patterns of transition

In summary, the records of transition countries differ across regions and over time within regions. Different criteria also paint different pictures of success. In the early reform years, East Asian transition countries clearly perform the best during the first years of reform in terms of both output and productivity.

However, after an initial few years, several CEE countries begin to experience rising productivity, measured either as labour productivity (ALP), yields, or TFP. Productivity measures rise throughout the later transition period (years 4 to 10) in both Central Europe and East Asia, even though the direction of output in the two sets of countries moves in opposite directions. Productivity in Central Europe rises even as output falls, primarily because inputs fall even faster. Hence, when critics of the transition in CEE nations point to the collapse of output as an indicator of poor economic performance, it is not clear that they always have a valid point. According to the TFP measures, the efficiency of producers of a number of CEE transition nations improves significantly a few years after transition. Such a pattern not only characterizes Central European countries but also several Baltic and some Balkan countries.

The record is less positive in the CIS. Output and labour productivity fell sharply in almost all CIS countries during most of the first decade of reform. Hence, according to both partial and most full measures, productivity during the first ten years of reform fell in most CIS nations. Despite this, there is evidence that TFP increased in some Transcaucasian countries, such as Armenia and Georgia. Moreover, some studies indicate that TFP may have increased in Russia and Ukraine, especially in the second half of the 1990s. The findings of these studies contradict those from the rest of the literature. Interestingly, and an early sign that productivity trends were beginning to turn even in the late 1990s in some of the slower-moving CIS, indicators in some nations show that although productivity fell with output during a significant part of the first decade, there is evidence of the beginning of improvements in productivity since the late 1990s (EBRD 2002).

Notes

1. Many transition economies also have a relatively small share of the population in the agricultural sector so rising output will not lead directly to higher incomes for much of the population.
2. Official data on labour use in transition agriculture are prone to measurement errors and statistical problems and should be interpreted with care. Different data sources often provide different numbers and do not always distinguish between full-time and part-time employment. Hence, in those countries in which more part-time work is being done, but which continue to report all producers involved in agricultural production as full-time labour units, labour productivity trends will be understated. Also, the aggregate data hide important other reallocations of labour. For example, while overall labour use in agriculture in China rose slightly during the first five years after reform (10 per cent), major efficiency gains in cropping occurred from the reallocation

of labour from crops to livestock production and other sideline activities (e.g. various self-employed enterprises—Lardy 1983; Fan 1991; Jin et al. 2002). Also, in other transition countries official labour data hide important changes in effective labour input. For example, in some of the CIS countries where former collective and state farms have survived, labour is often underemployed and members of rural households are officially still employed on these farms, even though they often spend a considerable part of their time working on their own household plots and are engaged in a myriad of other sideline activities (Lerman, Csaki, and Feder 2004). In such countries, the effects of these misreportings are ambiguous and depend on whether or not the output produced on their own plots are included in output figures. If private plot output is included, we, in fact, will be measuring rising productivity when it is actually rising. If the output of these plots is not included in reported output, labour productivity measures will be underreported like those in countries in which agricultural labourers are shifting from full- to part-time farmers. We use data from the Asian Development Bank for Azerbaijan, Kazakhstan, Kyrgyzstan, Moldova, Tajikistan, Turkmenistan, and Uzbekistan because for most of these countries there are no consistent data in the database of the International Labour Organization for the full period.

3. A number of factors increased the size in terms of labourers of the agricultural sector in countries such as Romania, Armenia, and several Central Asian nations. Policy, demographic and macroeconomic pressures, and other factors contributed to the rise of agricultural labour use in many countries: for example, in countries where the agricultural sector worked as a buffer after a collapse of the industrial economy (e.g. Romania, Kyrgyzstan), and in fact absorbed labour from other sectors. As in Vietnam, rapid population growth also contributed partly to the labour inflow in several Muslim countries, such as Uzbekistan and Turkmenistan. Finally, other events also contributed to rising agricultural labour. For example, in Armenia a regional conflict disrupted critical imports and industrial production, and many people migrated to rural areas.

4. In Table 2.3, the only exception is Romania where strong increases in dairy yields more than offset declines in crop yields.

5. As we will explain in Chapter 5, the inconsistent results for Russia are probably due to differences in sampling and reflect variations in the performance of different farm structures with the countries. An update of the Lerman and Brooks (2001) calculations indicates that TFP increases in Russia and Ukraine are due mostly to increases after 1995, as TFP declined before then.

3

A Model of Agricultural Transition

3.1. Introduction

Modelling agricultural transition is complex for several reasons. Socialist farm decision making and the system of allocating goods and services involved a complex set of incentives and institutions. Transition also included many reforms that were frequently implemented simultaneously with one another. Finally, there were many differences among countries. The danger in trying to address all of the nuances is that one could easily become bogged down with details and miss the first-order issues.

For these reasons, we consciously only present a set of simple conceptual models. Although simple, when taken in conjunction with the research of others, we believe that our modelling framework is tractable and sufficiently rich to help clarify some of the essential characteristics of agricultural transition policies and the economic trade-offs faced by reformers. Our analytical framework, however, is not made to stand alone. Several other authors have done excellent work over the past years in developing transition models and models of agricultural development. Above all, Roland (2000) and Blanchard (1997) build several sets of theoretical models useful for studying economies in transition, although none is directed explicitly towards agriculture. Bardhan and Udry (1999) have produced an advanced textbook with a number of models that can be used to describe relationships that are important for understanding agricultural development. The serious student of agriculture and transition also should consult both of these and the wide range of other material that are available. In addition, there are more sophisticated models of transition, such as one for labour adjustment (Dries and Swinnen 2002; Swinnen, Dries, and Macours 2005).

In this chapter, we develop a series of models that seek to explain the impact of agricultural transition policies on the behaviour and performance of farms and on the agricultural sector as a whole. To do so, we have decided to start off with the most basic models of farm input and output relationships and then gradually add several complexities. One important reason for starting with a simple model is that some essential characteristics and effects of transition in agriculture are strikingly consistent with the predictions of such a simple model. In other words, although it is possible to adopt a more complex modelling framework, some of the strongest points we want to make can be made by examining a basic set of economic trade-offs. In this chapter we also use simple empirical examples to illustrate some of the consistencies that exist between our predictions and the empirical literature. In some sense, the examples in this chapter are included to help the reader better understand our conceptual points. Although we believe our empirical examples also validate our modelling approach, the full empirical analysis of the effect of reform on behaviour and performance is presented in the next two chapters.

3.2. The basic model for illustrating Socialist inefficiencies

Consider a simplified Socialist farming system in which farms produce the output and the state determines the allocation of a subset of the inputs, all input and output prices, and the nature of the farm organization (including property rights). For each farm i, output, q^i, is produced with two types of inputs, x^i, and l^i:

$$q^i = f^i(x^i; l^i) \tag{3.1}$$

Under the Socialist regime, farms are subject to government control on the allocation of some of their inputs. Here we assume that x^i represents inputs which the farm can allocate itself given government-set prices (for example, farm chemicals or tractor time and the petroleum products to drive the machinery), while l^i represents production factors over which the farm has no authority (for example, land allocations or the other services that are needed for efficient operations of the farm). The state also determines the nature of the farm organization and in the basic model we assume production takes place in large-scale state or collective farms (on state-owned land).

Technical (in)efficiency

The first characteristic of the Socialist farm is its inherent technical inefficiency. Faced by virtually all farms in Socialist economies, the inefficiencies are well documented (for example, Brada and Wädekin 1988;

29

Gray 1990; Johnson and Brooks 1983; Putterman 1992; Lin 1991; Rozelle and Swinnen 2004). The technical inefficiency of a Socialist farm is reflected in a production possibility frontier which is below that which would exist in a private farm operating in a market environment.

This inefficiency is caused by two policies. First, the government is typically less efficient than the market in the way that it allocates l^i. If the government's allocation of l^i is not timely, provided in a lower quantity or lesser quality, or is offered in a way that poorly complements the farm's use of x^i, the output of the farm from the input of x^i will be lower. Second, by imposing a certain farm organization and property rights, the government sets the incentives faced by the manager of the farm. Assuming that the main contribution of the manager is 'effort', then the nature of the farm organization will determine the incentives for the manager to allocate appropriate effort. With production organized in collective farms and land in state ownership, managers had few incentives to allocate sufficient effort which, holding constant the level of the government-provided input l^i, led to lower output from the input of x^i.

More specifically, we can show this technical inefficiency as follows. Focusing on the second source of technical inefficiency (farm organization and property rights), and ignoring for a moment the impact of inefficient allocation of l^i—which can be analysed analogously—we define:

$$q^i_o = f^i_o(x^i) \tag{3.2}$$

as the production function facing the Socialist farm within the government-controlled system, and:

$$q^i = f^i(x^i) \tag{3.3}$$

as the production function facing the same farm operating as a private entity within a market system. Given these two definitions, the technical inefficiency of Socialist farming versus private farming in the market system is shown as:

$$f^i_o(x^i) < f^i(x^i) \text{ for all } x^i > 0, \text{ and} \tag{3.4}$$

$$\frac{d[f^i(x^i) - f^i_o(x^i)]}{dx^i} > 0 \tag{3.5}$$

The technical inefficiency, which is assumed to be due to poor incentives that do not elicit sufficient effort to use inputs in the most effective way, can be illustrated graphically. In Figure 3.1, the production functions are $q = f(x)$, for the farm household that was operating privately in a market economy, and $q_o = f_o(x)$, for the Socialist farm. The inefficiency can be seen by noting that for all levels of input x the output is higher for the private farm than for the Socialist farm.

The government can increase the technical efficiency of the farm by introducing changes in the farms' property rights and organization which provide better incentives for the manager. In the rest of the analysis we will refer to this action by the government as 'property rights reform'. For simplicity, we limit our graphical and mathematical expositions on technical efficiency effects in the rest of this chapter largely to property rights reforms.

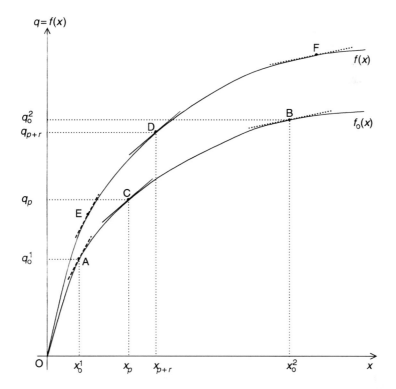

Figure 3.1 Reforms, initial conditions, and production allocations during transition.

Note: The iso-price line for market prices w^m and p^m is the solid line that passes the points C and D; the iso-price line for planner-set prices for a country that taxes agriculture is a heavy dotted line that passes through A and E; the iso-price line for planner-set prices for a country that subsidizes agriculture is a slightly dotted line that passes the points B and F. The production function, $f_o(x)$, is the Socialist production function; the function, $f(x)$, is the Reform production function.

However, another way in which the government can increase the efficiency of producers is by providing the government-provided input in a way that is more consistent with the production needs of the farm, e.g. by improving the performance of the input supply channels. We will refer to this decision as 'market liberalization'.[1] Even though, in the strictest sense, only improved incentives lead to technical efficiency increases, we refer also to market liberalization policies as a source of change in technical efficiency. If the increase of farm output from the same level of input, x^i, comes from higher levels of (or a higher quality of) the government-provided input, l^i, from the farm's point of view (and in the terminology of production economics), the higher output can be said to come from the rise in the farm's fixed factor. From the point of view of the relationship between inputs and outputs, however, it acts in a similar way to an increase in technical efficiency. Hence, for the sake of convenience, we refer to such actions as efficiency increasing. In the next sections, the discussion of l^i is limited, but we should stress that it is still one of the sources of changes in efficiency.

Allocative (in)efficiency

The second form of inefficiency, allocative inefficiency, is created when the government imposes its preferences on the farms by subsuming the price-setting functions of markets. The inefficiency occurs when the prices set by the government for inputs, w, and output, p, deviate from world market prices that are assumed to reflect the long-run scarcity values of the inputs and outputs. In order to illustrate this source of inefficiency, we assume that Socialist farm managers are conditionally profit maximizing. Conditional profit maximizing occurs when the manager allocates inputs up to the point in which the marginal revenue of the farm's output (which is equal to the government-set output price times the farm's marginal product) equals the government-set input price. Although the profits of the Socialist farm are at the maximum point, given the government-set prices, if profits for the Socialist farm's input and output levels were evaluated at market prices, it would be found that farm profits were lower. Clearly, blame for the inefficiency in this case is wholly due to the government's price-setting behaviour.

More formally, we demonstrate this by assuming that within the government-controlled farming system the government chooses two things: first, as before the government chooses the form of the property rights which determines that organization of the farm (as well as the level of allocation of government-controlled inputs). In our immediate discussion of allocative inefficiency, we hold the organization of the farm constant. Second, the government chooses two prices, the price of output, p_o^j, and the price, w_o^j, of the farmer-allocated input, x^i, where j is an index that will allow us to identify set of prices set in different Socialist economies (for example, $j = 1$ will be illustrative of the case of a country such as China that taxed its agriculture—henceforth Country 1—and $j = 2$ will be illustrative of the case of many countries in CEE or CIS that subsidized their agriculture—henceforth Country 2). We also define the market price for input x as w^m and for output q as p^m.

Given these definitions, we can now use Figure 3.1 to illustrate the allocative inefficiency of Socialist agriculture by focusing only on the Socialist production function, $q_o = f_o(x)$. In Figure 3.1, output is represented by points on the vertical axis that are in association with points A, B, and C. The input levels are represented by points on the horizontal axis (X_o^1, X_o^2, and X_p). The optimal allocation of a Socialist farm facing market-based prices is point C. At point C, given market prices, w^m and p^m, conditional profits are maximized, since:

$$\frac{df}{dx} = \frac{w^m}{p^m} \qquad (3.6)$$

However, planning ministries in Socialist countries did not use market prices when setting prices in their economies (see Chapter 4). In some cases (for example, Country 1, or in reality China and Vietnam), planners set output to input price ratios so they were less than those determined by the market. In these countries, planners are said to 'tax' producers. In other Socialist nations (for example, in Country 2, or in reality in countries in CEE and the CIS), planners set price ratios higher than market-based ratios and were said to 'subsidize' producers. In these economies, Socialist farm managers also maximize profits, but do so using government-set prices:

$$\frac{df}{dx} = \frac{w_o^j}{p_o^j} \qquad (3.7)$$

In Figure 3.1 can we illustrate two forms of allocative inefficiency by considering two representative Socialist countries: Country 1 taxes agriculture and sets prices equal to w_o^1 and p_o^1, and Country 2 subsidizes agriculture with prices set at w_o^2 and p_o^2, such that:

$$\frac{w_o^1}{p_o^1} > \frac{w^m}{p^m} > \frac{w_o^2}{p_o^2} \qquad (3.8)$$

The resulting allocation of resources is point A for Country 1, the country that taxes agriculture. In contrast, allocation is point B for Country 2, the country that subsidizes agriculture. In both cases, although farm managers are conditionally maximizing profits, the allocative inefficiency appears since the allocations at points A and B are far removed from the efficient allocation and true market prices (given the Socialist production function) at point C.

3.3. Modelling reforms

In this section, we illustrate the effect of economic reforms on farms in transition countries. For tractability, the analysis is restricted to two stylized reforms, property rights reform and price reform.[2] Although we look at how each reform would affect farm behaviour and performance separately, as will be seen in Chapter 4, in reality the two reforms often occurred simultaneously. Moreover, as the next chapter will discuss in great detail, the reforms were implemented differently in different countries. Therefore, we will first explain the impact of the two reforms separately and afterwards we will examine their effect when they are implemented simultaneously.

Using our modelling framework, it is easy to see that one of the most fundamental transition policies, *price reform*, can have large, but varying, effects in different transition nations. For example, in Country 1, price reform means that planners remove the implicit tax and the government-set input to output price ratio, w_o^1/p_o^1, falls as it moves to the market one, w^m/p^m. In Figure 3.1, this is represented as the move along the production frontier, $f_0(x)$, from point A to point C. Outputs and inputs rise due to these reforms. The farm managers remain on the Socialist production function in our simplified world because although price reform removes the price distortions, the farmers are still technically inefficient since there are no property rights reforms. In Country 2, the farm managers also respond to price reform. In this case, however, price liberalization reduces the input to output price ratio as subsidies are removed and the farm moves from point B to point C. Output and inputs both fall. Hence, price reform acts differently, depending on the initial conditions.

In the other transition policy shift, *property rights reform*, the farm manager is allowed to determine his or her own organization (e.g. they begin to work on a private farm, which is identical in all other respects to the original Socialist farm) and is given the rights to the residual income produced by the farm. As seen in Figure 3.1, increased effort shifts the production function from $f_o(\cdot)$ to $f(\cdot)$. Without considering the effect of price liberalization, the reform has similar effects on producers in Country 1 and 2: in both countries output goes up, but the magnitude differs. In Country 1, the farm moves up from point A to point E. In the case of Country 2, the farm moves up from point B to point F.

Modelling the *simultaneous implementation of both reforms* allows one to identify which part of the effects is due to each reform and to gain insights about the complex relationship between observed outcomes and reforms, and what role initial conditions play in these effects. This can be seen in Figure 3.1. If both price reform and property rights reforms are implemented successfully, Countries 1 and 2, although starting at different points, both end up at point D. For example, Country 1 first moves from A to C in response to price reform and then from point C to D in response to property rights reform.[3] In contrast, Country 2 first moves from A to C in response to price liberalization and, once at point C similarly to Country 1, from point C to D in response to property rights reform.

Using Figure 3.1, the analysis yields several conclusions. First, it immediately becomes clear that 'successful reform implementation' can have different effects on output depending on the initial conditions. In Country 1 output goes up: from q_o^1 (point A) to q_{p+r} (point D). In Country 1 the positive output effects from the property rights reform from q_p (point C) to q_{p+r} (point D) are reinforced by the positive output effect of the price reform from q_o^1 (point A) to q_p (point C). However, in Country 2 output may decline: from q_o^2 (point B) to q_{p+r} (point D). This is because in Country 1, with the initial subsidization of agriculture, the positive output effects from the property rights reform from q_p (point C) to q_{p+r} (point D) are more than offset by the negative output effect of the price reform from q_o^2 (point B) to (point C).

Second, not only do the combined reform effects differ in terms of output between Countries 1 and 2, they also may differ in terms of productivity changes. This can be seen from Figure 3.2. To avoid cluttering the graphical illustration in Figure 3.1, we show the average productivity effects, q/x, which are represented by the slopes of the OA, OB, OC, OD, OE, and OF lines in Figure 3.2. It is clear that when both reforms are implemented successfully, i.e. when both countries are at point D, the changes in productivity are different. Country 1, moving from point A to D, witnesses a decline in its average productivity (illustrated by a pivot of the average productivity line from OA to OD). This is because the increase in average productivity from property rights reforms (from OA to OE) more than offsets the reduction in average productivity due to the

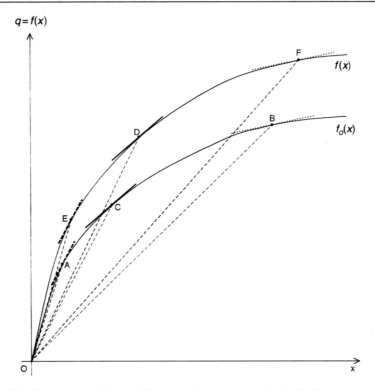

Figure 3.2 Reforms, initial conditions, and average productivity during transition.

price reform from OA to OC (or from OE to OD depending on the sequencing of the reforms). Since the marginal product is less than the average product in Country 1, given the assumed form of our production function, price reform, which removes the tax and stimulates an output and input increase, actually decreases the average product in Country 1. In contrast, in Country 2 when moving from point B to D average productivity increases (illustrated by an aggregate pivot of the average productivity line from OB to OD). In Country 2 both reforms reinforce each other in terms of average productivity effects. Property rights reforms increase average productivity from OB to OF and price reform increases it further from OF to OD (or first from OB to OC and then from OC to OD if the sequencing of the reforms is the other way around).

Third, to what extent are these results general or do they depend on the specific shapes used in the graphs? The answer is in Table 3.1 which summarizes all the effects. Table 3.1 shows that *all the partial effects which we have just discussed hold in general* (see rows 1, 2, 4, and 5). For the aggregate

Table 3.1 Summary of effects of price liberalization and property rights reforms on output, inputs, and average product of farms in Socialist countries

Row	Country	(1) Pricing policy environment during pre-transition period	Reform scenario		Impacts		
			(2) Price liberalization	(3) Property rights reform	(4) Output, Δq [a]	(5) Inputs, Δx [a]	(6) Average Product, $\Delta(q/x)$ [b]
1	1	Taxed	Yes	No	+	+	−
2	1	Taxed	No	Yes	+	+	+
3	1	Taxed	Yes	Yes	+	+	? [c]
4	2	Subsidized	Yes	No	−	−	+
5	2	Subsidized	No	Yes	+	+	+
6	2	Subsidized	Yes	Yes	?	?	+

[a] See Figure 3.1.
[b] See Figure 3.2.
[c] (?) means the sign is ambiguous.

effects (rows 3 and 6) this is not generally the case: the effect depends on whether the partial reform effects reinforce or mitigate each other. In those cases in which the reform effects reinforce each other, the aggregate effect is unambiguous and obviously the same as the partial reform effects. When the price reforms and property rights reforms have opposite effects, the net aggregate effect is ambiguous.

Fourth, property rights reforms and their associated rises in technical efficiency (rows 2 and 5) can have large and positive effects on farms in transition economies. Moreover, successful property rights reform, regardless of whether or not the country is being taxed or subsidized by pre-transition price policy, increases both output and productivity unambiguously. Assuming the property rights reforms are effective in raising technical efficiency (that is, assuming they are not offset by other disruptions that might come along with transition, a subject to which we return in the next section), in Country 1 the inputs and output of farmers rise when moving from point A to point E. The same is true for farmers in Country 2 (moving from point B to F). According to Figure 3.2, average product also rises when property rights are reformed in both Countries 1 and 2.

Fifth, the impact of price reform is more complex (rows 1 and 4). Successful price reform leads to rising allocative efficiency. However, the impact on output and average productivity depends on the pre-transition price policy. While in the case of successful property rights reform, whether a country is being taxed or subsidized by pricing policy, higher efficiencies will lead to higher inputs, output, and average product, it is not true in the case of successful price reform.

Sixth, because of the differences in the direction of some of the impacts, when two policies are implemented together, the net effects are sometimes ambiguous (Table 3.1, rows 3 and 6). For example, if Country 1 simultaneously implements price reform and property rights reform, according to our modelling framework, although input and output effects are unambiguous (they both rise), the same is not true for average product. It is unclear whether the rising average product associated with property rights reform is large enough to offset the falling average product associated with price reform. For example, if the price effect is large compared to the property rights reform effect, the net effect for Country 1 on aggregate productivity could be negative—unlike the situation in Figure 3.2. Inversely, in Country 2, the ambiguity of the effect of simultaneous price reform and property rights reform works in the opposite way. While average product unambiguously increases, the input and output effects are ambiguous. In Figure 3.1 the net impact of the combined reforms on output for Country 2 was negative, but this net effect depends on the shape of the production function and on the relative size of the technical inefficiencies and the subsidies. With different assumptions on these one could draw a situation where q_{p+r} would be above, rather than below, q_o^2, implying a net increase in output for Country 2.

3.4. Model extensions

The analysis so far has assumed a simple model of the effects of transition policies on farm behaviour and performance. In reality, price liberalization and property rights reforms have been more complicated and have occurred in an environment that is characterized by imperfect information and poor institutional support. Writing about the environment of nations in CEE and in the CIS states during the early years of transition, Blanchard and Kremer (1997) title their paper on transition 'Disorganization'. In fact, many in the literature have described how the process of property rights reform and market liberalization in some countries, especially in the beginning years of reform, was associated with the breakdown of institutions of exchange and the rise of transaction costs (Rozelle and Swinnen 2004). Property rights reforms did not only involve the granting of income and control rights to farms, but also necessarily entailed fundamental restructuring, which has been associated with temporary, and in many cases considerable, disruptions. Also, the process of transition was not immediate and was not completely orchestrated from the outside. In many places it has been a dynamic process, and in some cases very much a start and stop process. While we do not at all pretend to rigorously model these effects, in the rest of this section we do discuss and attempt to characterize how disruptions, rising transaction costs from market breakdown, and the dynamics of transition shaped the way reform policies affected farm behaviour and their performance.

Disruptions and farm restructuring

One way of modelling the temporary disruptions of the reform process when the policies reduce the ability of the farmer to fully utilize his inputs to their maximize potential is to treat it as a downward shift in the production function. While successful property rights reforms may unambiguously induce the farmer to increase input use, and raise the level of output and average productivity, by increasing incentives and raising technical efficiency, in the short run there could be offsetting effects. In the process of changing property rights regimes, there are many circumstances in which the necessary restructuring and dismantling of institutions could lead to at least temporary falls in productivity. For example, restoring land to private land holders in the long run will undoubtedly give farms greater incentives to produce more efficiently since the owner/manager become the residual claimant of farming activities. However, in the initial years of the implementation of reform policies there were often many uncertainties. For example, in the first years after the land reform in Central and Eastern Europe many producers were not certain that by the end of the cropping season they would be operating the land that they were in charge of at the beginning of the season. Under such circumstances, of course, farm managers and owner-operators may have been less willing to put out effort and/or invest in their farming activities for fear that the output would not accrue to them. After the land reform, rental markets were slow to develop and frequently there was an initial mismatch between those that received land and those that wanted to farm it. The delays in making these matches may have led to lower productivity because of lack of effort or investment, or because farmers could not plan sufficiently or apply inputs in a timely fashion.

Building on the models from Figures 3.1 and 3.2, we can model the disruptions of restructuring as the appearance of technical inefficiency. In Figure 3.3, we focus on the property rights reform (by assuming that the price reform is completed already and we are already at point C). Well-defined property rights reform would induce a shift from point C to D.

However, if the rights reform process initially causes severe disruptions one may not arrive at point D. Instead, if the disruptions are large enough to offset the gain from increased incentives, the initial impact of rights reform could actually induce a move from point C to E: instead of increasing inputs and output, property rights reforms could lead to falling inputs and output.

Such negative effects of the initial disruptions were real and important, as we will document in the next chapter. However, the negative disruption effects relative to the positive incentive effects may differ by country. In the short run in some transition countries the negative impact of the initial inefficiencies may outweigh the efficiency gains. For example, in countries with capital-intensive agricultural systems that are part of a complex network of input supply chains and output procurement or processing channels, the disruption effects may be relatively large compared to the incentive effects, making the overall effect of the property rights reform initially negative. This is the situation illustrated in Figure 3.3.

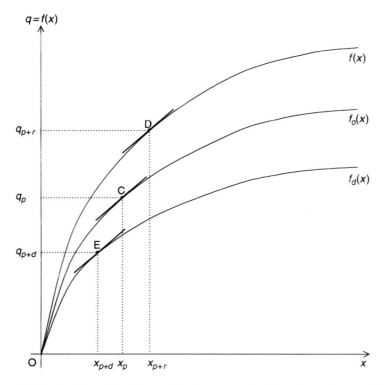

Figure 3.3 Production allocations with strong production disruptions and weak incentive effects.

In other countries, the disruption effect may not be as large. For example, for a variety of reasons, countries with labour-intensive agricultural systems, ones that use relatively simple inputs and technology, the incentive effects may be strong and disruptions less severe. In such a case, there could be an overall positive effect. Such a situation is illustrated by Figure 3.4. The incentive effect increases output from q_p (point C) to q_{p+r} (point D), but the disruptions have a negative output effect, equivalent to the distance q_{p+r} (point D) $- q_{p+d'}$ (E'). Hence, although the disruption effect reduces the output of the farmer, the incentive effect is relatively larger, and there is an overall gain to property rights reform with the aggregate shift from C to E', and a net increase in output of $q_{p+d'} - q_p$.

Transaction costs and market disorganization

Another source of technical efficiency gains can come from 'market liberalization', policies that seek to improve the quality, quantity, and timeliness of

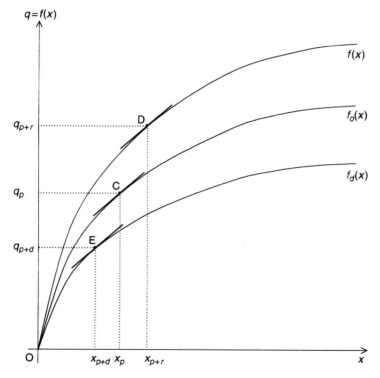

Figure 3.4 Production allocations with weak production disruptions and strong incentive effects.

government-controlled input supplies, l^i. However, this source of technical efficiency gain may also be associated with disruptions. In addition to the disruptions caused by initial property rights reforms, the disorganization of institutions of exchange caused by rapid market liberalization and the elimination of planning in some countries is also important to model. For example, to the extent that companies that supplied inputs, such as fertilizer, seeds, and credit, or processing companies, such as dairies and cotton gins, are simultaneously privatized and have somewhat diminished capabilities to (at least temporarily) procure the input and output of farms, there could be serious problems faced by farms. Unlike the disruptions associated with property rights reform which primarily affect the incentive to put out effort, the breakdown of institutions of exchange in the wake of market liberalization may be more appropriately modelled by changes in transaction costs.

To do so, we first define p and w as the effective prices facing the farm, P as the price which the processor pays for its supplies, and W as the price the input company gets for the inputs that it supplies to the farm. We define θ_p as the transaction costs (including transport, enforcement, monitoring, etc.) in the output market and define θ_w as the transaction costs in the input market. These transaction costs cause a difference between the price of the input suppliers (output procurer) and the farm's input (output) price. Hence:

$$p = P - \theta_p \tag{3.9}$$

$$w = W + \theta_w \tag{3.10}$$

Given this modelling framework, then, it is easy to see that when market liberalization occurs, relative price shifts are not only caused by officials encouraging prices to move towards those of world market prices (that is from price reform), but may also be affected by institutional disruption caused by increased transaction costs associated with market liberalization. Simply put, disruptions caused by changes in the institutional structure in the upstream and downstream sectors during market liberalization can be modelled as an increase in transaction costs. As a consequence, even in the circumstances when P and W reflect world prices and do not change (at least after the initial price reform), farm input use and realized output could be affected by rising transaction costs which depress the output prices faced by farmers and raise farm gate input prices of materials that farmers need to produce their crops. In other words, rising transaction costs lead to deteriorating terms of trade at the farm level.

While the mechanism is different from that caused by the disruptions associated with property rights reform, the effect is the same: a fall in input use and output.

The effect of rising transaction costs is illustrated in Figure 3.5. We assume that p and w initially reflect pre-transition transaction costs and that price reform has already occurred (P and W are world prices). The farmer is producing at point C in Figure 3.1, instead of at point A or B. The impact of increasing transaction cost due to market disruptions and the induced changes in terms of trade for farms is illustrated by the shift from point C to point G. This causes a decline in output from q_p to $q_{p+\theta}$.

Taking into account the efficiency gains from market liberalization, represented by a shift in the production function to $f(x)$, implies a move from G to point F. As with the property rights reform with disruption, here also we have the situation that the initial gains from market liberalization, represented by the output increase from $q_{p+\theta}$ to $q_{p+\theta+r}$, may not be

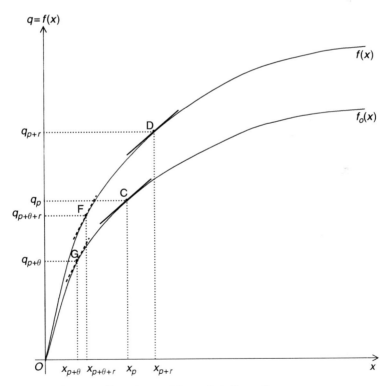

Figure 3.5 Production allocations with market disruptions.

sufficient to overcome the output decline due to the disruptions, and the net effect of the market liberalization is initially an output decline from q_p (point C) to $q_{p+\theta+r}$ (point F).

In several countries leaders undertook the entire basket of reforms, price reform, property rights reforms, and market liberalization. The combination of these three contributed to important efficiency gains but also to strong disruptions. In several countries (in the first years of reform) disruptions in farm management from property rights reform and the disorganization caused by the breakdown of the institutions of exchange and rising transaction costs from market liberalization occurred together. According to our modelling framework, this would combine the negative effects of both sources of disruptions into a large output decline. The sharp drop in inputs and outputs by farms in many countries in CEE and in the CIS nations, especially in the first years after reform, suggest that this simple conceptual framework may be consistent with the observed facts. We provide an empirical illustration of this in the next section, and a more detailed empirical analysis in Chapter 4.

Dynamic aspects

The reforms also may have important dynamic effects as the disruptions are likely to have a different time effect from the efficiency gains. In the words of Kornai (2000) transition calls 'for creative destruction. Because destruction is rapid, whereas creation proceeds more slowly, the two processes led to deep recession.' The implication is that if there are likely to be disruptions and disorganization in the early phase of transition and inefficiencies in some countries, the disruptions should be temporary. If so, the impact of reforms can change importantly over time as the impact of a certain policy can initially lead to lower efficiency, while ultimately it can improve efficiency.

Thought of in this way, in addition to the cross-country comparison our modelling framework can also be used to track the record of the effect of the reforms in a single country over time (Figure 3.6). Several points on Figures 3.1–3.5 can be thought of as snapshots at different moments of the reform process. To illustrate this, Figure 3.6 summarizes key parts of the previous analyses. For example, before transition Socialist farms in Country 2 are subsidized, are allocatively inefficient, and are operating on the technically inefficient Socialist production function, $f_0(x)$. Hence, prior to reform they are at point B. With price reform, output declines and farms move towards the allocatively efficient point C. Property rights reform

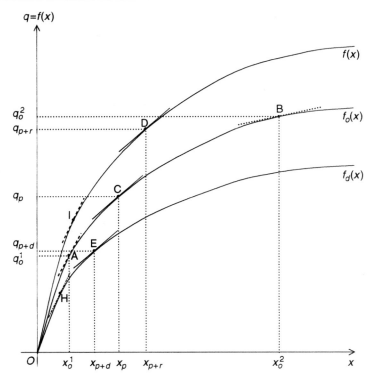

Figure 3.6 Production allocations with a combination of various reforms and disruptions.

initially mainly creates disruptions and in the early phase of transition farms actually become more inefficient (point E). Market liberalization also creates initial disorganization and the rising transaction costs exacerbate the falling terms of trade, inducing farms to move to point H. As point H in Figure 3.6 illustrates, during the early phases of reform farms can possibly be inefficient in both an allocative and technical sense. However, as the reforms proceed and succeed, property rights reforms improve incentives and the reorganization of input supply chains and output procurement and processing channels improves the provision of inputs that originally were supplied by the government, allowing farms to increase their technical efficiency by moving from point H to point I. In this process of improving marketing and input supply channels, the disorganization of markets is replaced by emerging institutions of exchange that are more effective, and transaction costs fall, improving the real terms of trade and improving allocative efficiency, inducing a shift from I to D.

In this dynamic process, which started in point B and ended in point D, output and productivity have been affected by various reform effects. The dynamic output effects are summarized in Figure 3.7, where the letters refer to the points in Figure 3.6. In the final point, output may be somewhat higher or lower than in the starting position. Importantly, technical and allocative efficiency will have increased unambiguously. Hence, in the longer run, productivity will improve.

That said, the disruptions and initial output decline associated with them have induced many scholars, and policy makers, to question the wisdom of taking this reform approach. Some argued that the aggregate output decline in the early transition was too heavy a price to pay to arrive at point D. Some also argued that it would be possible to arrive at point D without having to go through the output decline associated with 'radical reforms' by taking a more 'gradual approach' to the reforms. This issue was hotly

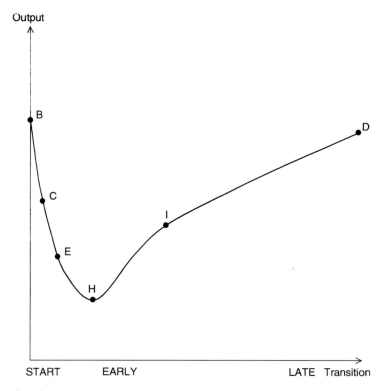

Figure 3.7 Output changes during transition with a combination of reforms and disruptions.

debated in the transition literature (see our introductory chapter). The gradualist school often referred to China as an example of the gradual approach and how a different reform approach would not need to lead to a decline in output. However, as our next chapter will show, the starting point of China in agriculture was much closer to point A (or even point H) on Figure 3.6 than to point B. Hence, going from point A to D would be associated with much more output growth *even with the same reforms* than if one started at point B. The next section demonstrates how the reform impacts illustrated in the graphical patterns are consistent with some basic indicators for China, Russia, and Central Europe. A more detailed empirical analysis follows in Chapter 4.

3.5. Reform and efficiency: an empirical illustration

Observations on changes in crop output, fertilizer use, and average productivity from three transition countries, China, Russia, and the Czech Republic, illustrate the relationship between agricultural reforms and efficiency (see Table 3.2). First, in response to the price and property rights reforms, our model predicts that the output and input level should rise in 'Country 1', a nation in which the farmers were taxed by pricing policies during the pre-transition era. The effect on average productivity is ambiguous. In the case of China, an example of a nation in which leaders heavily taxed farmers with pricing policy during the Socialist era, price reform induced a strong increase in the grain to fertilizer price ratio (37 per cent over the first five years of transition). After this price reform fertilizer use rose by 68 per cent and cereal output rose by 27 per cent. Average productivity,

Table 3.2 Changes in price ratios, fertilizer use, grain output, and average productivity in China, Russia, and the Czech Republic during the initial five years of transition

	Δ Grain to fertilizer price ratio (%)	Δ Fertilizer use (%)	Δ Grain output (%)	Δ Average grain productivity of fertilizer[a] (%)
China	+37	+68	+27	−7
Russia	−73	−89	−40	+103
Czech Republic	−50	−71	−17	+61

Note: The initial five years of transition are 1979 to 1984 in China and 1991 to 1996 in Russia and the Czech Republic.

[a] Average grain productivity of fertilizer is grain output divided by fertilizer use.

Sources: Tables 2.3 and 2.4.

however, fell by 7 per cent. This is consistent with the hypothesis that the average productivity decline due to the price effect was slightly stronger than the average productivity gain due to the technical efficiency gains with the property rights reforms.

Second, our model predicts that the aggregate reform effect is positive on average productivity for 'Country 2', a nation in which the farmers were subsidized by pricing policies during the pre-transition era. The impact on output and input levels is conditional on the relative partial effects: output should decline due to the price reform but increase with technical efficiency gains due to property rights reforms. Table 3.2 shows how in Russia and the Czech Republic, two nations that heavily subsidized agriculture in the pre-transition era, the grain to fertilizer price ratio declined by more than 50 per cent due to the price reform. Average productivity rose more than 60 per cent in both countries, consistent with the predictions.

Table 3.2 also shows that farmers in Russia and the Czech Republic sharply reduced input use: fertilizer use declined by more than 70 per cent in both countries. Moreover, cereal output fell by around 20–40 per cent after price reform. These numbers suggest that the reductions in inputs and output due to the dramatic price effects (−50 per cent and −71 per cent) were much stronger than the gains due to technical efficiency gains over the first five years of the reforms.[4]

In summary, these aggregate figures in China, Russia, and the Czech Republic, as reported in Table 3.2, move in a way consistent with the theoretical predictions in Table 3.1. In the next chapter we will provide more substantive and detailed empirical evidence to document the reform differences and their effects.

Notes

1. Market liberalization reforms in our framework are distinctly different from price liberalization, actions taken by the government to bring the relative input and output price of the domestic economy into closer alignment with international relative prices, which are assumed to reflect the long-run scarcity value of the goods. Pricing reform policies, as we note below, primarily affect allocative efficiency. We recognize, however, that in reality, the reform policies that affect the operation of input supply chains and output marketing channels often also affect relative prices, and are in this sense affecting both technical and allocative efficiency.
2. As explained above, 'market liberalization', as defined in Section 3.2, has similar effects to 'property rights reform'.

3. Alternatively, Country 1 could move from point A to C to D and Country 2 could move from point B to F to D. If the policies are implemented and become effective simultaneously, the order of movement is purely arbitrary.

4. Comparing the results of Russia and the Czech Republic shows that output fell much further in Russia than in the Czech Republic. Our model offers several hypotheses for this. One possible cause is that the decline in terms of trade was larger in Russia (-73% compared to -50%) Another possible reason is that although in both Russia and the Czech Republic there was considerable disruption that may have obscured gains from property rights reform, it is well known that progress in property rights reform occurred more rapidly in the Czech Republic than in Russia. If so, this means that during the first five-year period, the upward rise in the production function for the Czech Republic should have been greater than that of Russia (which was arguably zero, since few property rights reforms were implemented rigorously). Hence, one should be careful about assigning causality on the basis of such simple data (see next chapter for a more careful analysis with data for more years from more countries); the fact that both fertilizer use and output fell less in the Czech Republic than in Russia also suggests that the data are consistent with the predictions of the model.

4

Policy Reforms

Research on the determinants of growth and decline in transition economies has identified a number of important factors: for example, the initial level of development at the time of reform (Sachs and Woo 1994; Macours and Swinnen 2000*b*); the speed of reform (McMillan and Naughton 1992); the political economy and regional tensions (Roland 2000; de Melo and Gelb 1996); and the management of public investments (Huang and Rozelle 1996; Csaki 1998; Fan, Zhang, and Zhang 2002). In this chapter we focus on three key policy reforms in agriculture and the food industry. We examine shifts in price and subsidy policy, property rights reform and farm restructuring, and market liberalization because they have played a crucial role in most transition economies. Because of complicated ways that the policies and interactions of policies affect performance, we first review the policies in this chapter and we defer the examination of their effects to Chapter 5.

4.1. Prices and subsidies

The administration of prices by the Socialist planning apparatus is one of the most distinguishing characteristics of pre-transition countries. While in some countries leaders allowed subsets of goods to be traded out of the plan, for most high priority commodities—which almost always included food and fibre—planning ministries in most nations allocated goods and services mostly on the basis of quantity-based plans. Prices mostly served accounting functions.

Despite the similarities, there were several critical differences among nations. In setting the prices of agricultural goods, inputs, and services, the ratio of input to output prices faced by producers differed greatly among the countries. For example, in China and Vietnam before reform authorities used administrative prices to impose a heavy tax on agriculture by requiring farmers to deliver their output at artificially low prices (Lardy 1983; Sicular 1988*a*; Green and Vokes 1998). In contrast, leaders in most of the CEE and the CIS nations supported agriculture with heavy subsidies, typically setting artificially low prices for inputs and relatively high prices for output (Cook, Liefert, and Koopman 1991; Kwiecinski and Pescatore 2000; Liefert et al. 1996; USDA 1994; Tomich, Kilby, and Johnston 1995). As Chapter 3 showed, the extent to which prices were above or below the market price prior to an economy's transition almost certainly would have different consequences for the sector's performance as reformers tried to bring the nation's price structure closer to that of the rest of the world.

In East Asia, perhaps one of the least appreciated moves of the early reformers was their bold decision to *administratively* increase the price of farm goods that were to be received by farmers (Lardy 1983; Sicular 1988*b*). Between 1978 and 1983, in a number of separate actions, planners in China increased the above quota price, the payment farmers received for voluntary sales beyond the mandatory deliveries, by 41 per cent for grain and by around 50 per cent for cash crops (Sicular 1988*b*). According to the State Statistical Bureau's data, the relative price of grain to fertilizer rose by more than 60 per cent during the first three years after reform (see Figure 4.1).

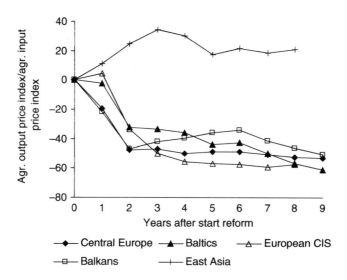

Figure 4.1 Change in agricultural terms of trade index (grain to fertilizer price ratio) during first 10 years of reform in transition countries.

Note: Balkans exclude Albania and Bulgaria; Baltics exclude Latvia; European CIS exclude Moldova; East Asia include China and Vietnam only.

Sources: OECD and national statistics for China.

During the early reform years, the rise in above-quota price represented a higher output price at the margin to farmers, since until 1984, state-run procurement stations regularly purchased all grain sold by farmers at the above-quota price as long as they had already fulfilled their mandatory marketing delivery quota which was purchased at a state-set quota price, which for the case of rice, for example, was 50 per cent below the above-quota price (Sicular 1995).[1]

The important contribution of China's pricing policy is the timing and breadth of the policy change. The first major price rise occurred in 1979, almost at the same time when reformers were deciding to decollectivize. However, given the leadership's decision to gradually implement the household responsibility system (HRS), beginning first in the poorest areas of China, the price increases immediately affected all farmers, both those in areas that had been decollectivized and those that had not. By 1981, the time of a second major price increase, according to Lin (1992), less than half of China's farmers had been allowed to dismantle their communes. Hence, as long as there was some, albeit weak, link between the output price and production, the *plan-based* price rise would have led to increases in China's farm output.

During its first years of reform, Vietnam followed an almost identical path (Tran 1997; Wurfel 1993). As in China, almost a decade before Vietnam's leaders abolished the state's procurement system and formally allowed private traders to purchase agricultural goods directly from farmers, leaders raised prices administratively and increased the profits earned by the farmers (Rana and Hamid 1996). According to official data from Vietnam, during the first five years of the reforms, the output-to-input price ratio rose more than 35 per cent above its pre-reform level. Like, China, the price rise occurred at a time when Vietnam was just beginning to push its Doi Moi decollectivization policies and more than ten to fifteen years before land titles were issued.

During the entire pre- and post-reform period, input prices—especially that of fertilizer—were still mostly controlled by the state's monopoly agricultural inputs supply corporations in China and Vietnam (Stone 1988; Pingali and Khiem 1995). Although it was in short supply, the governments in both countries controlled the price of fertilizer and other inputs (such as pesticides, diesel fuel, and electricity) as well as their distribution (Solinger 1984). Communes received low-priced fertilizer from the state, but almost all of it was inframarginal. In other words, the government-supplied, subsidized fertilizer was not sufficient to meet the needs of most farmers. Producers in both the pre- and post-reform periods typically purchased additional fertilizer from the state at a higher price (Ye and Rozelle 1994). Hence, unlike other transition and developing countries, at the margin, farmers in China and Vietnam were not able to purchase fertilizer at highly subsidized rates. In fact, according to Huang and Chen (1999), during the 1980s the real price of China's fertilizer was above the international price. Vietnam was in a similar position early during its reforms (Pingali and Xuan 1992). Although both nations raised the price of fertilizer somewhat under rising foreign exchange and budgetary pressures in the mid-1980s, the rise was not large enough to eliminate the positive incentives created by higher output prices (World Bank 1997).[2]

Although price and subsidy reforms were much bolder in CEE and CIS countries than in East Asia, there were differences among regions. In Central Europe, for example, governments immediately dismantled the planning system by decontrolling agricultural prices and dramatically reducing subsidies (Hartell and Swinnen 1998; Trzeciak-Duval 1999). For example, Estonia, the most radical reformer of countries previously belonging to the Soviet Union, totally liberalized output and input prices between 1990 and 1992. However, in most CIS countries, reformers decontrolled prices more gradually (Csaki and Nash 1998; Csaki and Zuschlag 2003). Russian reformers liberalized output prices in the early reforms, but certain key input subsidies have continued. On the other hand, in countries like Belarus, Uzbekistan, and Turkmenistan (the least radical reformers), price controls on both outputs and inputs continued far into the 1990s.

Yet, the main difference between CEE/CIS and East Asian transition countries is not in their administration of price reform; rather, it is in the direction of the price adjustments (see Figure 4.1). In East Asia pro-urban policies that used low procurement prices during the planning era to subsidize consumers (who also were workers on the front line of East Asia's heavy industry-led development strategy) led to artificially low farm gate prices. Price reforms that sought to set more realistic prices (that is to say, those that in some sense reflected the market value of the commodities) raised prices. In CEE and in the CIS nations, since output prices had previously been supported above equilibrium prices and input prices had been heavily subsidized, price liberalization caused substantive declines in agricultural terms of trade. In the first five years of transition, for example, output-to-input prices in agriculture fell more than 30 per cent in Hungary, 50 per cent in the Czech Republic, and at least 70 per cent in Slovakia, Poland, Russia, Ukraine, and some of the Baltics. In these countries the combination of the fall in the real price of output and the sharp rise in the real price of inputs led to a severe drop in production in most agricultural sectors and food crises in a number of them (OECD 1998).

4.2. Property rights reform and farm restructuring

Although there were many differences among countries in the organization of their agricultural sectors prior to reform, in most cases farm production units shared several key characteristics (Lardy 1983; Pingali and Xuan 1992; Lerman, Csaki, and Feder 2004). Prohibiting private farming, Socialist ideals favoured large, corporate organizations. In some nations state-owned farms dominated the landscape. Those that worked the land on state farms typically were paid a wage, drew a pension, and performed work assignments handed down by managers, which were often part of a larger national or regional plan. Farms were theoretically organized on the same principles as factory enterprises and farmers became workers. The state made investments, set planting plans, purchased inputs through planning channels and remitted profits up through the ministerial system. In other countries, farms were run as collectives. Like state farms in most respects, the main difference was that instead of drawing a wage, collective members earned work points that entitled them to a share of the harvest that was left over after deductions were made for input purchases, taxes, quota deliveries, and investment retentions.

Whatever the exact organizational form, wage- and point-earning farm workers typically faced few incentives to work hard since their compensation was at most only loosely tied to either their effort or the farm's profitability. Unlike industrial factories, however, monitoring farm workers was difficult. Logistics often compounded the problems. Planning necessities (for example, arranging for the procurement of inputs and disposal of output) meant that farms in most countries were quite large. The large scale of farms, in turn, meant that managers were often charged with trying to direct work of many individuals who on a day-to-day basis were physically spread out over a spatially dispersed area. In almost all studies of pre-reform agriculture collective and state farms were found to be inefficient (Brada and King 1993; Brooks 1983; Mead 2000; Lin 1990; Putterman 1992).

Searching for ways to make their economies more productive, reformers had several options for eliminating inefficiencies. First, they could try to provide better incentives to elicit more effort. Second, leaders could try to reduce the operational size of the farming unit to improve information about on-farm production needs. In this same spirit, it was thought that if planning was reduced by giving more decision-making authority to producers (that is to say, giving them better control rights), producers could produce more efficiently. Finally, reformers could try to facilitate the reduction or better allocation of inputs, including labour, that were being wasted. All countries, albeit with differing degrees of emphasis, tried to tap these sources of productivity gains.

In fact, the recognition of the shortcomings of the system and the launching of the wave of reforms in the 1980s in East Asian nations and in the 1990s in CEE and in the CIS nations was not new. Some CEE countries had attempted market-oriented reforms before 1989, mostly in the form of measures that increased enterprise autonomy (Roland 2000). For example, Poland introduced reforms in the management of their cooperatives and state-owned enterprises in the early 1980s.[3] Gorbachev followed later in the 1980s.[4] Hungary's leader had gone considerably beyond this by abolishing mandatory planning even earlier in 1968. Yugoslavia had also begun to introduce self-management in 1965. In contrast, Czechoslovakia and Romania had little or no history of significant reforms prior to 1988.

Most of the pre-1989 reforms in CEE and CIS nations, of course, did not achieve their objectives (Roland 2000). Communist leaders had hoped that if enterprise managers were given more autonomy in determining output and prices, they would show more profit awareness and increase enterprise performance. Instead, in many cases enterprises started distributing most of any rising value added to workers and managers in the form of wages. With soft budget constraints, enterprises started bargaining with the central authorities for more resources, contributing to macroeconomic imbalances.

In the light of the earlier failures and in response to the mounting pressures caused by the poor performance of agriculture (among other sectors), reformers after 1989 in most CEE and CIS countries—and earlier in East Asia—decided to make fundamental changes in property rights. Consisting of control rights (that is, who gets to decide on what to plant and what inputs to use) and income rights (that is, who gets the residual income generated by the productive activity), the final form and mix of property rights differed greatly across different countries. In some cases reformers only granted partial property rights to farmers. For example, reformers sometimes provided income rights, but few control rights. In other cases leaders provided nearly full control rights with only partial income rights. Ownership changes (that is, who received alienation rights to land and other farm assets) were often considered separately from questions of farm restructuring; likewise, restructuring sometimes occurred independently of changes in rights.

Almost always, the reforms to property rights in the new wave of the policy changes in the 1980s and 1990s were accompanied by a reduction in the propensity of the state to planning (gradually in the case of China and Vietnam; and more rapidly in the case of the CEE and CIS nations).

Rights reform in East Asia: incentives, individualization, and incomplete privatization

East Asia's reformers, more than anything, have followed a strategy based on providing incentives through property rights reforms, even though in China and Vietnam the shift to private ownership is today far from complete (see Table 4.1). The reforms in China started with the household responsibility system (HRS), a policy of radical decollectivization that allowed farmers to keep the residual output of their farms after paying their agricultural taxes and completing their mandatory delivery quotas. Farmers also began to exercise control over much of the production process (although in the initial years, the local state shared some control rights and in some places still does today). In this way the first reforms in the agricultural sector reshuffled property rights in an attempt to increase work incentives and exploit the specific knowledge of individuals about the production process (Lin 1992).

In executing the property rights reforms, leaders also fundamentally restructured farms in China and Vietnam. Within a few years, for example, reformers completely broke up the larger collective farms into small household farms (see Figure 4.2; Table 4.2). In China today there are more than 200 million farms, the legacy of an HRS policy that gave the primary responsibilities for farming to the individual household. There are more than 10 million farms in Vietnam.

The process of planning also began to take on a less important role (Sicular 1988*b*). In the case of China, for example, the marketed surplus delivery quotas were divided into basic and above-quota quotas. In addition to being given higher payment for above-quota quota deliveries, farmers were given more scope in deciding what they wanted to produce. Planners gave more discretion to farmers over a variety of products, such as eggs, certain meats, fish, and horticultural goods. Vietnamese reformers carried out similar reforms. In the rest of the book when reference is made to decollectivization or the implementation of HRS, we are referring to a process of the transfer of income and control rights to farmers *and* the initial reduction of planning (although not its immediate elimination).

The collective did not disappear, however. A companion set of reforms in the mid-1980s transformed communes into townships, the lowest level of

China's formal government hierarchy. Brigade leadership committees (a sub commune level of organization) were turned into village committees, which became the government's representative in China's villages (Oi 1999). Villages and the small groups below them (formerly production teams)

Table 4.1. Scope of property rights reform for agriculture in transition countries (1998)

	Land reform procedure	Individual use rights	Transfer of use rights	Individual ownership rights	Transfer of ownership rights	Progress in land reform	
						After 5 yrs	After 10 yrs
East Asia							
China	Dist	X	X	—	—	7/8	8/9
Vietnam	Dist	X	X	—	—	7/8	8/9
Laos	Dist	X	—	n.a.	n.a.	8	n.a.
Myanmar	—	X	X	n.a.	n.a.	8	n.a.
Central Asia							
Mongolia	Dist	X	—	n.a.	n.a.	n.a.	n.a.
Kazakhstan	Share	X	X	—	—	5	5
Kyrgyzstan	Share	X	X	X	—	6	7
Tajikistan	Share	X	X	—	—	2	5
Turkmenistan	Share	X	—	X	—	2	3
Uzbekistan	Share	X	—	—	—	1	2
Transcaucasus							
Armenia	Dist	X	X	X	X	8	8
Azerbaijan	Dist	X	X	X	X	6	8
Georgia	Dist	X	X	X	X	7	6
European CIS							
Belarus	Share	X	—	—	—	1	2
Moldova	Share	X	X	X	X	6	7
Russia	Share	X	X	X	—	5	5
Ukraine	Share	X	X	X	—	5	6
Baltics							
Estonia	Rest	X	X	X	X	6	8
Latvia	Rest	X	X	X	X	9	9
Lithuania	Rest	X	X	X	X	8	8
Central Europe							
Czech Rep.	Rest	X	X	X	X	8	8
Hungary	Rest+Dist+ Voucher	X	X	X	X	9	9
Poland	—	X	X	X	X	8	8
Slovakia	Rest	X	X	X	X	7	8
Balkans							
Albania	Dist	X	X	X	X	8	8
Bulgaria	Rest	X	X	X	X	7	8
Romania	Rest/Dist	X	X	X	X	7	8
Slovenia	—	X	X	X	X	9	9

Note: Dist = Distribution, Share = Distribution in shares, Rest = Restitution.

Sources: Csaki and Tuck (2000); Lerman, Csaki, and Feder (2004); and Macours and Swinnen (2002).

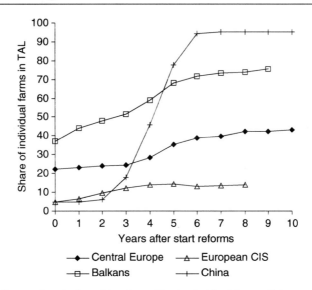

Figure 4.2 Share of agricultural land used by individual farms (%).
Note: Balkans exclude Albania; European CIS exclude Moldova; East Asia includes only China.
Source: see Table 4.2.

retained legal ownership rights over land and are the entities that were charged with contracting land to the farmers and setting rules for land management.

Doi Moi, Vietnam's reform programme in the 1980s, closely followed China's strategy (Pingali and Xuan 1992; Pingali and Khiem 1995). Faced with large food deficits and declining productivity, Vietnam switched from collectivized production to a household-oriented contract system in 1981. Designed to provide farmers with better incentives, the reforms stipulated that individual households were to enter into a contract with the former collective. In return for maintaining productivity and selling a portion of their crop to the state at below-market prices, farmers could keep all of the output from their land. Within a few years of the initial reforms, millions of new household-based farms were established.

Only a few countries outside East Asia followed China's model of reforming property rights and farming organizations (see Tables 4.1 and 4.2). Several countries in the Balkans and Transcaucasus region distributed land rights for specific plots of land to individual households in rural areas.[5] For example, in moves that were even more radical than China, reformers in Albania and Armenia gave households almost complete, private ownership rights to their land (Cungu and Swinnen 1999; Lerman et al. 1999).

In Georgia, land use rights were transferred to individual farms by Presidential Decree in 1992, a process that contributed to the individualization of farming. Four years later these use rights were converted into private ownership rights. Azerbaijan, the third Transcaucasian state, followed the same reform strategy, although the policy moves were made after 1996

Table 4.2 Restructuring of farming organization and general reform indicators

	Individual land use			Individual production		Agr. reform after 10 yrs
	Pre-reform	After 5 yrs	After 10 yrs[a]	Pre-reform	After 7 yrs	
East Asia						
China	5-10	98	99	n.a.	n.a.	n.a.
Vietnam	5	99	99	n.a.	n.a.	n.a.
Laos	54	99	99	n.a.	n.a.	n.a.
Myanmar	99	99	99	n.a.	n.a.	n.a.
Central Asia						
Mongolia	n.a.	n.a.	n.a.	n.a.	n.a.	n.a.
Kazakhstan	0	5	24	28	38	5.6
Kyrgyzstan	4	34	37	34	59	6.4
Tajikistan	4	5	9	23	39	4.2
Turkmenistan	2	3	8	16	30	2.0
Uzbekistan	5	13	14	28	52	2.0
Transcaucasus						
Armenia	7	95	90	35	98	7.2
Azerbaijan	2	5	n.a.	35	63	6.2
Georgia	12	50	44	48	76	6.0
European CIS						
Belarus	7	16	12	25	45	1.8
Moldova	7	12	20	18	51	6.0
Russia	2	8	13	24	55	5.6
Ukraine	6	10	17	27	53	4.0
Baltics						
Estonia	4	41	63	n.a.	n.a.	8.4
Latvia	4	81	87	n.a.	n.a.	8.4
Lithuania	9	64	85	n.a.	n.a.	7.6
Central Europe						
Czech Rep.	1	19	26	n.a.	n.a.	8.6
Hungary	13	22	54	n.a.	n.a.	8.8
Poland	76	80	84	n.a.	n.a.	7.8
Slovakia	2	5	9	n.a.	n.a.	7.6
Balkans						
Albania	3	95	n.a.	n.a.	n.a.	6.8
Bulgaria	14	44	56	n.a.	n.a.	7.6
Romania	14	71	82	n.a.	n.a.	6.6
Slovenia	83	90	94	n.a.	n.a.	8.0

[a] Due to data limitations, data are for eight, nine, or ten years after the start of transition.

Sources: Csaki and Tuck (2000); Lerman, Csaki, and Feder (2004); and Macours and Swinnen (2002).

(Lerman, Csaki, and Feder 2004). What makes the reforms in these nations so special is that outside of Asia, the rest of the transition world followed a different path in their policies and rights reforms.

Rights reform in CEE: restitution and restructuring

In contrast to East Asia, rights reform went much further than the transfer of use rights in CEE (Lerman, Csaki, and Feder 2004; Swinnen 1999). The dominant land reform procedure in Central Europe, the Balkans, and the Baltic countries was restitution of land to the former owners that had lost their rights during the collectivization movement in the past (see Table 4.1). If the original owners were not alive, reformers restored ownership rights to their closest heirs. Typically, land reform laws restituted land to the historical boundaries. If restitution to the original boundaries was not possible, former owners received rights to a plot of land of comparable size and quality. In some countries restitution was combined with other land reform programmes, for example, voucher privatization (Hungary), distribution of state land (Romania), or the leasing of state-owned land (Czech Republic). If successful, the new form of farming theoretically would be more efficient since land would become a marketed input that could be transferred to the most efficient producers and would provide operators with better incentives. The new farm managers would be free to adopt a more efficient mix of inputs. Initially, however, there was a danger that restitution would result in a fragmentation of farms and a fall in efficiency (or at least a period of adjustment) since the pre-Socialist distribution of land differed from the distribution of operational farms in the immediate pre-reform period.

While the restitution process resulted in the fragmentation of ownership, for several reasons it did not necessarily lead to a fragmentation of farms (see Figure 4.2). Mathijs and Swinnen (1998) illustrate how the nature of transaction costs in land markets actually led to a consolidation of land. Restitution in many countries gave land back to individuals that were no longer active in agriculture, most commonly to either former farmers or their heirs. Except for the case in some of the poorer countries, the new landowners did not return to farming and primarily were interested in renting their land. Because the search and negotiations costs of identifying individuals that were willing to rent the land were so high, the easiest way for the new land owners to find a renter was to contact those that were already using the land. Consequently, in most cases the new lessees became those that had been involved with farming on the large pre-reform farms.

Transaction costs also favoured the large farmers from the point of view of their search for land to rent. Almost all of those that farmed after reform were those that were active in agriculture prior to reform. Most were farm workers or cooperative members. Since land was restituted to people outside agriculture, if they wanted to stay in farming, they were forced to search for the owners of the land and strike a rental contract. However, since the management of the large farms was closely involved in the restitution process, they had an information advantage in identifying the new owners. Transaction costs on both the supply and demand side gave an advantage to large farms. As a result, after restitution, farm size did not fragment as much as had been feared. Although a small farming class did emerge everywhere, many large farms did not disappear and the agricultural sector in several CEE countries remained characterized by a dual farm structure (Sarris, Doucha, and Mathijs 1999).[6]

In the course of transition, however, different mixes of farm structures emerged in different nations in CEE (see Table 4.2). Analyses of CEE farm restructuring often distinguish between individual family farms (that is, a farm operated by an individual family) and corporate farms (that is, a farm that is managed by a manager, whether acting as a manager of a shareholding corporation or acting as a manager of a cooperative). The main characteristics of an individual family farm are twofold: one, it is the family that has almost complete say over the operation of the farm (that is, the individual family has full or nearly full control rights); and, two, it is the individual family that is the residual claimant to the farm's profits (that is, the individual family has complete income rights to the farming operation).

Individual farming dominates now in several Baltic and Balkan countries. In contrast, large-scale, privatized corporate farms still use most of the land in Central European countries, such as Slovakia and the Czech Republic. The corporate farms, all of which resulted from organizational restructuring of the collective and state farms, are also far from a homogeneous organizational form. Observers in CEE find joint-stock companies, limited-liability partnerships, and agricultural cooperatives operating in the same economic environment.

Although decollectivization did not result in a complete shift to individual farming, in several countries in CEE incentives improved significantly. The reforms basically gave control and income rights to the managers of the various organizational forms. The new organizations no longer guaranteed employment to their shareholders. Moreover, they were forced to operate under hard budget constraints with a real threat of bankruptcy proceedings in the cases where they defaulted on their loans. This radically changed the organizational behaviour of farm enterprises. Many of the large farms turned into market-driven corporations (Lerman, Csaki, and Feder 2004). With such incentives managers set out to improve the efficiency of the farms. One result of the changed incentive structure is that many of the farms cut back substantially in their labour use by laying off workers (Swinnen, Dries, and Macours 2005). And, as we will see, in these countries production rose as output per worker rose.

Rights reforms in CIS countries: paper shares and poor incentives

In most CIS countries, such as Russia, Ukraine, Belarus, and most of Central Asia, land reform proceeded more gradually and procedurally in a different way from in East Asia or CEE (see Table 4.1).[7] Unlike restitutions, reformers in CIS nations were generally supposed to follow a two-step process, although in practice the process was not always followed completely (Lerman, Csaki, and Feder 2004). In the first part, reformers transferred land from state ownership to ownership by the collective, which typically consisted of people that were living and working on the collective farms. In the second part, ownership rights were then supposed to be given to the individuals. In fact, in many nations individual households only received certificates of entitlement to land that had been shifted to the protective care of the collective. Although the certificates were frequently called land shares, they were, in fact, 'paper shares' that did not establish a direct link between a specific plot of land and an individual. As a result, land reform in most CIS nations often resulted in the large-scale shift of landownership to the collective, not to individual owners.

At least in the first decade of the reform, the share distribution system created major obstacles for restructuring CIS farms and did not always provide strong incentives to the producer (Prosterman and Hanstad 1999). Leaders in almost all of the countries that used share distribution also banned agricultural land from being sold or purchased during the first decade of reform (Lerman, Csaki, and Feder 2004).[8] Several of the countries have also created additional restrictions on land rights. For example, farmers in Belarus, Turkmenistan, and Uzbekistan cannot transfer use rights among themselves. Potential users of land also face high transaction costs in accessing land since the property rights on specific plots are unclear (Uzun 2000). As Uzun (2000:8) observes: 'land share owners do not know where their land shares are located; managers of agricultural enterprises have an opportunity to use the land owned by citizens freely and without controls; and workers, still, after nine years of reforms, do not clearly understand their choices.'[9]

The limitations on access to land also clearly dampen incentives to use it efficiently. Weak rights reduce pressure for restructuring of existing farm organizations by shielding them from competition for land use. Under such a system, few individuals have strong incentives to undertake any substantial investment in the physical land, equipment, or management reorganization.

The partial effect of the adoption of the share distribution on outcomes in farm restructuring can be best illustrated by the case of Russia and Ukraine. The shift towards individual farming of land was limited (see Table 4.2). During the first decade of transition most of the land remained in use by large-scale former collective and state farms. Although, as in Central Europe, former collective and state farms have taken on new names, such as joint-stock companies, limited-liability partnerships, agricultural cooperatives, and collective enterprises, the restructuring was often superficial, and traditional functions and inefficient allocation of production factors continued (Lerman and Csaki 1997; Sedik 1997). According to Lerman, Csaki, and Feder (2004) the main change appeared in the abolition of production plans. However, because of continued dependency of farms on political authorities, the production plans of the local government continued to influence production behaviour. In some countries explicit intervention through the issuance of production plans continues in case of strategic commodities, such as cotton in Turkmenistan and Uzbekistan.[10]

Despite the pessimistic record of rights reform in CIS nations, some reports suggest that by the end of the 1990s there may have been more changes than were evident in traditional statistical sources (see Table 4.2). In many of the CIS countries the share of output from individual farms was much larger than their share in land use. This partially reflects the fact that, on average, individual farming may be more productive and that farmers typically produce a different set of more labour-intensive, high value added commodities on their own plots. Moreover, at least in some regions, household farms, operating on their own small plots, but sometimes with some rented land, were able to make progress in adapting to new market conditions. In Russia this is especially the case in some of the more reformist regions in which regional policies allowed more experimentation with private agriculture (O'Brien, Patsiorkovski, and Dershem 2000). However, as in the pre-reform period, the higher productivity can also be explained by the symbiotic relationship that continues to exist between large-scale farms and many individual farms. Amelina (2000) shows that even in the reform era, households frequently

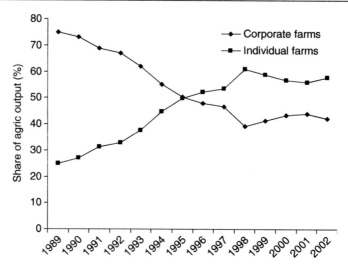

Figure 4.3 Agriculture output by farm organization in Ruzzia,1989–2002.
Source: Goskomstat.

use the large-scale farms as a way to access inputs and market their goods. Despite 'help' from inputs that leaked out from the formal system, the record also clearly demonstrates that in places where reform was allowed, the improved incentives contributed to productivity growth and this in turn has encouraged greater shifts to private holdings. In Russia, for example, the share of land farmed by individuals increased from 25 per cent in 1989 to 60 per cent in 1999 (see Figure 4.3).

In some of the slowest reforming countries, such as Turkmenistan and Uzbekistan, policy changes in the second half of the 1990s have strengthened the development of so-called intra-farm leasing (Kandiyoti 2003; Lerman and Brooks 2001). Within the framework of the former collective farms land is leased to family groups. Control rights are still limited; the leases are subject to state orders for strategic products, such as grains and cotton. In Uzbekistan, the former collective farms provide a range of services to the farms, including access to inputs and access to water. However, these are as much used to enforce production plans and extract rents from the farms as they are to assist them (Pomfret 2000, 2002*b*).

4.3. Liberalization and the development of market institutions

In addition to property rights reform and transforming incentives, the other major task of reformers is to create more efficient institutions of exchange.

Markets—whether classic competitive ones or some workable substitute—increase efficiency by facilitating transactions among agents to allow specialization and trade and by providing information through a pricing mechanism to producers and consumers about the relative scarcity of resources. But markets, in order to function efficiently, require supporting institutions to ensure competition, define and enforce property rights and contracts, ensure access to credit and finance, and provide information (McMillan 1997; World Bank 2001). These institutions were either absent in the Communist countries or, if they existed, were inappropriate for a market system. For example, in most countries central planning agencies directed production and other economic transactions and their directives served to enforce contracts involving exchanges among various agents in the chain. Market liberalization requires the elimination of central planning, but to do so successfully requires the process to be executed in a way that will allow producers to continue to have access to inputs and marketing channels while the necessary market-supporting institutions are emerging. In this section in order to document how transition countries have taken different paths in market liberalization, we consider three types of ways institutions of exchange have emerged: through the process of market liberalization; by the increased ability to enforce exchange contracts; and on the basis of how well reformers or some alternative institutions were able to guarantee access to input and output markets during transition.

Market emergence in CEE and CIS: the collapse of exchange, institution rebuilding

On the eve of transition, the agro-food systems in CEE and the CIS countries were organized much as in the West with specialized companies at various stages of the chain, such as food-processing and marketing companies (downstream firms) and fertilizer, machinery, and feed-producing and supply enterprises and agricultural banks (upstream firms). While there was specialization on a functional basis, the companies at various stages of the production and marketing chain operated in an environment that was centrally planned and vertically integrated.

The reform path taken in most of the CEE and CIS nations, although implemented with variations in speed, was predicated mostly on removing central planning and privatizing the up- and downstream companies. Reformers in the most aggressive countries began to liberalize markets at about the same time that they privatized farms, liberalized prices, and cut subsidies. Control and ownership of tens of thousands of firms shifted.

While such actions are part of the rapid market liberalization scheme, the removal of the central planning and its system of allocation and control, in the absence of new institutions to enforce contracts, distribute information, and finance intermediation, caused serious disruptions throughout the food economy (Blanchard and Kremer 1997; Gow and Swinnen 1998; Roland and Verdier 1999; Stiglitz 1999). One of the most serious problems for farms was access to credit for investment and working capital (Hobbs, Kerr, and Gaisford 1997). With farm profitability collapsing due to the falling terms of trade, internal financial resources became limited. External finance was difficult to obtain during early transition (OECD 1998). Formal sources of credit, such as agricultural banks, were themselves facing restructuring and macroeconomic reforms. Financial market liberalization made external credit scarce and expensive. When there was credit from formal or informal sources, it was directed towards more profitable activities, such as trading, which frequently returned high and quick profits.

Problems accessing physical inputs appear mostly in fertilizer use for crop production and feed use for livestock production. Disruptions in supply contributed to the dramatic fall in input use over the first years of transition. Fertilizer use collapsed to around 30 per cent of its pre-transition level in virtually all CEE and CIS countries (see Table 2.4). Unable to buy feed, livestock operations slaughtered large fractions of their herds (Bjornlund et al. 2002). The feed scarcity-induced cullings contributed to a massive decline in the animal stock during the first five years, from around 30 per cent in Central Europe and the European CIS to more than 50 per cent in the Baltic countries (see Table 2.4).[11]

One of the clearest manifestations of the institutional disruptions in the agro-food chain is the contract enforcement problems that resulted in delayed payments for product deliveries and labour. A survey of food companies in Central Europe identified payment delays as one of the most severe barriers to growth (Gorton, Buckwell, and Davidova 2000). Data from East European farms show that payment delays are correlated with profitability problems (Gow and Swinnen 1998). A 1997 survey of Hungarian agricultural enterprises found that 61 per cent of farms suffered contract breaches in the form of delayed payments and that these negatively affected profits (Cungu and Swinnen 2003). These delays, in the presence of high inflation, contributed importantly to the cash flow problems throughout the agro-food chain and ultimately created serious financing constraints.[12]

Contract enforcement and non-payment problems contributed to the widespread use of barter exchange in CIS countries, such as Russia and

Ukraine. For example, in the early years of the reforms estimates put the share of barter transactions at 75 to 85 per cent in Russia (Bruszt 2000). In several countries, the government was as much part of the problem as it was part of the solution, since farms used barter to avoid taxation that could occur because the government could monitor formal bank transactions. Furthermore, as the government did not impose hard budget constraints (for example, it did not allow bankruptcy procedures to occur), farms continued their practice of not paying bills and accumulating debts in several CIS countries, including Russia, Kazakhstan, and Ukraine until the late 1990s (Csaki et al. 2002; Von Cramon-Taubadel, Zorya, and Striewe 2001).

Finally, the absence of market-supporting institutions constrained the process of farm restructuring. Households, in weighing their prospects of farming on their own, frequently opted to stay with the collective farms, or in some of the new forms of farmer associations that had appeared, in order to retain access to inputs and to marketing outlets (Lerman et al. 2003; O'Brien and Wegren 2002; Rizov et al. 2001; Sabates-Wheeler 2002). Institutions of exchange, no matter how poorly they functioned, in many nations were still largely organized around the former structure because of the absence of reform in the up- and downstream sectors.

Furthermore, in an environment in which there are no organizations that want to deal with supplying inputs to small farms—either because the existing organizations had no incentives to do so or because new companies targeting small farmers did not emerge—political lobbying and bureaucratic connections began to play a role in facilitating change and act to discourage restructuring. In countries such as Russia and Ukraine, governments discriminate openly against independent private farmers (Csaki and Zuschlag 2003). For example, to obtain fertilizer Russian farms usually need the help of political authorities, such as the regional government. Farms get fertilizer at low prices in exchange for the commitment to sell their output to the authorities (Liefert, Gardner, and Serova 2003). Amelina (2000) documents how in many Russian regions local governments use so-called commodity credit schemes to support former collective farms, irrespective of their profitability.[13] These 'soft' outside funds allow the collective farm management to continue to subsidize inputs for their employees under the form of in-kind payments. The funds are also used to provide funds that collective employees can use to buy inputs for their household plots. The system, however, discriminates against independent, individual farms as it excludes them from such credit access and from having access to the lower input prices. Moreover, the commodity credit scheme had another, equally harmful effect (Csaki and Zuschlag 2003). Because commercial credit sources cannot compete against the subsidized credit schemes, the attention of alternative sources of finance dried up for individual farmers. The result is that only a small share of the output from 'individual farming' in Russia (see Table 4.2 and Figure 4.3) comes from registered individual 'private farms', and most from so-called 'household plots'.[14] Similarly, in countries, such as Kazakhstan, most grain farms continue to depend on local authorities to supply key inputs and for finance for these inputs through the issue of local authority guarantees for the provision of seed and fuel by suppliers on a barter against the season's production (Gray 2000).

Although, in its initial years after transition, the food economy in much of CEE operated within a setting of incomplete input and output markets, a combination of public policy measures and private initiatives facilitated the emergence of market-supporting institutions. Those nations that implemented market liberalization reforms fastest were the first to recover (de Melo et al. 2001; Wyplosz 2000). Besides general institutional and macroeconomic reforms, which were important prerequisites, various CEE governments have also implemented public policies targeted at reducing institutional constraints in the agro-food chain. For example, in some CEE nations, leaders began warehouse receipt and loan guarantee programmes to overcome the problems faced by farmers in finding collateral for their farm loans (OECD 1999).

A number of private initiatives have also been able to overcome market imperfections and institutional constraints (Gow and Swinnen 1998, 2001). The most successful ones frequently depend on private enforcement mechanisms within the framework of specifically designed contracts or other arrangements (Johnson, McMillan, and Woodruff 1999; McMillan and Woodruff 1999). In other cases firms have turned to vertical integration. Such contracts with private agents, and other moves to vertically integrate, act as substitutes for missing or imperfect public enforcement institutions (Klein and Murphy 1997). As a result of initiatives from both the public and private sectors, the agro-food chain's financing problems in some cases have been overcome by the actions of new and restructured food-processing firms and input suppliers (Pospisil 2001; Szekelyhidi 2001). For example, restructured food-processing companies provide inputs to farmers and even set up programmes to fund investments. In return, producers deliver products to the firms.

The input provision programme also assists farmers with gaining access to physical inputs, such as seeds, fertilizer, and pesticides. The most straightforward approach is pre-payment of inputs and working capital loans. For example, processors of oilseeds and grains provide advanced payments for chemical inputs and fertilizer. Dairy processing companies pre-finance feed for farms that deliver milk to them and provide loans for milking equipment. Input supply firms in some countries also provide payment guarantees for farm input purchases. The rise of equipment leasing services provided by machinery suppliers is another example of how an institutional innovation helped mitigate the farm's collateral problems in financing new equipment.

In CEE firms that were taken over by foreign investors initiated many contractual innovations. For example, foreign managers of food processors typically provide technical and financial assistance to farms as part of supply contracts in order to ensure a stable and minimum quality supply of produce from their suppliers (Dries and Swinnen 2004a). Empirical evidence suggests that there are important spillovers from these contract innovations on domestic companies that quickly start imitating successful contracting and vertical integration programmes introduced by foreign firms (Foster 1999; Gow, Streeter, and Swinnen 2000).

Currently in the countries that have most successfully created a system of market institutions, a complex of public and private and formal and informal institutions has emerged that is capable of enforcing contracts and supporting access to inputs and output markets. For example, recent surveys of farmers in Poland found that almost three-quarters used formal bank loans and trade credit from processing companies to finance investments in equipment and technology (Dries and Swinnen 2004b). While there was a significant difference in investments and product quality of farms supplying to foreign-owned dairies compared to local dairies in 1996, this difference had all but disappeared by 2001, reflecting important convergence in standards, contracting, and management practices in the agro-food chain—a combination of private actions and public policies both imposing tougher standards and securing the emergence of market-supporting institutions.

The emergence of markets has progressed considerably more slowly in most CIS countries because slow policy reforms have constrained both the development of public institutions that facilitate trading as well as private institutional innovations (Csaki and Tuck 2000; EBRD 2002). Since the late 1990s, however, there are signs of a turnaround in some CIS countries. For example, in Russia, after the 1998 financial crisis, important new developments have occurred in the food economy. A combination of enhanced policy credibility under the Putin government, minimal reforms, a more stable macroeconomic framework, and increased profitability of domestic food production has induced significant investments in the Russian food economy. An important share of the investments has come directly and indirectly from local financial groups. As in CEE, investments in the food industry have affected farm performance by reducing the financial constraints that producers face through contractual arrangements (Rylko 2002). Similarly, in Kazakhstan, recent downstream investments and contracting of grain traders with the farms have alleviated cash flow problems and relaxed input constraints at the production level (EBRD 2002; Gray 2000). That said, much remains to be done in building market institutions in transition countries and particular so in CIS countries.

Market emergence in China: a gradual shift from plan to market

In contrast to the CEE and the CIS countries, leaders in China did not dismantle the planned economy in the initial stages of reform in favour of liberalized markets (Rozelle 1996). Sicular (1988*a*, 1988*b*, 1995), Perkins (1988), and Lin (1992) all discuss how China's leadership had little intention of letting the market play anything but a minor supplemental guidance role in the early reforms period in the early 1980s. In fact, the major changes to agricultural commerce in the early 1980s almost exclusively centred on increasing the purchase prices of crops (Sicular 1988*b*; Watson 1994). The decision to raise prices, however, should *not* be considered as a move to liberalize markets, since planners in the Ministry of Commerce made the changes administratively and the price changes were mostly executed by the national network of grain procurement stations acting under direction of the State Grain Bureau.

An examination of policies and the extent of marketing activity in the early 1980s illustrates the limited extent of changes in the marketing environment of China's food economy before 1985. It is true that reformers did allow farmers increased discretion to produce and market crops in ten planning categories, such as vegetables, fruits, and coarse grains. Moreover, by 1984, the state only claimed control over twelve commodities, including rice, wheat, maize, soybeans, peanuts, rapeseed, and several other cash crops (Sicular 1988*b*). However, while this may seem to represent a significant move towards liberalization, the crops that remained almost entirely under the planning authority of the government still accounted for more than 95 per cent of sown area in 1984. Hence, by state policy and practice, the output and marketing of almost all sown area was still directly influenced by China's planners.

Reforms proceeded with equal caution when reducing restrictions on free market trade. The decision to permit the re-establishment of free markets came in 1979, but initially only allowed farmers to trade vegetables and a limited number of other crops and livestock products within the boundaries of their own county. Reformers did gradually reduce restrictions on the distance over which trade could occur from 1980 to 1984, but as Sicular (1988*b*) and Skinner (1985) point out, the predominant marketing venue during the early 1980s was mainly local rural periodic markets. Farmers did also begin to sell their produce in urban settings, but free markets in the cities only began to appear in 1982 and 1983. In addition to these being small and infrequent, traders could not engage in the marketing of China's monopolized commodities that were still under strict control of the state procurement stations.

The record of the expansion of rural and urban markets confirms the hypothesis that market liberalization had not yet begun by the early 1980s. Although agricultural commodity markets were allowed to emerge during the 1980s, their number and size made them a small player in China's food economy. In 1984, the state procurement network still purchased more than 95 per cent of marketed grain and more than 99 per cent of the marketed cotton (Sicular 1995). In all of China's urban areas, there were only 2,000 markets in 1980, a number that rose only to 6,000 by 1984 (deBrauw, Huang, and Rozelle 2004). In Beijing in the early 1980s, there were only about 50 markets transacting around 1 million yuan of commerce per market per year. Each market site would have had to serve, on average, about 200,000 Beijing residents, each transacting only 5 yuan of business for the entire year. In other words, it would have been impossible for such a weak marketing infrastructure at that time to even come close to meeting the food needs of urban consumers.

After 1985, however, market liberalization began in earnest. Changes to the procurement system, further reductions in restrictions to trading of commodities, moves to commercialize the state grain trading system, and calls for the expansion of market construction in rural and urban areas led to a surge in market-oriented activity (Sicular 1995). For example, in 1980, there were only 241,000 private and semi-private trading enterprises registered with the State Markets Bureau; by 1990, there were more than 5.2 million (deBrauw, Huang, and Rozelle 2004). Between 1980 and 1990, the per capita volume of transactions of commerce in Beijing urban food markets rose almost 200 times. Private traders handled more than 30 per cent of China's grain by 1990, and more than half of the rest was bought and sold by commercialized state grain trading companies, many of which had begun to behave like private traders (Rozelle et al. 2000).

China moved equally slowly in its liberalization of input markets (Stone 1988; Ye and Rozelle 1994). During the pre-reform era, the state distributed all key inputs such as chemical fertilizer through the government-controlled network of agricultural input supply stations. During a time when many inputs in many regions were scarce, local officials were issued coupons that gave communes that right to purchase at least part of the inputs they needed. In the initial years of reform when decollectivization was occurring, leaders did virtually nothing to limit the role of the state in input allocation. Indeed, private sales of nitrogen fertilizer were restricted and the state continued to completely control all chemical fertilizer distribution.

Even after the start of liberalization in both output and input markets in 1985, the process was still partial and executed in a start and stop manner (Sicular 1995). For example, in the case of fertilizer, Ye and Rozelle (1994) show that after an early attempt at market liberalization in 1986 and 1987, perceived instability in the rural economy in 1988 led to sharp retrenchments. Agricultural officials only took controls back off fertilizer marketing and began encouraging private trade in the early 1990s. Lin, Cai, and Li (1996) argue that leaders were mainly afraid of the disruption that would occur if the institutions through which leaders controlled the main goods in the food economy (such as fodder, grain, and fertilizer) were eliminated without the institutions in place to support more efficient market exchange.

However, it was only after twenty years of market liberalization that the state had largely abdicated its responsibilities for grain and inputs trade. By the mid-1990s, about 50 per cent of fertilizer was sold by private traders. In 2000, according to a survey of 1,200 households in six provinces, fertilizer sales at the farm gate level were almost exclusively handled by the private sector. Likewise, despite the failed attempts by the government to remonopolize grain trade in the mid-1990s, by 2001, the State Grain Bureau commercialized its remaining grain trading divisions and tens of thousands of private traders dominate grain trade. For example, according to a survey by Xie (2002), in 2001 there were more than 2,000 private rice wholesalers trading in Beijing, more than 3,000 in Shanghai, and more than 5,000 in Guangzhou. Nearly all rice moves through their hands, completely bypassing the state. Hence, China's markets have become more integrated, transaction costs have fallen, and there are increasingly fewer arbitrage opportunities left unexploited (Park et al. 2002).

Notes

1. Although the statistical bureau did report a 'market' price at that time (which actually was about the same level as the above quota price), such a small amount of grain (and less of fibre and oil seeds) was sold on markets, since rules still tightly controlled the distance of shipment and the goods that could be bought and sold, that most farmers did not consider the market price as their opportunity cost.

2. To the extent that access to fertilizer improves during the reform (Stone 1988), the shadow prices of fertilizer would also have fallen, which would also encourage higher output.

3. In Poland and Yugoslavia the farm sector remained dominated by private family farms throughout the Communist regime. Hence, reforms targeted other parts of the agro-food system.

4. Gorbachev also launched a major investigation into corruption in the Uzbekistan cotton regime.

5. Romania used a mixed land reform strategy, combining both land distribution and restitution.

6. In general, the new corporate farms are smaller than the former collective and state farms, and the individual farms larger than the pre-reform household plots. The average corporate farm in CEE today is between 500 to 1,000 hectares, compared to 2,000 to 4,000 hectares for an average collective or state farm before 1990. At the same time, however, the average size of individual farms increased (Lerman et al. 2003). For example in Hungary the average size of the large scale cooperative and corporate farms declined by 50% during the first five years of reform; the average size of the family farm doubled between 1991 and 1996 (Mathijs and Vranken forthcoming).

7. The main exceptions are Armenia and Georgia (see above).

8. However, changes have been emerging in some countries in recent years. For example, Russia introduced a new land law in 2002 allowing sales of agricultural land, with some restrictions.

9. O'Brien, Patsiorkovski, and Dershem (2000) document important regional variations within Russia in land rights (e.g. in leasing), associated with differences in regional policies, and show how these have had important impacts on output and productivity variations among household farms in different regions.

10. The important role of cotton in the economy of Uzbekistan, Turkmenistan, and Tajikistan as a source of foreign exchange and tax revenue is essential to understanding the transition and the special nature of the reforms in the agricultural systems of these countries (Pomfret 2000, 2002b).

11. For example, in Russia the relative price of mixed feed more than doubled in comparison to prices of livestock products during the first years of transition and remained around that level for most of the decade (Bjornlund et al. 2002). This

contributed to the decline in the animal stock to less than half of pre-transition levels. The main exceptions to this decline in livestock are Turkmenistan, Uzbekistan, and Albania. In Albania, growth in livestock resulted from a combination of an (atypical) strong increase in relative prices of livestock over grain and the shift to small-scale livestock production with the fragmentation of the collective farming system (Macours and Swinnen 2002). In Turkmenistan and Uzbekistan, growth came about because much livestock production was already in private households, and the availability of large areas of pastures in those countries (e.g. more than 90% of agricultural land in Turkmenistan is in pastures) allowed households to switch to less feed-intensive forms of livestock production. However there also livestock productivity and herd quality declined because of diminishing availability of mixed feed (Pomfret 2000).

12. While early discussions of the finance problems focused mostly on the institutional problems, later empirical studies emphasize the profitability and cash flow problems. For example, Pederson, Brooks, and Lekhtman (1998) identify the importance of profitability and cash flow problems in the perceived 'excessive debt burden' of Russian farms. As Csaki, Lerman, and Sotnikov (2001) show, farm debt in most CIS countries increased during the 1990s because farms did not pay their obligations to government, suppliers, banks, and even workers. Another example is a 1997 Romanian survey, where farmers identify insufficient income as the key reason for their loan application being rejected (52% of the cases), much more than lack of collateral (18%) or outstanding debts (11%) (Davis and Gaburici 1999).

13. Under this 'non-cash' system, input suppliers provide goods directly to farms during the sowing season, but are not paid by the farms. Rather, the debts are assumed by the government, and written off against taxes owed to the government by the input suppliers. Farms, in return, are obliged to deliver their products (often grain) to the government, often for its use in food reserves. In the autumn, when (grain) prices are low, regional governments try to collect payments sometimes by imposing barriers to sales of the commodities outside the region (Csaki and Zuschlag 2003).

14. In all CEE and CIS countries, rural households and farm workers had household plots under the Communist system. There was a certain symbiotic relationship between the collective farm and the household plots. The small-scale farms allowed workers to add to their income by producing both for own consumption and selling some farm output. By the 1980s these household plots produced a substantial amount of output, especially for labour-intensive products such as some fruits and vegetables. Farm workers got access to cheap inputs for their household plots as they got them as in-kind compensation on the farm, or simply stole them. After 1989, in CEE the shift to individual farms was a shift to independent individual farms. While 'hybrid' structures were important in some countries (e.g. in Romania), they were limited in CEE. Hence 'individual farms' includes a mixture of 'real' family farms and

household gardens in CEE statistics. However, in countries such as Russia the development of independent individual farms was quite limited (for reasons discussed here) and household plots which were strongly linked to the large farms (in complex and informal ways) grew in importance. Therefore, the Russian statistics have differentiated between (individual) 'private farms' and 'household plots'. For example, in 1998, 'household plots' used 59% and (individual) 'private farms' 3% of total output. For consistency, however, we combine, for all countries, both types of farms in the category of 'individual farms' in the tables and figures throughout this book.

5

The Effects of the Reforms

5.1. Introduction

In Chapter 4 we analysed changes in price and subsidy policy, reforms of property rights and farm restructuring, and market liberalization in the transition economies. In this chapter we will analyse the effects of these reforms on output and productivity, based on our own studies and other studies in the literature. The efforts to identify the sources of output and productivity growth of the agricultural sectors in transition economies range from purely descriptive to the use of time-tested methodologies. Unfortunately, most studies tend towards the descriptive end of the spectrum. In many studies researchers at most examine output and productivity trends and compare them to trends of prices and periods of implementation of property rights and market liberalization reform policies. Such casual attribution of the cause and effect, if anything, is the rule, not the exception. In the rest of this chapter, we discount this part of the literature and refer to only a small number of such descriptive studies.

A subset of studies, however, uses more rigorous methods. In some cases, carefully carried out growth accounting procedures control for changes in terms of trade and fixed factors and attempt to attribute the explained rise in output to policy changes (for example McMillan, Whalley, and Zhu 1989, in China). Others use regression-based methods to isolate the sources of the changes in output and productivity. After holding physical inputs constant, some studies use primal-side models to identify the rise in output that is associated with the reform period by including a time period or continuous time variable (for example, Pingali and Xuan 1992; and Benjamin and Brandt 2001, in Vietnam).[1] The parts of the rise in output associated with the institutional change (either property rights reform, market liberalization, or both) are assumed by these studies to be the productivity effect associated with reform (or the period during which the reform policies were implemented).

Other studies adopt dual-side approaches, holding prices and other factors constant, and similarly attribute the part of the output that increases over a reform period as the reform-induced change in productivity (for example, Kurkalova and Jensen 2003). Others use both approaches (for example, Lin 1992; Macours and Swinnen 2000*a*). The importance of reform is typically demonstrated in these studies by using a decomposition procedure which divides the rise in output or (the overall increase in the growth rate) to the various factors (for example, price changes, changes in fixed factors, and reform). A smaller group of studies (for example, Jin et al. 2002, in China) uses regression and decomposition analysis to determine the factors that explain over time changes in TFP trends. Because leaders in China and Vietnam launched their reforms earlier, the most comprehensive set of studies tend to be those studying East Asia.

Despite attempts carefully to match periods of reform to regression-based analyses, the results of most studies need to be carefully interpreted because the use of time trends and time dummies by definition captures *all* systematic change that is unexplained by the other regressors included in the equation. The implicit assumption of most analysts almost always seems to be that nothing else was changing during the time. In almost all cases, however, it is likely that the failure to capture other factors, such as traditional technological change in cropping and livestock operations, means that the estimates of the impacts of reforms may be biased. Finally, although interactions among the different components of reforms (for example, price reforms are more likely to matter more if property rights reforms have given producers greater incentives) are almost certainly important, little attention is given to them.

5.2. Effects of price and subsidy reforms

Several studies show that price changes had an important influence on the performance of the agricultural sector and in part help explain observed trends in output. Using simple measures of correlations, Macours and Swinnen (2002*a*) find a positive relationship (the correlation coefficient is 0.70) between changes in output and changes in relative prices across fifteen countries during the first five years of transition. Although only being used to motivate the changes, they show that output increased only in those countries in which terms of trade increased (for example, China, Vietnam, and Albania). Empirical studies using multivariate analysis on China confirm a strong impact of these price changes on output during the first years of transition (Lin 1992; Fan 1991; Huang and Rozelle 1996; Fan and

Pardey 1997). Lin (1992), for example, finds that 15 per cent of output growth during the first six years of reform came from the rise in relative prices. Huang and Rozelle's (1996) decomposition exercise for rice demonstrates that about 10 per cent of the output between 1978 and 1984 came from the price effects.[2] In contrast, the multivariate estimates of Macours and Swinnen (2000a) show that around 50 per cent of the initial decline in crop output in eight Central European and Balkan countries was due to deteriorating terms of trade.

The direction of these movements is exactly as predicted in Chapter 3. When agriculture was taxed before reform, price reform led to rising inputs and outputs. In contrast, when agriculture was subsidized, price reform led to falling inputs and outputs.

5.3. Effects of property rights reforms

While the speed and nature of rights reform and restructuring has varied greatly across the reforming world, in those places that have carried out decollectivization, land restitutions, control rights transfers, and farm reorganization, a robust positive effect appears on output in some areas and productivity has risen in all of the areas that carried out these multi-dimensioned reforms.

East Asia

In East Asia, the changes in incentives that resulted from the property rights reforms and farm restructuring triggered strong growth in both output and productivity. In the earliest study of the reforms, McMillan, Whalley, and Zhu (1989) document that the early reforms in China sharply raised productivity, accounting for 90 per cent of the rise of output (23 per cent) between 1978 and 1984. While the strong positive link between the reforms and output has been confirmed by many other studies, the shortcomings of attributing the entire productivity rise to the reform movement generally is shown by subsequent studies. In the most definitive study on the subject, Lin (1992) estimates that China's HRS accounted for 42 to 46 per cent of the total rise in output during the early reform period (1978 to 1984). The lower effect due to property rights reform is undoubtedly due in part to the fact that Lin's estimates held other reforms measures constant—for example, pricing policy changes (accounting for 10 per cent) and nascent market liberalization policy shifts (accounting for less than 5 per cent). In addition to including independent measures of specific reform policies, the main strength of Lin's study is that he uses both primal- and dual-side models and his measure of decollectivization is a continuous variable.

Subsequent studies of China's growth, however, showed how even Lin's seminal work both over- and underestimated the impact of the early reforms on agriculture. The reform effect falls to only about 30 per cent in both Fan (1991), who uses a primal-side approach, and Huang and Rozelle (1996), who mainly use a dual-side approach. The fall in the return to decollectivization is explicitly shown in Huang and Rozelle (who use Lin's measure of the shift the HRS as well as controlling for prices and most of the other factors that Lin controlled for) to be due to the inclusion of variables that hold constant technological change. In contrast, a number of researchers have suggested that the effect of the reforms exceeded the direct impact on the agricultural sector. Rises in surplus in the agricultural sector created by HRS triggered a number of subsequent growth dynamics, providing labour for rural industry's take-off in the mid-1980s (McKinnon 1993), fuelling the nation's overall industrialization drive later in the reforms (Chen, Jefferson, and Singh 1992), and creating demand for the products of firms in other parts of the economy (Qian and Xu 1998).

Similarly, the Vietnamese Doi Moi reform induced strong growth in both output and productivity. Rice production, the nation's primary crop, grew on an annual basis at the rate of 3.14 per cent between 1982 and 1987 up from less than 0.5 per cent between 1976 and 1981 (Pingali and Xuan 1992). Econometric analysis showed that productivity-led growth boosted output by around 15 per cent during the early post-reform period. Noting that both technological change and market liberalization in Vietnam's agricultural sector were virtually absent during the early 1980s, Pingali and Xuan assert that almost all of the growth should be attributed to the property rights reforms. Clearly in the case of China and Vietnam, property rights reforms have been associated with the rise of output and productivity. This means that the positive effects were greater than the negative ones. This is exactly what the theory will predict.

CEE and the CIS

In contrast, in the CEE and the CIS countries in which effective reforms had been implemented, privatization of farming has generally produced two different effects on output, although one must be careful in attributing causality, due to the complex links between rights reform, restructuring, and output and the interactions with the other reforms that are occurring in many countries. For example, the hard budget constraints imposed on producers by reformers reduced subsidies and led to falling inputs and output disruption. On the other hand, greater incentives increased effort, raised technical efficiency, and increased output. Calculations based on the multivariate analysis of Macours and Swinnen (2000a), which also holds constant the price effect, indicate that in CEE the disruption created by the reduced subsidy effect dominated in early transition. The negative output effect due to reductions in input (a −70 per cent fall) was mitigated, but not fully offset, by the increase in output from gains in technical efficiency (a 45 per cent rise). The net effect was negative (−25 per cent) and explains around a quarter of the total output fall in CEE agriculture in early transition.

However, in countries in which rights reforms and farm restructuring did not improve productivity, the negative output effect of the decline in input use was reinforced by a fall in efficiency. Estimates by Kurkalova and Carriquiry (2002) and Kurkalova and Jensen (2003) indicate that in Ukraine falling input use and declining efficiency reinforce each other during early transition. Both studies estimate company-level (or corporate farm-level) efficiency using stochastic production frontier analysis. They then go on to explain differences in inefficiency levels over time as a function of price changes, input adjustments, and year effects. Although somewhat ad hoc (in that they use relative prices to explain technical efficiency differences among companies), their results are persuasive in showing that the decline in the use of inputs accounts for about the half of the total output decline in collective farms. They also blame a decline in technical efficiency (of 15 per cent) between 1989 and 1992 on general reform matters.[3]

Total factor productivity estimates on the FSU countries between 1992 and 1997 by Lerman et al. (2003) are also consistent with the significant impact of rights reforms and restructuring on productivity. Their analysis indicates strong productivity growth in Baltic countries in which reforms were implemented most strongly. Total factor productivity also increased strongly in Armenia and Georgia, two Transcaucasian countries which implemented strong individualized land rights and dramatically shifted to individual farming even though the nations were recovering from a series of natural disasters and war-related incidents. In contrast, TFP declined in the Central Asian republics in which reforms lagged most. While this is the most comprehensive study of productivity in the CIS nations, their link between the rise in TFP and reform should be interpreted cautiously. Using one observation per state per year, the authors estimate a production function and implicitly assume that the unexplained change in the output over time (or productivity changes) is due to transition policies. Unfortunately, a paucity of data makes it impossible for Lerman and his co-authors to create a model explaining TFP, an approach that would enable them to identify more precisely the exact causes of the changes in productivity.

The importance of distinguishing between ownership types in studies that are seeking to link reforms with productivity is perhaps best illustrated in the cases of Russia and Ukraine.[4] Whatever growth occurred during the first decade of transition in Russia and Ukraine seems to have occurred on household plot production, the only place where rights were effectively in private use. Johnson et al. (1994), Kurkalova and Carriquiry (2002), Sotnikov (1998), and Sedik, Trueblood, and Arnade (1999) find declining productivity on corporate farms in Russia and Ukraine. Trueblood and Osborne (2002) discover that productivity on corporate farms declined by 2.1 per cent annually after 1993 and continued to decline until 1998. Their analysis does not find any indication of a productivity rebound in Russia in the late 1990s. Interestingly, all studies that find a negative effect of rights reforms on TFP exclude household farming. In contrast, Lerman et al. (2003), who include both corporate and household farming in their analysis, find that productivity in Russian agriculture increased by 1.4 per cent annually between 1992 and 1997. Similarly in Ukraine, Lerman et al. (2003) and Murova, Trueblood, and Coble (2004) find that TFP in production improved slightly during transition when they include both corporate and household farms in their analyses. Their results suggest that the positive effects come mostly from the shift to household farming.[5]

Technology, endogenous farm restructuring, and the nature of productivity gains

Looking inside transition regions in CEE and the CIS nations, as in the case of East Asia, illustrates a link between technology, policy and performance. Although gains in productivity have come from both rights reforms and organizational restructuring, the relative importance of each component differs between countries reflecting technology and policy differences (Macours and Swinnen 2002). In countries with labour-intensive technologies the shift from large-scale collective farming to small-scale individual farming caused dramatic gains in technical efficiency with relatively small losses in scale efficiency. In capital- and land-intensive regions, gains in labour productivity, if any, came primarily from large farms shedding labour with privatization of the farms.

These different sources of productivity gains are not coincidental. Technology has an important impact on the relative efficiency of different farm organizations, and thus on the incentives for farm restructuring. Technology affects both the costs and benefits of the shift to individual farming, as summarized in Figure 5.1. An important factor in the optimal scale of farming is transaction costs in labour management. Large operations in agriculture face transaction costs because of principal–agent problems and monitoring costs in labour contracting, which are typically large in agriculture (Pollak 1985; Schmitt 1991). Hence, individual farming will improve labour effort and a farmer's control over farm activities and this will lead to efficiency gains. However, the importance of these efficiency gains vary with specialization and technology (Allen and Lueck 1998). Since the greatest improvement in efficiency from farm individualization is attributable to rising effort from better incentives, the benefits will be relatively greater for systems in which labour plays a greater role.

However, there are also costs that are incurred when collective or corporate farms are broken up into individual farms. In many cases there are

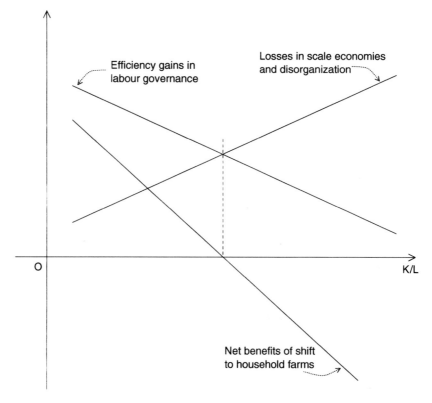

Figure 5.1 The impact of technology on the costs and benefits of the shift to individual farming.

two major types of costs. First, there is one set of costs that could arise due to the loss in scale economies. As in the case of the incentive effects, the impact on scale economies will be sensitive to the nature of the technology. The economy of scale losses may be considerable in the case of capital-intensive production systems, systems in which we would expect economies of scale to be relatively significant since there are many fixed expenses and many large assets used in farming activities. In countries in which farming is labour intensive and few capital inputs are used, however, such losses could be minimal.

Second, there also may be costs associated with disorganization that will occur with the restructuring of farms. The costs will arise from the mismatch that can occur between the farm's needs for inputs, services, and equipment and the infrastructure that has been set up to provide those inputs and services. Initially designed for large-scale farming, the inputs and services that the nation's agricultural input supply chain is set up to provide are not always suitable for individual farms. Hence, newly formed individual farms may require an entirely different set of inputs, services, and equipment. The disorganization and economies of scale costs could be high (initially) if such inputs, services, and equipment play an important role in the local farming systems. Again, this is affected by technology. These disruption costs are more likely to be lower in labour-intensive systems than in more advanced, integrated, and capital-intensive agricultural systems.

The importance of technology in the growth of individual farming is illustrated empirically by Figure 5.2, which shows a strong positive

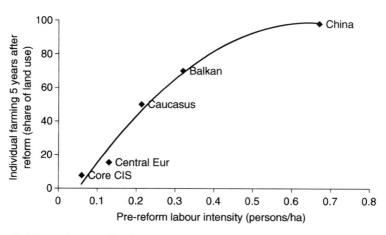

Figure 5.2 Pre-reform technology and the growth of individual farming.

relationship between the pre-reform labour intensity of farming and the importance of individual farming five years after the start of transition.[6] As such, the farm restructuring process, in particular the growth of individual farming, is at least partially endogenous in this transition process.

Table 5.1 Selected initial condition indicators for immediate pre-reform period in transition countries

	Share of agr. in employment (%)	GNP/capita (PPP$ 1989)	Labour/ land (Pers./ha)	Agr. land in individual farms (%)	CMEA export (% of GDP)	Years central planning
East Asia						
China	69.8	800	0.672	5–10	0.01	42
Viet Nam	70.2	1,100	2.298	5	0.05	21
Laos	n.a.	n.a.	n.a.	54	n.a.	16
Myanmar	66.2	n.a.	0.970	99[a]	n.a.	38
Central Asia						
Mongolia	32.7	2,100	0.002	0	0.17	n.a.
Kazakhstan	22.6	5,130	0.008	0	0.18	71
Kyrgyzstan	32.6	3,180	0.054	4	0.21	71
Tajikistan	43.0	3,010	0.185	4	0.22	71
Turkmenistan	41.8	4,230	0.015	2	0.34	71
Uzbekistan	39.2	2,740	0.109	5	0.24	71
Transcaucasus						
Armenia	17.4	5,530	0.218	7	0.21	71
Azerbaijan	30.7	4,620	0.203	2	0.33	70
Georgia	25.2	5,590	0.217	12	0.19	70
European CIS						
Belarus	19.1	7,010	0.105	7	0.45	72
Moldova	32.5	4,670	0.269	7	0.25	51
Russia	12.9	7,720	0.044	2	0.13	74
Ukraine	19.5	5,680	0.118	6	0.25	74
Baltics						
Estonia	12.0	8,900	0.072	4	0.27	51
Latvia	15.5	8,590	0.085	4	0.31	51
Lithuania	18.6	6,430	0.098	9	0.34	51
Central Europe						
Czech Rep	9.9	8,600	0.122	1	0.10	42
Hungary	17.9	6,810	0.131	13	0.10	42
Poland	26.4	5,150	0.258	76	0.17	41
Slovakia	12.2	7,600	0.139	2	0.10	42
Balkans						
Albania	49.4	1,400	0.627	3	0.02	47
Bulgaria	18.1	5,000	0.132	14	0.15	43
Romania	28.2	3,470	0.204	14	0.03	42
Slovenia	11.8	9,200	0.116	83	0.07	46

Note: Pre-reform indicators are from 1978 for China, 1981 for Vietnam, 1986 for Laos, 1989 for the CEECs and Myanmar, and 1990 for the FSU and Mongolia.

[a] Own estimation.

Source: Macours and Swinnen (2002).

In countries with labour-intensive technologies there is a strong shift from large-scale collective farming to small-scale individual farming and with it strong gains in technical efficiency with relatively small losses in scale efficiency,[7] as we documented above. For example, in countries such as China, Vietnam, Albania, Armenia, Georgia, and Romania, the gains in productivity came mostly from the shift to household farming when land was distributed to rural households (see Table 4.2). In all these countries the man/land ratio was over 0.2 persons per hectare (see Table 5.1) and TFP increased strongly during early transition (between 4 per cent and 9 per cent annually) when individual farming grew from 8 per cent of total land use on average to 84 per cent on average. [8]

In contrast, in capital- and land-intensive regions, large-scale corporate farming remained important and productivity gains came primarily from large farms shedding labour with privatization of the farms. For example in the Czech Republic, Slovakia, and Hungary, countries in which farming was more capital and land intensive (man/land ratio of 0.14 or less), gains in labour productivity came primarily from large farms shedding labour with privatization of the farms.[9] During the first five years of transition, labour use declined by 44 per cent on average in these three countries, yielding an annual increase in labour productivity of 7.5 per cent on average, while individual farms used only 15 per cent of the land.[10]

5.4. Effects of market liberalization

Few authors have attempted to quantify the gains from market liberalization. Part of the problem may be the short period of analyses, the inability of standard methodologies and measures or indicators of market liberalization to separate efficiency gains of market reform from overall gains in the reforming economy, and the breadth of the studies. For China, Wen (1993) found total factor productivity (TFP) growth had stopped in the post-1985 period, a trend he blames on the failure of the market liberalization stage of reform. There are two shortcomings of Wen's conclusions. First his analysis ends in 1990, a period that might be too early to have allowed the liberalization reforms to take effect. Second, he is only examining the net change in TFP and does not account for other factors that could be affecting productivity. Holding the effect of technology constant and using data up to 1995, Jin et al. (2002) find that TFP growth restarts in the 1990s, a finding that they claim could be linked to increased liberalization of the economy. Like Wen, however, they do not explicitly examine the improvements in efficiency that are associated with market development. Fan (1999) uses stochastic frontier production decomposition analysis to isolate the efficiency gains of Jiangsu provincial rice producers in the late reform era, a time when most of the property rights reforms had already been implemented and when market liberalization was just getting started. Fan finds that there have been only limited gains in allocative efficiency since 1984, a result that he suggests is due to the partial nature of China's market liberalization. Unfortunately, Fan does not explicitly model the interactions between property rights reform and market liberalization. Also, his study examines only one crop in one province, a fact that limits the generalization of his study, since it is possible that many of the gains from market liberalization may come from shifting among crops (and between cropping and non-cropping activities).

The only truly systematic attempts at trying to measure the returns to market liberalization in China are deBrauw, Huang, and Rozelle (2000, 2004). These papers develop measures of increased responsiveness and flexibility within a dynamic adjustment cost framework (as developed by Epstein 1981) to estimate the return to market liberalization reforms, holding the incentive reforms and other factors constant. The authors find that the behaviour of producers in China has been affected by market liberalization, but that the gains have been relatively small. Small gains in responsiveness (measured by price elasticities of factor demand for variable inputs—in this case, fertilizer) between the early and late reform periods are attributed to the gradual market liberalizing changes of the late 1980s. Farmers also have increased their speed of adjustment of quasi-fixed factors (which in the case of China's agriculture includes labour and sown area) to price changes (and other shifts in exogenous factors) between the early and late reform period. The magnitude of the gains in efficiency from increased responsiveness and flexibility in the late reform period, however, is substantially less in percentage terms (less than 1 per cent per year) than that from the incentive reforms in the early reform period (up to 7 per cent per year or about 40 per cent over the whole period). But, although the gains are small, they are still positive, and China's gradual market reform policy appears to have avoided the collapse that was experienced throughout CEE and CIS nations. Unfortunately, the results of the deBrauw paper cannot shed light on the interactions among property rights reform and market liberalization since it relies on the assumption that the time period of the reform identifies the effect of individual policies (that is, all of the property rights reforms were complete before 1984 and market liberalization did not begin until after 1985). The analysis also only examines the effect of market liberalization.

In contrast to the research in China that demonstrates the success of the gradual market liberalization measures, scholars have differing views outside Asia. Without much quantitative support, several authors have pointed to the negative impact of the early market policies on output and productivity in CEE and the CIS nations (Roland 2000; Wehrheim et al. 2000). Other studies explain how the emergence of market-supporting institutions has been crucial in the agricultural recovery and growth and improved access to input and output markets in several CEE countries, and that their absence hampered recovery in other, mainly CIS, transition countries (EBRD 2002; Swinnen 2002*b*; World Bank 2001).

Unfortunately, the only studies that try to quantitatively examine market liberalization effects use rough time period indicator variables. These studies provide some support for a J-shaped impact of radical market liberalization. For example, Macours and Swinnen (2000*a*), after holding constant property rights reform, farm restructuring, and other factors, measure the impact of the breakdown of exchange systems between farms and input suppliers and processing companies with a time period dummy variable for the first two years after major restructuring. They find that the breakdown of exchange has a negative effect on output and productivity in CEE. Evidence on subsequent recovery with the emergence of new institutions for contract enforcement in CEE is limited, but growing.

Transnational, systematic evidence of the impact of market liberalization is still missing. There have been a growing number of papers on single industries and small groups of firms in transition nations (Beckmann and Boger 2004; Gow and Swinnen 2001). These studies, often case study in nature, find strong positive effects on firm performance of the emergence of institutions that help in contract enforcement and the provision of credit and other inputs.[11] For example, Gow, Streeter, and Swinnen (2000) for sugar and Dries and Swinnen (2004*a*, 2004*b*) for dairy, document how enterprises have used contracting to help producers gain access to inputs and sell their output in the absence of well-functioning wholesale markets.

Despite the appearance of these case studies, most of which tell a similar story, there is still relatively little systematic, econometric-based evidence of these dynamic market liberalization effects. Macours and Swinnen (2002), using a rough measure of the overall liberalization of the economy developed by de Melo and Gelb (1996), do find in their regression results explaining agricultural productivity in fifteen transition countries, that over the first five years of the reforms the coefficient on the indicator of market liberalization was significantly positively related with productivity growth. This positive correlation between the emergence of markets and productivity was found even after holding constant property rights reforms, farm restructuring, and prices. This conclusion is consistent with findings of Swinnen and Vranken (2004) who calculate farm-level efficiency indicators based on representative surveys in five CEE countries and show that, after the initial transition period, the average farm efficiency in the five countries is strongly positively correlated with the level of economic reforms and market liberalization as measured by EBRD and World Bank indicators.

In summary, the transition countries have taken vastly different roads in market liberalization. The empirical evidence suggests that there is not a single successful path in establishing a market economy. In several CEE countries a rapid and radical approach to full-scale market liberalization of the entire agro-food system contributed importantly to output declines in early transition, but within five years after the start of transition market institutions were emerging and after a decade robust productivity growth.

In contrast, the success of China's liberalization policies is due to an entirely different, much more gradual approach that ultimately contributed to positive productivity growth, while avoiding catastrophic disruption. In the short run, planning with all of its inefficiencies was retained for the nation's major agricultural commodities. Even though the maintenance of the system of planned procurement and supply in China almost certainly caused substantial allocative irrationalities during the interim (although these have never been measured), the benefit of such a strategy was that it did provide farmers with access to inputs and product outlets during the period of property rights reforms and farm restructuring and avoided the economic collapse experienced outside Asia (Rozelle 1996). With improved farm productivity (initially from other policies, such as HRS), the planning system actually increased farm incomes and allowed an increasing supply of food to urban consumers. In the longer run, China's market liberalization strategy depended on creating an environment that allowed new entrants. The gradual policies at the very least allowed space for traders to slowly develop networks and figure out ways to finance commodity trade (Watson 1994). In the longer run, as these traders began to take advantage of profitable trades, they attracted new traders and forced the state to commercialize the trading divisions of the grain bureaux in a way that is described more generally by McMillan and Naughton (1992). Ultimately, this competition forced policy makers to formally remove most of their market-restricting policies, mainly because they were not effective. The gradual deregulation of the input and output marketing also ultimately produced its own successes.

5.5. The effects of interactions among reform policies

Although discussions of optimal sequencing and precise measurement of returns to reform policy depend heavily on the ability to identify and disentangle interaction effects that may occur when leaders implement more than one policy during a single time period, almost no empirical work has addressed the challenge. The biggest problem is certainly data. Lack of long enough time series with explicit measures of the reform policies makes the task almost impossible in most countries. Although most studies that use time dummies to identify reform impacts point out the multiple effects that are occurring simultaneously as well as working together, nothing more is (or can be) done with most studies.

The only two studies that have generated any formal empirical measure of the magnitude of the interaction effects are Lin (1991) and Huang and Rozelle (1996). In these two works, although the authors try to isolate the behavioural effects of the HRS first-stage reforms from the effects of market liberalization, they show that in reality the two are quite related. Their analyses show that China's agricultural sector has experienced both positive and negative interactions between market improvements and improved incentives. For example, own-price output elasticities of farm producers rise after HRS, but the total output shows a secular drop due to the demise of some centrally planned policy functions that free market agents do not take over. In other words, the papers show that increased responsiveness is conditional on having good incentives and relatively full decision-making authority. Moreover, the authors realize that given these interactions, when using time period indicator variables to capture the returns to a specific reform, the results will be biased.

Despite the lack of rigorous empirical evidence, our understanding of transition economies suggests that interactions are important. If state government procurement and sales channels have collapsed and market liberalization has not created new ways for producers to purchase inputs or sell out, it is almost certain that the effectiveness of improved incentives from property rights reforms will be attenuated. Likewise, market liberalization without improved incentives is likely both to slow down the emergence of markets (there will be little supply or demand for the newly marketed goods and services) and reduce the impact on output and productivity growth. As a result of these strong and important interaction effects, it is likely that studies that use time period indicators to measure effects of reforms on outcomes will be over-attributing the effects to a single policy if there is more than one reform being undertaken by reformers.

Notes

1. Only Lin (1992), and those that were able to use Lin's data were able to create a measure of reform that was more finely graded than a time trend. Lin was able to create a variable that measured the number of villages in each year that had adopted decollectivization reforms.

2. It is more difficult to measure the effect of price changes on productivity, since, as in McMillan, Whalley, and Zhu (1989) and Jin et al. (2002), the price effects are removed before explaining TFP changes. In Lin (1992) and Huang and Rozelle (1996), however, there is evidence that higher prices are associated with higher rates of technology adoption, which has contributed positively to the rise in TFP during the reform era. Hence, price changes may have an indirect effect on TFP.

3. Kurkalova and Carriquiry (2002) attribute the rest of the decline (−35%) to weather effects. Weather effects caused 10% of output decline in the Macours and Swinnen (2000a) study.

4. The importance of accounting differences in the ownership status of plots (especially in distinguishing between private collective plots) is less important for the cases of East Asia and CEE. In China and Vietnam, farm households had small private plots—about 5% of total cultivated area—both before and after reform (Brandt et al. 2002). But, except for in some villages that allocated more land in the form of private plots to households at the beginning of the reforms, a vast majority of households saw no difference in private plots with the onset of reform. As the reforms have proceeded, the importance of the distinction between private plots and the rest of collectively allocated plots has decreased. Moreover, all studies of the effect of the reforms on farm output and productivity include both private and collectively owned plots. The work in CEE by Macours and Swinnen (2000a) also includes all types of plots. Moreover, although there was a clear distinction in the pre-reform era, after reform the importance of private plots diminished markedly.

5. The study indicates that labour measured in hours employed contracts significantly more strongly than 'agricultural employment', suggesting significant underemployment remaining on the large farms.

6. However important, technology is not the only factor affecting farm individualization. Mathijs and Swinnen (1998) show how several other factors, including land reform policies and government regulations regarding farm privatization, also matter.

7. An important factor in the optimal scale of farming, besides scale economies in some technologies, is transaction costs in labour management. Large operations in agriculture face transaction costs because of principal–agent problems and monitoring costs in labour contracting which are typically large in agriculture (Schmitt 1991; Pollak 1985), although the importance varies with specialization and technology (Allen and Lueck 1998).

8. In Azerbaijan this productivity effect is not captured in the data in Tables 2.2–2.5 because the land distribution and farm individualization process only started in 1996. Average yields increased by 13% annually between 1997 and 2002 (Republic of Azerbaijan 2003).

9. On average, the man/land ratio was more than five times higher in East Asia than in Central Europe or Russia (see Table 5.1).

10. In contrast, agricultural labour use increased in many of the transition countries where individual farming grew strongly.

11. See Swinnen (2005) for a survey of the case studies and survey-based evidence.

Part II
The Political Economy of Agricultural Transition

6

Basic Determinants of Reform Strategies

In this chapter we discuss several of the forces that we believe had an import-ant impact on the choices leaders made regarding their reform strategies. In doing so, we first build a vocabulary that will aid in the understanding of our arguments in the following chapters. For expediency and ease of pre-sentation we divide the factors into four main categories: initial levels of technology; the level of wealth of an economy and its associated economic structure; the degree of decentralization of the economy; and the historic legacy of a country and path dependency.

6.1. Initial technology

The initial level of agricultural technology plays an important role in explaining several of the reform decisions in the following analysis mainly because it is so important in determining the size of the benefits and costs of property rights reform and farm restructuring and because it differs so significantly among nations (see Chapter 5). There are two main differences among nations. First, there are differences among nations in their factor ratios. The man to land ratio in China is more than five times that in CEE and seven times that in Russia (see Table 5.1). When labour plays a larger role in the production process, the returns to incentives that boost effort, ceteris paribus, will be larger. Also when farms are more labour intensive, the losses of economies of scale are lower when farms are restructured. Labour-intensive agriculture means that land can be divided more evenly without a loss of efficiency. Hence, labour-intensive agricultural systems tend to have higher benefits to effort-increasing incentives and have the lower costs associated with diseconomies of scale when farms are restructured.

Second, most farms in the Soviet Union and Eastern Europe were not only more labour intensive than those in East Asia, they were also more integrated into an industrialized production system and vertically integrated with an agro-food supply chain. Under the Soviet system, the tasks of providing inputs to farmers and managing their operations, storage, processing, transport, and road infrastructure were allocated to different agencies, and local authorities had little control over these activities. Warehouses and processing plants were sometimes hundreds of miles away. The organizational problems inherent in this structure led to waste and inefficiency during the pre-reform era. In the early 1980s, the Soviet agro-industrial complex was managed by eleven different ministries and at least three state committees, contributing to bureaucratic infighting, poor coordination, and inefficiency (Wegren 1998). Several studies argue that these inefficiencies were the most fundamental problem of agriculture in the Soviet era, even more so than the low productivity of the farms, and affected the willingness for and feasibility of reform (Johnson and Brooks 1983; Wädekin 1988). In contrast, prior to reform, producers in East Asia were more self-sufficient and produced staple commodities that required little processing and travelled from farm to consumer through much simpler marketing channels.

Given the importance of agricultural technology and the environment within which the technology is used, and the differences among nations, it is not surprising that these elements play at least a partial role in explaining the political processes and reform strategies of different transition nations. Hence, factor intensities, economies of scale, and the complexity of the agro-industrial chains on which agriculture relies will be discussed in almost every subsection. In order to avoid repetition in the rest of the analysis, we will use the term *technology* as a shorthand way to refer to all of these processes; in summary, technology refers to both factor intensities and the nature of the input supply chain and agroprocessing complex within which farms have to interact in order to carry out the business of farming.

6.2. Wealth and structure of the economy

The wealth of an economy can have both direct and indirect effects on the choice of reform strategies. If agents in an economy are below or near the poverty line, reforms that seek to change the system that in part caused the poverty will be welcome or at least not resisted. In contrast, if the original system, no matter what its macroeconomic costs, has bestowed a high level of benefits on a subset of individuals, those individuals should be expected to resist reforms that seek to dismantle the system that is providing the benefits.

In addition, it is well known that the structure of the economy and the nature of institutions in it are highly influenced by a nation's wealth. One example is that wealthier countries invariably have a lower share of their population in the agricultural sector. Another example is that poor nations almost never choose to invest their scarce financial resources in a welfare system. In gauging the costs and benefits of a reform policy in agriculture, reformers in poorer countries with large parts of the population in the agricultural sector almost certainly will have more to gain if the reforms are successful than leaders in wealthier nations. In contrast, when considering restructuring policies that threaten to lay-off farm workers, the relative cost to poorer nations will be higher since those that are laid off will take a direct income cut and have little recourse. Those that are laid off in richer countries, while certainly not happy, may be somewhat mollified if they are able to collect unemployment insurance or have access to other benefits. As with technology, in order to streamline the analysis, in the rest of the chapter, when we refer to *wealth*, the word can embody these several different dimensions.

6.3. Degree of decentralization

Decentralization can both enhance and constrain reforms. For example, when there is a high degree of decentralization, top-down policy implementation is more difficult since incentives embedded in the reform policies have to be compatible. In more authoritarian regimes, bureaucrats can be more readily controlled by strong and clear policy directives. Otherwise, local leaders may have to be bought off to ensure their compliance. Hence, decentralization can make reform more difficult.

In contrast, decentralized systems can also facilitate reform. Because the different parts of their economies are isolated from one another, they are more amenable to experimentation, a valuable tool to be able to exploit during the process of reforms that were almost always untried (Qian and Weingast 1997). Decentralization also allows local leaders to be able to benefit more directly (and indirectly) from the growth that accrues to their regions if reforms trigger local growth.

While we consider factors associated with decentralization that both enhance and constrain reform, we necessarily must simplify. The impact of decentralization on transition policies can be multi-dimensional and complicated. However, while the topic of government decentralization and policy efficacy is important and currently widely debated, we restrict our attention to a subset of issues.

6.4. Historic legacy and path dependency

Long historic legacies of the institutions that were used to promote Communism are thought to slow down reform. Part of the reason is that it is thought that when individuals spend many years in Communist systems they lose the social capital and human capital skills that are needed in market economies. Rules and regulations also most likely have emerged which are often incompatible with running modern, market economies. However, having a long history of Communism can also have benefits for implementing complex property rights reforms. For example, ties to previous property rights are more likely to have been erased and reformers are not faced with difficult issues of restitution of property.

The determinants of certain reforms, at times, may be somewhat path dependent. That is, because a certain set of actions were taken at some time in the past, there is more of a likelihood that a future course of reform will unfold. For example, because Communist officials in Poland decided to stay with individual farming even during the Socialist period, their farm restructuring problem was trivial. The implementation of one reform could also eliminate the pressures that were building to push forward other reforms. It is in this sense that we use the term *path* dependency. It should be recognized that the presence of the forces of path dependency may increase the likelihood of a subsequent event or action, but this should not be equated with inevitability. Indeed, the forces of path dependency should be treated as one of many factors that can affect the decisions of reformers.

6.5. Other factors

There are also countless other factors that could affect reform choices. Experience with law and legal institutions; political coalitions; connections with other nations and networks of people that can help form new institutions and support reform policies; cultural and religious differences; geopolitical factors; and many others could affect the decision of one nation to choose one path while another could decide on another. In Swinnen (1997) we have analysed several of these factors in detail for a more limited set of political economy questions. In this book, we will introduce these *other factors* into our analysis when needed. However, in order to narrow the focus of our enquiry, we put heavy emphasis on the effects on reform strategy choice of technology, wealth, decentralization, and historical legacy and path dependence.

7

Why did the Communist Party Reform in China, but not in the Soviet Union?

7.1. Introduction

In this section we seek to explain why China was able to reform agriculture in its pre-reform economy, but the Soviet Union was not. The logic of our explanation depends on several related arguments. First, we show how in China there was a confluence of interests of the leadership at the top and those at the grassroots, both farm households and local officials. In implementing such radical policies as decollectivization and market liberalizing reforms, if there is resistance or lack of will of one party then it is likely that the reforms will stall.

Second, we provide evidence of how the support of grassroots in absence of support of the top leadership led to failed reform. For this we turn to China in the early 1960s during the years after the famine caused by the Great Leap Forward. During those years, farmers and local leaders in China broadly supported moves to decollectivize agriculture; in the early 1960s, however, the top leadership resisted. Reform failed.

Third, we also have to show the reverse case: when the top leadership supports reform in the absence of grassroots support reform fails. For this we turn to the Soviet Union in the late 1970s and early 1980s. During this time, the top leadership pushed the reforms but those at the grassroots resisted. Reform also failed. Based on these arguments we conclude that the empirical evidence suggests that for major reforms to proceed under Communist rule, a nation needs to have two key conditions fulfilled *simultaneously*: strong grassroots pressure for reform and the support of the top leadership. See Table 7.1 for a summary of these hypotheses.[1]

Table 7.1. Conditions for agricultural reforms under Communism

		Grassroots pressure for agricultural reform	
		NO	YES
Support of top leadership for agricultural reform	NO	NO REFORM Example: USSR 1970s	NO REFORM Example: CHINA early 1960s
	YES	NO REFORM Example: USSR 1980s	REFORM Example: CHINA late 1970s and 1980s

Note: Reform refers to major changes in pricing policy, property rights and farm restructuring, and/or market liberalization.

Identifying the need for both upper- and lower-level support, however, is only half the explanation. We also look for the fundamental causes. More specifically, we attempt to answer a more basic question: why is it that although the leaderships in both China and the Soviet Union supported reform, it was only the farmers and local cadres in China that pushed for reform while those at the grassroots in the Soviet Union resisted? The last part of this section attempts to answer this question. First, we argue that while the leaderships of both Communist countries would benefit from reform, China would benefit more because of the nature of its technology and level of wealth. The nature of technology in China, in addition, allowed for the realization of efficiency gains without a deterioration of income distribution. In other words, in China since land could be given to virtually everyone in the farm sector without much disruption and with a substantial increase in efficiency, leaders did not need to deal with the efficiency–equity trade-off, a tension that would have created different resistance in any country, but was especially a sensitive issue in a Communist country.

Finally, we examine the forces that affected the grassroots and helped build support among the rural residents. We show that the same forces of technology and wealth (though in a somewhat different sense) are two factors that contributed to the support of the grassroots in China, among both households and local officials. In addition, it is also the decentralized nature of China's economy that allows leaders to enact a set of complementary policies that can in essence buy off local leaders. In contrast, we show that the nature of technology and the relative wealth levels of farm households and local leaders in the Soviet Union mean that they would have singularly lost in a pre-transition agriculture reform effort. This loss explains their resistance.

7.2. Political changes, grassroots pressure, and agricultural reform in China

Full credit for the reforms in China is often attributed to the new leadership that came to power after Mao died in 1976. These initiatives are primarily associated with the new leader, Deng Xiaoping. However, a careful analysis of the reform discussions and decisions that took place at the top of the Communist Party and the changes that took place in the rural areas suggest a more nuanced picture of the reform decisions, and their implementation. When property rights reform and decollectivization started in China's countryside in 1978, those that were in favour of reform at the top of the Communist Party were still in the midst of a power battle with conservative forces and not yet in charge. The power struggle among different factions continued throughout the 1978–82 period (Yang 1996). Most poignantly, although top leaders debated the pros and cons of decollectivization on both sides of the issues, official party policy still had not openly encouraged the HRS during the period. While strong signals were being officially sent out of Beijing by reformers in support of decollectivization, it was not until the summer of 1982 that a central policy document was drafted which formally praised the HRS. At this time, 68 per cent of all households had already adopted the HRS in agriculture. By the time the document made decollectivization official dogma in 1983, more than 90 per cent of China's villages had decollectivized.

Hence, instead of being seen as a policy solely emerging from the political bag of Deng, property rights reform, or decollectivization, in China should be seen as a process that was encouraged by grassroots pressure. In fact, the pressure by farm families to return to family-based production not only occurred during the late 1970s and early 1980s, but had actually begun to emerge during the decades preceding the HRS reforms.[2] Because of this, we believe that grassroots pressure was a key element of the reform movement. Interestingly, however, while there has been pressure at different periods of time during the 1960s and 1970s, it should be noted that the pressures were not constant, but fluctuated both by region and over time. Over time, the pressure to decollectivize was most strong in the aftermath of the Great Leap Forward policy in the late 1950s and the famine that it created in the early 1960s. The ideological pressure and the associated radical collectivization during those periods intensified the problems of the collective farming system and with that negatively affected the welfare of rural households. Similarly, in times of drought, the problems intensified. With such crises, the pressure to shift to household-based production systems was strong at the grassroots levels.[3] It is well documented that what are now called the household responsibility system (HRS) reforms started in some of more drought-prone rural areas of China several years before they began to be openly allowed (or encouraged) by even the more reform-minded leaders in Beijing in the late 1970s. In other words, grassroots pressure, in addition to policy movements in Beijing, was crucial for launching the reforms.

One of the clearest indications of this is that HRS had spread to more than half of China's villages before it became the official policy of the national government. Yang (1996) documents how the willingness of rural households to risk punishment by the party traditionalists because of the actions that they took by decollectivizing agricultural production is positively related to the intensity of famine that followed the Great Leap Forward.[4] In the second half of the 1970s, household contracting started clandestinely in several regions in China, especially those regions that suffered heavily during the famine. The best-documented case is that of a village in Anhui province where a severe drought in 1978 induced several households to secretly distribute the work among themselves. Although farming on their own, the members of this group of farmers agreed to continue to fulfil the commune's output demands and to let each member keep the rest of the harvest from his own land (Zhou 1996). Despite the oath of secrecy among the participating village members, the dramatic yield effects became known and induced neighbouring households and villages to replicate their actions. The spread of HRS in parts of Anhui initially occurred despite official Communist Party prohibition of household contracting.

While the gains in output and productivity caused increasing numbers of poor villages to shift to the household contracting system despite the risk of punishments from the party at the highest levels, local initiatives could not have happened without the support of local leaders. Local cadres in these areas often tolerated the practices. In many case they were active collaborators. The collusion went on in some areas even though certain factions of middle and top party officials came out explicitly against the practice. Most likely if local leaders had been found to cognitively go against the demands of upper-level leaders, they would have been dismissed from the party. Therefore, to the extent that party membership conveyed benefits to its members, the local leaders were acting at the risk of losing these benefits.

The environment of uncertainty and risk can only be imagined now, but statements in the media and policy documents make it clear that local leaders and farmers faced possible consequences for their actions. While there was an attitude gradually emerging at the central level that reform was to be tolerated in the late 1970s, for those officials far from the capital and out of direct policy discussion that relied on the media there were many ominous signs for local reformers. For example, official policy statements strongly condemned the practice once Beijing got word of the changes in some rural areas. Doubtlessly, middle-level cadres in many places must have used these statements to crack down on reform, whether out of commitment to their Communist beliefs or for some other gain. However, the main point to be made here is that while there was policy support by some factions at the top of the government to reform in the late 1970s and early 1980s, the evidence also shows that there was strong grassroots pressure to decollectivize in China in the late 1970s and that the presence of this local support may have helped tip the scale towards the reformers.

Ultimately, however, the presence of grassroots pressure, while perhaps necessary for reform in a Communist nation, is clearly not sufficient. Specifically, grassroots support by itself cannot explain why the reforms took place in the late 1970s. Research by Yang (1996) and others (for example Lardy 1983) shows that grassroots pressures to decollectivize also existed in the aftermath of the Great Leap Forward. At that time China failed to decollectivize. So the additional question must also be asked, why is it that the grassroots pressure in the late 1970s succeeded in pushing through the reforms while they failed in the early 1960s?

The crucial difference between the periods is what was happening at the top of China's Communist Party. Earlier grassroots attempt to move to household-based production were resisted by the Communist regime under Mao (Lardy 1983). There was a large contingent in China, including Liu Shaoqi and Deng Xiaoping, that were pushing for decommunization and the return of decision-making power to smaller groups—such as the mutual aid and production teams that had been the main decision-making entity in the mid-1950s. Although individuals may have favoured household farming, most of the documented debate in the early 1960s revolved around whether or not the nation should move the basic unit of production from the commune to the team. Moving entirely away from collective agriculture in the 1960s was anathema.

The situation changed substantially by the late 1970s. Although many of the proponents of collective agriculture, such as Hua Guofeng and Chen Yonggui, were still in power and those that surrounded them continued to officially struggle against the HRS, the balance of power was soon to change. Mao died in 1976. The Gang of Four, a group of four of

Mao's protégés that ruled briefly in the mid-1970s, was jailed. In such an atmosphere there was room at the top for a return of those that wanted changes in the nature of agricultural production. It did not happen immediately, however. There were still many against reform.

Gradually, however, the reformers began to emerge. Although the reformers were not totally in charge of agricultural policy and not fully committed themselves to a precise blueprint for reform, there was support in upper-level governments and party cells for more fundamental reform in agriculture. In 1978 Deng had returned to assume important roles in the government and party. Wan Li had already got permission in the late 1970s from the top leadership to allow the naturally evolving experiments in Anhui to continue. In 1979 the State Council appointed Du Rensheng, a bold statesman who favoured household farming, to set up an office to study, support, and indeed direct the unfolding rural reforms. Many of the actors in these newly emerging power centres of reform supported HRS. Debates were commonplace and more open. Reflecting this emerging line of thinking, even in the late 1970s, the media carried positive statements about agricultural reform. In fact, according to interviews with local leaders by the authors more than twenty years after reform, in many areas it is often recalled that there was not much fear of reprisal. By the early 1980s, many local officials in China were comfortable with the idea of HRS because they believed that the top leadership supported this shift.

The main point of the preceding discussion is important and bears reiteration. The changes at the top—that is the rise of the reformers—and the existence of grassroots support were mutually reinforcing in China at the late 1970s. While support in Beijing helped spread the HRS, the grassroots support also help the pro-reform leadership win its case. When the news about the dramatic effects of the HRS spread, more reform-minded Communist officials

saw an opportunity to exploit the agricultural changes as part of their drive, following the death of Mao Zedong, to oust the Maoists. Provincial Communist Party officials visited the village and gave their blessings. It was not until after this that a high-level Beijing official travelled to Xiaogang and the neighbouring villages. The report of the official, which concluded that individual farming increased output and improved living standards, became influential when it was circulated among the national leaders. However, it was not until a Communist Party conference in 1982, four years after the meeting of the Xiaogang villagers, that China's paramount leader, Deng Xiaoping, formally endorsed the reforms. In 1983 the central government formally proclaimed individual farming to be consistent with the socialist economy and therefore permissible.   (McMillan, 2002: 93–94).

Hence, the decision to reform appears to have been a delicate balance between pressure from the grassroots and preference to reform from an important part of the top leadership. In the temporary leadership vacuum that existed after Mao's death, both reinforced each other in China's context. The success of the HRS reforms in increasing output, reducing poverty, and maintaining social stability in China's countryside reinforced the positions of the pro-reform groups in Beijing. Inversely, the enhanced position of the pro-reform groups created the policy space that was necessary for the grassroots initiatives to spread across rural China.

7.3. Grassroots resistance and failed agricultural reform in the Soviet Union

The story of China's reform seems to suggest that grassroots support for reform was important in triggering decollectivization in China. However, the question remains whether China's reforms could have been successful if they had only had the support of the nation's new reform champion Deng Xiaoping. Quite simply it is important to explore the question: if there had been no grassroots support, could China's agricultural reforms have succeeded? The lessons from the last years of the Soviet Union provide support for the hypothesis that despite the presence of a strong proponent of reform in the top leadership, grassroots pressure is also needed.

Although the reform process and its outcome differ greatly between China and the Soviet Union, the beginning of a state-led effort in the Soviet Union began shortly after the time that the HRS reforms started in China when Mikhail Gorbachev became the head of the agricultural department of the Central Committee of the Communist Party of the Soviet Union in Moscow in 1978. When Gorbachev began under the Brezhnev regime, his ability to influence policy was still limited. This continued during the short regimes of Andropov and Chernenko from 1982 to 1984.[5] However, in March 1985 Gorbachev became the General Secretary of the Communist Party. Gray (1990: 4) argues that at that point 'the top Soviet leader is the main proponent of economic reform' and that 'perhaps at few times in history has high authority been so responsive to new ideas from intellectuals, most of whom are acutely aware of foreign examples'.

To see the emergence of the preference of the state to reform, it can be shown that during the Gorbachev years several agricultural reforms were designed, debated, and eventually promoted, at least to the extent that they were allowed to be. The objectives of the reforms mainly included two themes: the reorganization of the state agricultural administrative apparatus and a revamping of the organization of production. Initially, the most important reform initiative was the introduction of the so-called agricultural collective contract (ACC) system in the early 1980s (Brooks 1990; Wegren 1998). In theory, under the ACC system, a brigade of farm workers negotiated with farm management to provide labour services on an assigned unit of land. The contract specified the inputs and services that farm management must provide and the price the brigade would receive for output delivered to management. In most cases, the farm management was supposed to provide specified quantities of inputs free of charge, and the brigade was supposed to receive compensation for value added through labour services. However, brigades did not buy inputs and sell output. In fact, they had little discretionary power except that of dividing up their collective earnings among their members. The collective contract essentially was an attempt to replace a wage-based system with one that based earnings on the farm's output. In summary, this innovation was an attempt to impose financial discipline on farm workers and to reward them by making remuneration more directly on the basis of their performance (Gray 1990).[6]

Although the reforms were tried across a widespread region, they largely failed because they were insufficient to solve the key problems. By 1987, 70 per cent of farm workers were officially under collective contracts. However, in practice instead of creating an economic miracle as in China, all of the old problems continued to affect farming. As a consequence, the impact of the reforms was disappointing (Lerman and Brooks 2001; Van Atta 1990).

In response to the shortcomings of the ACC reforms, Gorbachev attempted to introduce even bolder reforms in the late 1980s. In particular, new regulations in 1988 allowed individual farmers to lease land, hire labour, and own tractors, trucks, and other capital assets. Rental brigades (*arendnyi podriad*) had more discretionary power, and they increased in number in 1988 and 1989. As in the case of the ACC reforms, however, the effect of the reforms never materialized during the Soviet era.[7]

Although the reforms did not trigger a revitalization of agriculture as they did in China, what is remarkable is that the Soviet leadership under Gorbachev in the second half of the 1980s introduced a reform proposal similar to those of China's leadership almost a decade earlier.[8] In fact, the contract system that the Soviet leaders proposed is similar to the *lianchan daozu* (linking output to the group) reform in China, a policy reform effort which actually preceded HRS. Interestingly, the path chosen by Gorbachev (that is, a system close to *lianchan daozu*) was also preferred by a considerable faction of China's leadership as it was considered to be ideologically less radical than HRS. It was also still clearly collective-based farming.

In short, the substance of the reforms in China and the Soviet Union was remarkably similar. Reform in both the Soviet Union and China began as efforts to improve incentives to collective agriculture. The Communist leaderships in both nations quickly moved beyond their initial proposals and made an assault on the basic principles of collective agriculture. Deng and Gorbachev both proposed to allow households to lease land, gain access to factors of production, and claim rights to the residual income after certain payments were made.

So, how was it that two such similar reform initiatives should end up performing so differently? The main difference in the reform process appears to be less in the nature of the policies than in the dynamics of the relationships among the actors involved in the reforms. In the Soviet Union reform was driven primarily by a Communist leadership that was unsatisfied with previous reform attempts. The central leadership in the Soviet Union, however, had little support from farmers or local officials. In contrast, China's leadership, albeit supportive of reform efforts, at times seemed to be driven by force of the farmers. For example, in September 1980, a Chinese Communist Party document on the new agricultural policy still stated that '[t]he Collective economy is the rock-solid-foundation on which the advance of our country's agriculture towards modernization rests' (Yang 1996: 170).[9] Yet by the summer of 1980, 30 per cent of all rural households in China were already engaged in contracting output; the share of farms managed by the individual was even higher in some provinces, such as Guizhou (50 per cent) and Anhui (90 per cent). To be sure, powerful groups of leaders at the top were pushing their reform agenda and were sympathetic to what was going on in many rural areas. However, it also is true that by the time that China's leadership formally endorsed HRS, the system had already spread widely, and so by 1984 there were hardly any communes left that had not reformed (Lin 1992). This process was clearly different from the reforms under the Gorbachev regime where reforms were driven from the top and had to be supported by large-scale propaganda schemes. However, no matter what Gorbachev did, he met with resistance and lethargy rather than enthusiasm at the farm level.

In summary, then, according to the experiences of China in the 1960s and 1970s/1980s and those of the Soviet Union in the 1980s, the confluence of interests between *both* the central leadership *and* farmers was a key part of the process that let the Communist Party push a successful reform agenda without a fundamental change in the leadership regime. When there was grassroots support in China in the 1960s without support at the central leadership level, reform was stifled. When the top leadership in the Soviet Union in the 1980s pushed an aggressive reform agenda without grassroots support, reform was also stifled. It was only in the late 1970s in China when grassroots support emerged with a supportive top leadership that a Communist Party was able to fundamentally reform collective agriculture, one of its basic institutions.

7.4. Technology, wealth, and decentralization in China and the Soviet Union

While we believe that the confluence of central leadership and grassroots support is the proximate reason that China was able to reform agriculture while the Soviet Union was not able to, it still does not get to the fundamental reasons why China and the Soviet Union differed in this way. To identify the basic sources of the differences we need to back up one step and seek to answer a more basic question: why were the attitudes towards decollectivization of farm workers and local officials in China and the Soviet Union so different? To answer this question, we first examine the reasons why those at the grassroots, both farmers and local officials, in China might favour the reforms and why those in the Soviet Union would not. We also compare the motives of the leaderships in China and the Soviet Union, showing that, although there were differences in the motivations, both leaderships had an incentive to initiate reforms.

Motivations for farmers at the grassroots

HISTORIC LEGACY

It is tempting at first to blame the historical legacy of Socialism for creating the differences between China and the Soviet Union. By the 1980s rural households in the Soviet Union had been working on collective farms for nearly sixty years. As a result, all active workers had been born under the collective system and there was no memory of family farming. In contrast, when HRS was introduced in the late 1970s, households in China had worked on collectives for only around twenty-five years. Although most of the collective members under 40 could not recall the household farming days, there were still many older members that could. Because of these historical reasons, then, it is possible that farm households in China favoured a return to what they remembered while those in the Soviet Union feared what they were unfamiliar with.

While the long history of collective agriculture in the Soviet Union no doubt affected the attitudes of rural households to individual farming, this is unsatisfactory. Such an explanation is incomplete because it cannot explain the divergence between the attitudes towards reform of rural households in China and the attitudes of those in many CEE countries. For example, it is well documented that farm workers in countries such as Bulgaria and former Czechoslovakia were equally unenthusiastic about decollectivization. Older farm workers in CEE had worked on family farms until after the Second World War; many were collectivized only during the late 1940s and early 1950s around the same time that China's Communist Party was collectivizing. On this basis, it is clear that historical legacy, while perhaps a factor, cannot completely account for the differences between China and the Soviet Union.

WEALTH

While history may not provide a complete explanation, the differences in wealth levels between China and the Soviet Union and standard of living offered by pre-reform collective agriculture are most likely one of the more fundamental reasons that households in the two countries differed so sharply in their enthusiasm for reform. In China, rural households had faced famine in the recent past and more than 30 to 40 per cent of households lived below the one-dollar-per-day international poverty line (World Bank 1992). It is likely that nearly 70 per cent of households lived at less than the two-dollar-per-day international poverty line.

In stark contrast, farm workers in CEE and the Soviet Union had benefited greatly from large subsidies from the government budget and relatively high wages in agriculture since the beginning of the Brezhnev period.[10] This is not to say that farm performance was good in the Soviet Union. At the end of the Brezhnev era, although input use reached an all time high, agricultural productivity was falling. Yet, despite the poor performance, workers in the Soviet Union's state farms and collectives had standards of living far higher than those in China's rural sector. In fact, consumption and wages of those in rural areas were not that far below those in the urban areas in the Soviet Union under the Brezhnev regime (Ellman 1988). Most workers were also covered by social welfare benefits. Of course, high farm incomes amidst low productivity could only occur with extensive budgetary support.

And, indeed, after the mid-1950s unprecedented support had been given to agriculture (Wegren 1998).[11] In the ten-year period ending in 1965, 16 per cent of total Soviet investment was devoted to agriculture. This grew to approximately 28 per cent by the 10th and 11th Five-Year Plans (1976–80 and 1981–5). In fact, Soviet leaders boasted about their support of agriculture during the Brezhnev era. Of all the investment made in agriculture between 1918 and 1977, 72 per cent took place after the March 1965 party plenum on agriculture (Gray 1990).

And this situation was not confined to the Soviet state. Despite working on overstaffed and inefficient farms, in Central and Eastern Europe, farm workers lived relatively well due to large subsidies. Life on the farm was known to be one that could be lived comfortably with low work pressure. In several countries rural incomes were actually higher than urban incomes.

Given such high wages for such low effort, it is not surprising that farm workers in the Soviet Union and CEE would resist agricultural reforms. In the pre-reform system wages were guaranteed by the state; under a performance-based or contracting system, farm workers would have had to bear the risk of agricultural production. Hence, it is likely that wages would have fallen, effort would have had to rise, and risk would have been higher. Moreover, given the level of overemployment and pre-reform soft budget constraints, agricultural reform would almost certainly have triggered significant lay-offs (as it eventually did in many countries in the 1990s). Facing such changes, Gorbachev found that, unlike China's farmers who had little to lose, grassroots support in agriculture for significant reform was almost non-existent in the Soviet Union.

TECHNOLOGY

In the same way that wealth factors had opposite effects in China and the Soviet Union, the nature of technology also did. Specifically, it is likely that technology increased the support of farmers for reforms in China since they would have a higher probability of benefiting. Providing incentives to farmers in China would cause relatively little disruption in the nation's labour-intensive agricultural systems. Farmers in China purchased few of their inputs. Supply channels were simple. They sold relatively little of their output into the market. There were almost no farmers that used production processes that interfaced with processors. And, most importantly, given the high labour factor share, the potential for efficiency-enhanced output would mean significantly higher incomes for farmers. Knowing this, farmers welcomed reform.

The opposite was true in the Soviet Union. Farmers were aware of the nature of their production systems and the ties that they had to input and output networks. If reform meant radical changes to the input procurement channels and output marketing system, farmers surely understood that there would be disorganization costs.[12] Moreover, they must have anticipated that even if, as residual claimants, there could be some efficiency gains, such a gain would probably be relatively small, since labour played a relatively small role in Soviet agriculture. Hence, with such small upside gain, they could not be sure when, if ever, they could recover from the disruptions that would certainly accompany any set of bold reforms in the Soviet Union. Hence, the nature of the technology reinforced the will to resist the reforms that were proposed by Gorbachev.

Technology and the way it affected the distributive consequences of the agricultural reforms also contributed to the creation of a consensus among farmers in China and, if anything, would have created additional tensions among households in the former Soviet Union. Because economies of scale are relatively unimportant in China's labour-intensive farming systems, reformers were able to distribute land in kind to every rural household with little loss of efficiency. Since all households gained, naturally such a policy had broad-based support. In the Soviet Union, however, if contracting was to be successful, it would almost surely have meant large lay-offs. Efficient operation of farmers in the Soviet Union demanded that capital-intensive farmers required access to sufficiently large tracts of land. Hence, efficiency-oriented reform would have meant that the farm's management rights would have had to be concentrated in the hands of a few and the others either laid off or hired back as wage workers. In fact, this is precisely what happened in the early 1990s in many of the successful CEE nations. Faced with such prospects that are so different from China, it is easy to see how the technology-based uneven distribution of rights would have had trouble generating enthusiasm.

Motivations for local officials at the grassroots

Farmers are not the only actors at the grassroots. Being mass mobilization parties, during the entire histories of the Soviet Union and China the government and the party had established hierarchical networks down to the lowest levels of society. The reason for these bureaucracies was to implement policies, administer investments, operate commercial and social services, collect taxes, and impose discipline. In some cases they acted as careful guardians of state policy. But not always. As in all large bureaucracies, incentives for local officials to implement the will of the state are not always consistent with the interest of central policy makers at the top. In many cases the interests of lower-level officials are more closely aligned with individuals—for example, farm workers—than with the state. In some cases, due to the lack of a clear policy direction, local officials have to take their own initiative and make decisions that are needed to govern. Hence, local officials, whether playing the role of guardian of state interests or acting as an intermediary for the individuals under their jurisdiction, almost by virtue of their distance from the centre have a degree of latitude in decision making. As such, they often play an important role in promoting new policies or resisting them. At times, especially when there is a policy vacuum, local officials can also take actions to start grassroots movements without the direction of the state.

During China's Socialist period, local officials—commune, brigade, and team leaders—often found themselves closely aligned with the interests of farmers (Oi 1989), and this was also the case when trying to decide the way to organize agricultural production (Zhou 1996). Because of the close alignment of interests, in the same way that wealth effects and technology generated enthusiasm for decollectivization for farmers, local leaders almost certainly were likewise influenced (Putterman 1992). Indeed, Yang (1996) implicitly argues that poverty induced some local leaders in China to initiate their own version of agricultural production reforms. It is easy to see why. Teams and brigades in China were small so the local leaders were almost always close relatives, friends, or acquaintances of the rest of the members of their collectives. Team and brigade leaders were also farmers and indeed most of their income was derived from their own farming activities, not from the salaries paid by (or perks provided by) the collective or government, especially in poorer areas. Thus, when an area was poor, from the viewpoint of the local leader, there was little to lose in moving to individual farming. It is also possible that local leaders could earn rents as gate keepers for certain inputs in the collective era. However, if the whole village was mired in poverty, such rents certainly could not have been very large. In addition, if the reforms were consistent with the labour-intensive farming systems of the farmers, they would also serve to help local leaders—as farmers themselves, as headmen of their villages, and even if they were collecting rents, the scope for rent collection would increase with the level of wealth in the local economy. Indeed, according to Morduch and Sicular (2000), local cadres benefited more from the HRS reforms, albeit only moderately so, than the average farmer.[13]

But, while wealth and technology may have made local officials support the reforms in poorer areas, it is possible that local leaders in richer areas of China would not have been so enthusiastic. In fact, during interviews by one of the authors in the final days of collective agriculture in China in the early 1980s, commune and brigade officials in one rich suburban commune in Jiangsu province were still defiant, predicting that the new HRS policies would soon be reversed. They claimed that farming without the collective would be inefficient and lead to falling output. Hence, also in China, there were some local leaders that were not naturally supportive of the government's initial reforms.

While this might have been a problem in some parts of China (although it is not likely to have been a very large problem in too many areas), the decentralized nature of China's rural economy was one important factor that allowed leaders later to implement the rural fiscal reforms and encouraged the participation of local leaders in setting up township and village enterprises (TVEs) (Oi 1989; Walder 1995). Although these policies did not directly affect agriculture, they were implemented shortly after the formal initiation of the HRS policies (in 1983 and 1984), and were sufficiently beneficial to local leaders, especially for those in the richer areas, that they secured support for the overall reform agenda. Hence, even if local leaders in richer areas believed their interests were hurt by decollectivization, Walder (1995) and Oi (1999) show how the rural industrialization and fiscal reforms were instrumental in buying off local leaders and bringing their interests into alignment with those of the state.[14]

The support of local officials in the Soviet Union, however, was not forthcoming, in a large part due to the different wealth levels and different nature of technology. In more capital-intensive systems, breaking up the farms implied large losses of scale economies. Privatization and the imposition of hard budget constraints also implied the loss of benefits, not only for the farm workers, but also for the managers and local officials. If the Soviet Union's system of wage subsidies and upper level support of input supply and output procurement benefited the average farm worker, one can only imagine the benefits earned by those in charge of mediating the flow of funds and goods between the state and the farm. Moreover, as in the rest of the economy, local officials were aligned with the interests of state and collective farms and other state-owned enterprises and, as in the rest of the economy, would have been antagonistic to any move to privatize (Shleifer 1997).

There are also reasons why local officials in the Soviet Union would have resisted apart from the effect that such reforms might have had on their own salaries and status. The system of subsidies that supported the wages of farm workers actually had a much broader use. The collective or state farm in the Soviet Union was the unit that provided all social services to rural society. If there had been successful agricultural reforms without any supplementary help in the areas of social service provision, large holes would have opened up in the safety net for many rural residents. Hence, rent seeking aside, these were real concerns for local leaders since there were no alternative institutions available to provide local services, let alone help the unemployed (which, of course, did not officially exist). There also were few off-farm jobs to which laid-off farm workers could have gone. Hence, local officials had to be concerned about the wider effect of an aggressive reform policy. In many senses, the rural economy was not ready for such radical reforms.

Motives for the Central Leadership

We also need to address the motives for the central leadership for a number of reasons. First, in the case of the Soviet Union, after the discussion about the nature of the resistance of the grassroots in the previous sections, it is natural to wonder why it is that when there was no grassroots pressure to reform, the top leadership should ever try to initiate the reforms in the first place. Second, it is important also for the discussion in the next section; in analysing the determinants of sequencing we have to be able to understand the motives of leaders in order to understand why, after pushing one successful reform (for example, in the case of China, property right reform), they would not continue.

In a broad sense, wealth (as we have defined it) induced both Deng and Gorbachev to pursue economic reforms, although the precise wealth-based motives differed between China and the Soviet Union. In the aftermath of the Great Leap Forward and the Cultural Revolution, China's context as a nation in East Asia (where growth was occurring all around in Japan, Korea, and Taiwan) put pressure on Communist leaders in China to produce growth and begin to raise the standards of living of their people (Lardy 1983). Since nearly 80 per cent of China's population still lived in rural areas and depended on agriculture, Deng doubtlessly knew that if he could raise agricultural productivity he could improve the incomes of most of China's households. Economists must also have realized the multiplier potential for the entire economy if growth could be launched in rural areas.

It also is clear that in the mid-1980s, the leadership of the Soviet Union was feeling pressure to get the Soviet economy growing. The need for investing in new technologies, infrastructure, and other social welfare programmes was rising rapidly and creating the need for access to funding no matter what the source (Desai 1987). Although the earlier subsidies to agriculture helped alleviate some of the Soviet Union's food security concerns, given the size of the investment into agriculture, it is likely that Gorbachev would have liked being able to make agriculture more efficient so at the very least the financial ministry could stop (or even reverse) the increasing investments that were being directed to the agricultural sector.

Moreover, it was clear that the policy which appeared successful until the 1970s no longer worked. The large amount of roubles being invested in agriculture yielded increasingly low, and eventually even negative, marginal rates of return. This meant that the policy which during the Brezhnev years had led to increased output was no longer producing desired results. After thirty years of marginal adjustments to the Stalinist state and collective farm system, there was a growing understanding among Soviet leaders that an alternative approach was needed (Macey 2003).[15] Hence, even though the agricultural sector was much smaller in the Soviet Union, the leader of the Soviet Union looked to improving the performance of the agricultural sector as one source that could help economic growth get started.

Leaders in both China and the Soviet Union were not only concerned about stimulating growth when considering reforms to improve the efficiency of agriculture. They were also concerned about other possible effects. One was ideology, and the effect on the organization of social and political relations. We will not discuss this here. Instead we focus on two other concerns. The first was the reform's possible impact on equity. The equality of benefits (or costs) of reforms was important to make the reforms socially and politically sustainable (Hellman 1998). In fact, Yang (1996) argues that the effects on income distribution were as important as ideological arguments in the debate at the top of the Chinese Communist Party on whether to support the HRS in the 1978–83 period. Conservative leaders opposed the HRS arguing that it would increase inequality in rural areas. The second concern was disruptions caused by the reforms. Disruptions could reduce the existing rents collected by Communist officials and leaders and/or they could have important negative social effects, like unemployment or income falls. Hence, like unequal income effects, disruptions could create strong political opposition and backlashes against the reforms.

For both these concerns, the different nature of technologies in the two systems of farming meant that reform was less problematic in China than in the Soviet Union.[16] First, the labour-intensive nature of China's farming systems means that with less input of physical capital, reform policies that changed incentives could increase incomes with little danger of disruptions to the rest of the economy (see also Chapter 3). In contrast, the more capital-intensive and large-scale nature of Soviet agriculture, and the way that farming was embedded in a much larger and complex agro-food system, means that the initial gains from property rights reforms and market liberalization would be relatively less. To succeed, reformers in the Soviet Union would have to make structural changes in the input and output channels. The potential disruption and disorganization could be relatively widespread and severe. Hence, although grassroots pressure may have been pushing China's leadership to implement the reforms in the late 1970s, the relatively large gains that the leadership could expect from decollectivization must have made them more responsive. Likewise, given the potential difficulties and high cost of reforms in the Soviet Union, assuming that the leadership understood these costs, it could explain why there was more reluctance in pushing the reforms when they met resistance.

Second, technology also helped China's leaders by reducing the efficiency and equity trade-off that could have been caused by agricultural reform. Because of the absence of large economy of scale effects, reformers in China were able to provide land to all farmers. With better incentives, increased efficiency raised incomes substantially. However, there was another effect. Because China's farmers were all so poor, and because leaders could allow all farmers to participate in decollectivization, the reforms also helped improve equity (Putterman 1993; Rozelle 1996). Hence, there was no tension among China's leaders concerning the possible distributional impacts of an efficiency-increasing policy. In China, because of the nature of the technology, it was win-win.

In contrast, in the Soviet Union, technology would have meant that there were inevitably going to be winners and losers from reforms, because it demanded restructuring, restitution, lay-offs and other changes. Efficiency would have only come at the cost of equity. In a system like that in the Soviet Union, this would have caused tension among leaders who were willing to sacrifice efficiency for a relatively more fair distribution. This is another reason why leaders in China were more willing to push the agricultural reforms.

7.5. Communist organization and reform experimentation

The decentralized nature of China's economy may also have given China an advantage over Russia in being able to make the agricultural reforms more successful, although such claims are based on observations by researchers working on other sectors of the economy. Several authors have argued that the organizational and hierarchical different structure of the central planning systems of China and Russia allowed for more reform experimentation by Communist leaders in China, and therefore aided the reform process because China could take a trial-and-error approach (for example, Qian and Xu 1993). China's economy was organized mainly on a regional basis, with each region being responsible for a whole array of industries as well as the welfare of its residents. In contrast, the Soviet economy was organized differently. Planners created specialized or functional ministries, grouping similar activities into gigantic factory complexes.

Qian and Xu (1993) refer to these differences as a U-form (Soviet Union) versus an M-Form (China) hierarchy, based on typologies used by Williamson (1975). Roland (2000) argues that while China's planning system was based on the regional duplication of industries, the Soviet system was organized to exploit economies of scale and division of labour on a much wider scale. It is argued that China's planning structure allowed for much more flexibility for experimentation.[17] Qian, Roland, and Xu (1999) argue that the benefits from learning relative to the possible costs of reversal of a reform experiment were significantly higher in China's regionally organized system compared to the Soviet functional organization of central planning. By introducing reforms in one region, China's leaders could learn from experiments while limiting reversal costs, before extending them across the nation. The Soviet system, according to the theory, was not set up for this type of experimentation. Since the system was nationwide, if reformers made mistakes, the direct costs could be high and the costs of reversing the ill-designed reforms also high.

Although the arguments and empirical examples of the authors are cogent and convincing, we find little support for these arguments in the case of China's agricultural reforms in the late 1970s and early 1980s for several reasons.[18] First, although the introduction of China's HRS reforms was regionally concentrated, this had little to do with the design of planners. As argued by Yang (1996), it probably had more to do with grassroots initiatives. In fact, as we showed above, in many cases, the reforms that were initially discussed by China's leaders were considerably less far reaching than those implemented by the farmers and local leaders. Second, the location of the start of the reforms—often in remote outlying regions—was often determined by the relative absence of control of the planners (Yang 1996). This is the opposite of what would be expected from a government-designed experiment. Finally, the spread of the HRS system—across nearly a million brigades and more than 10 million teams in less than five years—could not have reflected the careful planning of experimental reflection. Instead, as one village official in China is quoted by McMillan (2002): 'HRS spread like the flu.'

In fact, if there was any tendency for experimenting with reform, it actually appears to have happened mostly in the Soviet Union. According to the literature, there was significant experimentation in the former Soviet agricultural system. For example, Van Atta (1990) discusses several experiments with brigade and team contracting in the late 1970s and early 1980s. Experiments with new forms of agricultural management also were tried out on a regional basis in the Soviet Union. For example, the agro-industrial district union (RAPO) was first established on an experimental basis in one region in Georgia in 1974 and was later progressively extended to all regions in Georgia. Parallel schemes were launched in Estonia and Latvia in the late 1970s. They became 'a testing ground for a new agricultural strategy' (Radvanyi 1988: 110).[19]

Hence, although it is possible that China's more decentralized system helped them to reform more successfully, the record does not support a contention in the case of the start of the reforms, i.e. the HRS, that decentralization acted through a more ready will to experiment. It appears that the decentralized nature of China played a more important role in the years afterwards, for example in market liberalization (see Chapter 8), in the implementation of the fiscal reforms, and in the emergence of TVEs, and other policies (Wong 1997; Nyberg and Rozelle 1999).

Notes

1. Earlier periods and other countries can also be introduced in this diagram. For example, after Nikita Khrushchev was deposed, largely because of failures in agriculture, in 1964, Leonid Brezhnev started giving much greater priority to agriculture and investments in agriculture were dramatically increased. However the impact was modest and disappointing as key reforms to address structural failures of Soviet agriculture were not introduced (Gray 1990; Johnson and Brooks 1983).
2. In this section, we draw heavily on the book of Dali Yang (1996).
3. Agricultural productivity was lower in 1978 than in 1949, when the Communists took over.
4. Yang shows a significant correlation between the number of people dying of hunger in preceding years and the spread of the HRS in the region.
5. Gorbachev began to have a freer hand under Yuri Andropov in 1982, but under Konstantin Chernenko the situation seemed to change again. For example, Gorbachev did not even speak at the November 1984 conference when Chernenko, who was Brezhnev's close associate, and others sought to expand Brezhnev's high-cost programme of land reclamation (Gray 1990: 4).

6. For a discussion and analysis see also various papers in the volume edited by Brada and Wädekin, published in 1988 with the ex post prophetic title 'Socialist Agriculture in Transition'.

7. It is interesting to note the similar developments occurring elsewhere in the Communist world (Wädekin 1990). The absence of radical reforms in agriculture also characterized the Communist countries of Central and Eastern Europe in the 1970s and 1980s. It is not that CEE nations did not try to implement agricultural reform policies. They did, frequently trying different approaches from those favoured by Gorbachev. Despite the differences in the reform strategies, however, the CEE agricultural reforms in the pre-transition era also met with, at best, only modest success. Many reforms were ineffective. In some cases the reform experiments also made things worse in CEE. For example, in the 1970s Bulgaria, in an apparent attempt to obtain more economies of scale, combined collective and state farms into huge agro-industrial complexes (APKs), averaging 24,500 hectares of land and 5,600 workers. It was soon clear that the inefficiencies increased rather than declined (Wyzan 1990). When the Soviet Union introduced its collective contract, the Bulgarians introduced a similar system (*akordna sistema*) at the brigade level in the mid-1980s. Yet, as in the Soviet Union, the impact was minimal due to a variety of reasons (Cochrane 1990).

8. In fact, there are other ways in which it can be seen that Gorbachev was influenced by China's reform process. In China groups were often organized along kinship lines, with six to ten households per group. Similarly, Gorbachev in a 1986 speech emphasized that family ties should be used to reinforce work solidarity. He even called for contracting plots of land to individuals and families in order to increase productivity. In December 1986, a Central Committee resolution explicitly endorsed family work teams (Van Atta 1990).

9. According to Wegren (1998: 64), this strongly resembles Gorbachev's 1988 statement that 'our collective farms remain the basis of Socialist agriculture production'.

10. Subsidizing agriculture was new under Brezhnev. The early Soviet Period's policies resembled Mao's more closely. From Lenin to Stalin and through most of Khrushchev's regimes, agriculture grew increasing neglected. Capital was drained from an impoverished countryside to finance urban industrial growth (Ellman 1988). The dramatic implications—millions of peasants who died of starvation—are documented in Conquest (1986).

11. The subsidy of the food-processing industry and trade network—which makes up the difference between fixed retail prices and the prices paid to farms—grew from 4 billion roubles in 1965 to 25 billion in 1980 and to over 50 billion in 1985. By the time Gorbachev took the helm, there was also approximately 40 billion roubles in state producer subsidies, consisting of 8 or 9 billion roubles for off-farm inputs—mainly machinery and mineral fertilizer—with additional amounts for state land amelioration and the remission of unpaid credit for farm wages and investment. The Soviet leadership

threw dollars, as well as roubles, towards the goal of increasing food consumption (Gray 1990).

12. In the former Soviet Union and many CEE countries, there was a symbiotic relationship between the state and collective farms and household plots. Household plots played an important role in adding to income and food security of farm workers' households. However, in many farms, many inputs for the household plots came from the large farms, including 'unregistered use' of fertilizer and pesticides, and labour shirking. Hence, reform of the large farms or input supplies would also affect household plot production.

13. McMillan (2002: 100) notes that '[w]hat is noteworthy, though, is not so much that officials abused their power, but that the abuse for the most part was contained'. He gives two arguments why China's bureaucrats resisted the temptation to abuse their power over the farmers—or how the hierarchy kept that temptation in check. First, while the Chinese Communist government faced no challenge, it had lost considerable legitimacy it might have once had and reform-era China was only 'Communist' in name. Its legitimacy as the ruling party of the government, and its ability to pre-empt any future political opposition, rested on its delivering of economic growth. Second, in order to deliver growth, paradoxically, the lack of political changes may have helped in China. The Communist Party had retained its disciplined organization and so was able to prevent self-seeking behaviour by low-level officials. The state motivated local officials to maintain agricultural output growth by rewarding them with bonus payments and promotion, and by firing them if output targets were not met. Sanctions for extreme misconduct could be severe: officials found guilty of corruption might be executed. As a result of this party discipline, bureaucratic control provided a property rights platform that was ad hoc but secure enough that market forces could operate reasonably well. The system was showing strains in the 1990s as riots erupted when farmers protested against corrupt officials imposing taxes and fees on them.

14. In the 1980s, the economic reforms in China were further sustained and broadened by reforms of the bureaucracy (Li 1998). First, in 1980 Deng imposed a massive mandatory retirement programme, effectively removing the old guard and moving up many younger and more pro-reform people in the bureaucracy (Lee 1991). Between 1982 and 1988, 90% of officials above the county level were newly appointed. As a result, the bureaucracy changed dramatically in terms of its support for reforms and its competency. (In contrast, little change took place in the Russian bureaucracy and local leaders remained the same as before the reforms (Shleifer 1997).) Li (1998) argues that these bureaucratic reforms were made easier by the ex post legacy of the Cultural Revolution which not only boosted Deng Xiaoping's credibility and authority as a reformer, but also left China with a weakened bureaucracy. The second major change took place in the mid-1980s when bureaucrats were allowed to quit their government positions to join the business community.

This was a 'bureaucratic revolution', according to Li (1998), and had a positive impact on China's reform process in the second half of the 1980s and later, as it stimulated the interest of bureaucrats in local economic growth and new enterprises.

15. Moreover, some of the moderate attempts at reform had made things worse. Giving more autonomy to farm management but not introducing hard budget constraints (to avoid unwanted social effects) leads to increasing debts but not to improved productivity (Roland 2000).

16. Of course, ideology and politics also played a role in the timing and motivation of the leaders in both the Soviet Union and China (Desai 1990).

17. Another reason emphasized by Weingast (1995) is that greater competition between regions in China stimulated reforms and constrained the re-emergence of state control.

18. It should be noted, however, that later in the 1980s and 1990s, officials from the central government experimented with new agricultural reform policies—such as grain marketing reforms in Henan and cultivated land contracting in Guizhou.

19. There are plenty of additional examples. Gray (1990) also refers to experiments with custom farming services in the Stavropol region in the North Caucasus when Gorbachev himself was the regional leader there. Finally, there was considerable variation in the agricultural systems in the Eastern European countries. The Socialist models of Hungary, Czechoslovakia, Poland, Yugoslavia, Bulgaria, etc. differed significantly, and formed a continuous source of information on how differences and changes in the agricultural systems affected farm performance and output. After the political changes experiments with farm restructuring also occurred in Russia: there were considerable variations in regional policies in allowing experiments with private agriculture (O'Brien, Patsiorkovski, and Dershem 2000). See also the discussions by Wegren (1998) and Macey (2003) of the Nizhniy model, a regional reform attempt in the 1990s to introduce a 'bottom-up' variant of land reform by giving decision-making power on production and organization to farm members.

8

Determining the Pace of Market Liberalization

8.1. Introduction

While there is a large literature on the optimal sequencing of economic reform policies (for example, McMillan and Naughton 1992; Sachs and Woo 1994), in this chapter we address a related, although more modest question: why is it that the agricultural reforms were implemented gradually in China, but implemented simultaneously in CEE and the CIS states? In fact, given China's success in being able to begin its reform agenda with HRS policies that reformed property rights and restructured farms—and the failure in CEE and the CIS states—we will actually be answering a much narrower question: what determined when and how transition nations liberalized their agricultural markets? While a full analysis of the fundamental determinants of how nations choose to implement market liberalization reforms could be undertaken, in fact, a simpler, and perhaps more convincing, explanation may be found by examining the effect of path dependency. Path dependency in this case means that some action taken (or not taken) by the government in the pre-reform (or an earlier) period may provide the best explanation for why they took a certain course later in the reform era.

The stories, however, vary somewhat for China and the nations of CEE and the former Soviet Union. Specifically, for the case of China we argue that the same factors that allowed China to implement HRS successfully in the late 1970s and early 1980s (for example the nature of technology, wealth factors, and decentralization) also made it unnecessary to immediately liberalize markets. The success of HRS (and the price reforms) at least temporarily achieved the goals of the Chinese Communist Party and met the needs of those at the grassroots by raising the efficiency of the agricultural sector and improving incomes in the rural sector. There was no immediate pressure from either the top or those at the bottom to push forward with market liberalization, the remaining part of the reform package.

In the case of CEE and the CIS states, path dependency is relevant also, but only in a somewhat different and more limited sense. Path dependency in this case means that the factors that had led to failed agricultural reforms in the 1980s were still present in the 1990s and, as such, made gradual reform difficult at any time for any reform-minded regime. Given the nature of technology and wealth factors, it is almost certain that agricultural reform would always be a challenge, since it was virtually impossible to align the interests of a top leadership that wanted to reform and the grassroots that would be hurt by reform.[1] Most simply, any reform programme by any government would, at least in the short run, inflict costs on farm workers and local officials and would create grassroots resistance. Hence, if reform was going to be able to happen at all, it seems that a consensus-based gradual approach was not going to work. Instead it took the dramatic political changes in the late 1980s and early 1990s to give leaders (in this case the reformers) a political basis on which they could launch economic reform. When deciding on their economic reform agenda, we argue that the nature of technology and wealth considerations meant that they had little choice on sequencing; they could only reform all at once. In fact, the once and for all reforms that the leaders in most nations pursued were much broader than agriculture; they occurred in almost all sectors, agriculture being just one of many.

In this chapter, we seek to flesh out these summary comments and take a more detailed look at these two stories, seeking to shed light on the question of why China could wait to liberalize markets and nations in CEE and the CIS states had to implement market liberalization at the same time that they implemented property rights reform and restructured farms. Later, in Chapter 9, we examine the difference among transition nations in their choice of how they reformed property rights and restructured farms.

8.2. Gradual market liberalization in China

The importance of path dependency can be seen by showing that the choice of China's leadership to gradually liberalize markets is due in a large part to its earlier actions. Specifically, once China had successfully implemented property rights reform and restructured its farms (as well as adjusting prices to reduce the implicit tax on farmers), it is clear the policy actions needed to continue the reform by liberalizing markets became less imperative. The diminished need to continue the agricultural reforms can almost certainly be traced to the fact that the early pricing reforms and HRS helped the reformers to meet their initial objectives. The HRS reforms increased agricultural productivity which led to higher farm incomes and food output. The agricultural pricing reforms also contributed to higher farm incomes and output. From the point of view of the leaders, the performance of the agricultural sector helped leaders achieve their goals by fuelling China's first surge in economic growth and reducing the concerns about national food security. The legitimacy that they sought as leaders of a government that could raise the standard of living of its people was at least temporarily satisfied.

Given this, there was no immediate necessity to launch into an entirely new set of reforms that would necessitate spending additional political capital as well as exposing the leaders to a new set of risks that reforms inevitably create. Most likely there were still those that recognized that the reliance on government input supply channels and state procurement agencies at set prices was imposing efficiency costs on the economy. Indeed, one of the first set of government-designed experiments in the mid- to late 1980s was to set up a market reform experiment in Henan province to determine how the market could be allowed to play a more important role in the procurement of farm output (Sicular 1995). But, at the time in the early 1980s, planners had erased, at least temporarily, the worst of the inefficiencies created by nearly thirty years of government policy. Not only had HRS policies improved incentives, the planning commission had implemented price reform by adjusting the mix of domestic output and input prices to levels that were more favourable to farmers and also improved incentives for rising input use and output expansion. Hence, with the urgency for additional reforms dampened for both the top leaders (since their goals were met) and farmers (since their incomes and control over the means of production had both improved), there was less policy pressure from the top and the grassroots.

If the gradual pace of reform taken by China is indeed due to the initial success of the price reform and decollectivization, then the fundamental determinants of market liberalization are essentially the same as those that are associated with decollectivization. As discussed in the previous section, wealth, initial technology, and decentralization created the environment within which decollectivization could succeed. According to our logic, then, the same factors—wealth, initial technology, and decentralization—are likewise the underlying causes of the gradual pace of market liberalization in China.

Wealth, or more accurately China's poverty, may also have directly contributed to the decision to delay market liberalization. Although the potential disruption effects due to market liberalization were relatively low (given the nature of China's farming systems), ex ante the leaders did not know how much disruption would be caused by complete market liberalization. In the early 1980s, China was still a net importer of food, had only small foreign exchange reserves, and had little means to make up food shortfalls through imports. The nation's per capita calorie level was still low. In short, China was living on the edge of a precarious food balance; it was mostly feeding itself, but barely. Hence, when considering whether or not to proceed with a reform that possibly (though maybe not even probably) could disrupt the nation's food supply, it is easy to see how the calculus induced leaders to proceed only gradually.

Besides, the decentralized nature of China's economy gave it a choice not only when to reform, but how. In addition to the indirect effects of decentralization on the pace of market liberalization in China, decentralization also affected the way that China reformed its markets. Because regions were relatively self-sufficient, China's grain system was built around thirty separate provincial grain bureau systems that each ran around 100 county-level grain bureaux. Each county grain bureau had its own network of ten to twenty township grain stations. Hence, in total there were more than 50,000 different units involved in the grain business. While vertically integrated into a nationwide hierarchy, the grain bureau in each individual jurisdiction also reported to the local government and part of their effort (as well as part of their funding) was spent in meeting the food goals of the local economy. Essentially what this means is that while each grain bureau sub-agency did retain ties to the grain bureaux in the level of government above them, they also had a certain degree of independence. An almost identical system existed in parallel with the grain bureau for distributing fertilizer.

As a consequence, when China's national leaders finally began to slowly relax the restrictions on inter-regional trade of grain and fertilizer they did not need to build a competitive market system out of nothing. Instead, grain and fertilizer marketing reform was actually started by partially commercializing the state-owned grain stations and fertilizer input supply corporate branches. In return for performing certain state policy functions (such as continuing to collect the state-imposed delivery quota or deliver ration-priced fertilizer), managers of the grain stations and input supply branches were allowed to engage in trading as long as it did not interfere with their policy duties. They were also allowed to keep part or all of their trading profits. Hence, as described by McMillan (1997), China liberalized grain markets using an approach that was used in other sectors of the economy: competition by entry. In this case, however, the competition was among quasi-commercialized grain bureau managers and the entry occurred because there were thousands of units all of which were provided with an incentive to trade. During most times, there were also few restrictions imposed by policy on who could trade where.

Fertilizer market reform: a case study of China's gradual approach

The effectiveness of such a system in giving control to China's leaders over the pace of reform is seen in the case of reform in the fertilizer sector (Stone 1988; Ye and Rozelle 1994; Rozelle 1996). In search of more efficient inter-regional allocations of chemical fertilizers, leaders partially commercialized the local branches of China's Agricultural Inputs Corporation (AIC) in the mid-1980s. Almost immediately, inter-regional trade sprang up to a level that had never before been experienced (albeit still relatively small from the point of view of a mature market economy), driven by managers that had an incentive to arbitrage price differences between fertilizer surplus regions and those in relative deficit.

The new fertilizer marketing channels, however, were still relatively new, and although the newly liberalized traders helped ease regional shortages, they did not eliminate them. In fact, they could not for two reasons. First, the marketing networks were still immature, having just started. Many transactions still depended on old relationships and not the forces of supply and demand through competitive wholesale markets. In addition, the nation was still in aggregate deficit; that is, aggregate fertilizer supply was insufficient to meet aggregate demand. Moreover, the aggregate deficit not only existed when output prices were relatively low in 1985 and 1986, but was even more evident as the demand for fertilizer rose with the rise of grain prices in the late 1980s.

It was the tensions caused by rising demand for fertilizer and a marketing system that was not ready to handle the pressures that ended up leading to a suspension of the first attempt at fertilizer reform. As the prices for grain began to rise sharply in late 1987, the demand for fertilizer across regions became increasingly intense. The media was filled with reports of hoarding, fertilizer hijacking, and price gouging. By early 1988, it was becoming clear to leaders that a system relying solely on the nascent fertilizer markets was not going to be able smoothly to handle the rising pressures. In response, China's government took immediate action by temporarily suspending the rights of AIC officials to commercially trade fertilizer and reverted back to the planned allocations. As during the time before the reforms, localities would depend mostly on production from their own local plants (which were built during the Mao self-sufficiency era) supplemented (often only minimally) by shipments supplied under a nationally planned inter-regional transfer matrix.

The actions of the leaders revealed their preferences and demonstrated that they had a choice in the pace of liberalizing markets. Despite the inefficiencies associated with the plan, at the very least local leaders and producers could make their production plans under a degree of certainty, even if the quantity of fertilizer was insufficient. Apparently, China's leaders believed the costs of allocative inefficiencies by not having market forces equilibrating prices across regions (and relying on planned fertilizer allocations) were less than the costs that would have been created by the uncertainty of access to fertilizer associated with imperfectly developed markets.

After the aggregate supply of fertilizer rose in the early 1990s, due to increased production capacity and imports, fertilizer markets were liberalized once again, this time with almost no market disruptions. Clearly, the gradual nature of China's fertilizer reforms benefited from the decentralized nature of China's economic and political system and the fact that there was no immediate imperative to reform. If it did not work the first time, a second attempt at reform could be started at some point in the future when conditions were more favourable.

8.3. Simultaneous reforms in CEE and the CIS states

As it turned out political events of a much greater magnitude overtook the agricultural reform debate in the Soviet Union and CEE states in the late 1980s and created an environment in which it was possible to reform, not only agriculture, but the entire economy.[2] The change in leadership dramatically strengthened the impetus to reform—not only for economic reasons, but also for political reasons. The anti-Communist political forces that came to power were determined to get rid of the Communist system and to introduce democracy and a market economy.

In those countries where anti-Communist forces came to power, for agriculture and the food economy, as for the rest of the economy, the implications were dramatic. Reforms were launched despite resistance by farm managers, workers, and local officials.[3] As before transition, many farm managers, workers, and local officials expected that they would lose from agricultural reform. However, in the wake of the dramatic political changes, even realizing there would be disruption and disorganization costs associated with property rights reform and farm restructuring and market liberalization (although almost certainly the reformers—and everyone else—underestimated the magnitude of the costs), reformers chose to push through as much of the economic reform agenda as possible at the time that they were (still) in charge. Hence, for political and economic reasons, radical reforms were introduced. Since the previous system had failed to result in efficiency improvements with marginal and slow reforms, a more radical and broad reform approach was inevitable in the view of the reformers. The nations could not continue to operate at the same old levels of inefficiency. Reform had to be done.

Determinants of the pace of agricultural reform

Therefore, the only real question facing reformers of agriculture in CEE and the CIS nations, as in other sectors, was in what order and at what speed should reform policies be implemented? On this, we argue also that pro-reform leaders did not have much of a choice. In the past the role of wealth and technology was so strong in creating stiff resistance at the grassroots level that it undermined reform. The post-Communist reform programme needed to be sufficiently radical to overcome the same strong forces that existed before the political changes: the resistance to reform at the grassroots because of large subsidies; the need to use an encompassing reform agenda in order to have a significant impact on productivity of the entire food system; and the administrative difficulties of implementing an optimally sequenced reform programme in such a complex and integrated agro-food system.

There were several reasons for implementing the reforms simultaneously. First, the more industrialized nature of the Soviet agricultural production system and the inefficiencies embedded in the agro-food supply chain required an approach beyond the farm sector. Several scholars argued that the organizational inefficiencies in the supply chain would strongly limit the potential impact of farm-level reforms in the Soviet Union, and that they were a more important problem in the agricultural efficiency problem than the low productivity of the farms themselves. They believed this was a fundamental problem of agriculture in the Soviet era and affected the willingness for and feasibility of reform. For example Wädekin (1990: 235) wrote that '[i]t has by now become general knowledge that the food crisis in the USSR is more one of distribution than of production and should therefore be primarily approached from the distribution side'. Similarly, Johnson and Brooks (1983: 57) argue that '[Soviet] agriculture cannot be efficient and productive unless the rest of the economy provides it with high quality inputs . . . and with a responsive service . . . [and] marketing sector. One of the great disadvantages of Soviet agriculture is that the rest of the economy . . . so poorly serves it.' Gray (1990: 6) agrees that 'the usefulness of farm production is greatly decreased by deficiencies in processing and distribution'. Maybe Wegren (1998) makes the point most forcefully, in saying that, given the degree of bureaucratic infighting and lack of coordination and other factors over which farms had no control, it is not surprising that farms did not produce efficiently. The real question, he argues (1998: 62), 'is how they produced at all and how they managed to improve food production during the 1960s, 1970s, and 1980s'.

All these authors agree that solving the problems of Soviet agriculture would require a broad reform approach, with many of the most crucial policy reforms occurring beyond the farms. As Wegren (1998: 62) summarizes: 'making Soviet farms more efficient [required] "getting prices right" and liberating wholesale, trade, distribution and marketing networks (as well as correcting deficiencies in infrastructure).' Hence, successful agricultural reforms—in contrast to China—needed to include not only price reform but also fundamental reforms of the up- and downstream industries and the entire marketing chain.

In addition, in terms of administrative feasibility, the nature of technology in CEE and the CIS states also makes it less likely that a gradual set of reforms could have been orchestrated. More complicated technologies mean that there is a more complex set of exchanges between a larger number and greater variety of firms. In such a system, to design a sequence of policy moves that would become the core of a gradual reform strategy, policy makers would have needed to have access to extensive information on a vast number of processes. Because of these nearly impossibly large informational requirements, most observers question the feasibility of plotting out a rational, systematically executed reform path ex ante. As McMillan (1997: 232) puts it: 'If it were possible to plan the transition it would have been possible to plan the economy.'

Finally, the importance of agriculture in the overall economy played an important role as well. Unlike in China, in which agriculture made up such a huge share of the economy at the outset of reforms, agriculture in the

Soviet Union and the CEE played a much less important role in the economy.[4] As a result, reformers took several decisions which had a major impact on agriculture and on the sequencing of the agricultural reforms as part of a broader reform agenda. For example, the decision to liberalize food prices was not part of an agricultural reform or poverty alleviation effort, but rather part of a macroeconomic reform to liberalize consumer prices. Similarly, the decisions to liberalize markets and privatize and restructure the food-processing and agribusiness sector were made as part of a broader industrial reform agenda. Obviously, however, these decisions had major impacts on the agricultural reforms.

Hence, for all of these reasons, reformers in CEE and the CIS nations did not have much of a choice if they were going to consolidate their reform agenda—either in what to reform or the pace of reform. The same factors that kept gradual reform from occurring in the pre-reform era made it imperative that the reforms happened all at once when the decision to reform was taken. In this way, like the case of China, there is an element of path dependency. The factors that put a country in a situation in which it was not able to reform during an earlier era, pushed it to reform all at once when other events triggered the reforms.

The importance of political reforms

In the arguments which we presented in this section on the reasons for simultaneous reform implementation, we started from the assumption that dramatic political reforms had changed the leadership in CEE and CIS after 1989. However, this assumption does not hold for all the transition countries in CEE and CIS. In several of the CIS countries no such leadership change occurred. For example, countries such as Turkmenistan, Uzbekistan, Kazakhstan, and Belarus are still run by more or less the same leadership as under the Soviet period.

Clearly, these differences in political reforms and leadership change have affected the likelihood of reforms and the pace of liberalization. In other words, the starting assumption of this section does not apply to these countries. To illustrate the importance of this, Figure 8.1 shows the correlation between an indicator of political reforms in the fifteen CIS countries and a composite indicator of agricultural reform. The correlation is positive and very strong.[5] The lack of political reform in several countries, in particular in the least reformed countries such as Belarus, Turkmenistan, and Uzbekistan, has been a major constraint on the progress of economic reforms in these CIS countries.

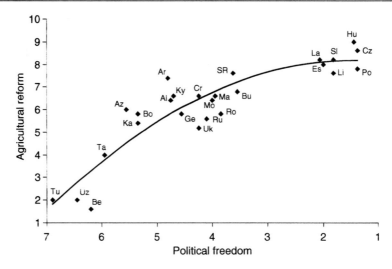

Figure 8.1 Political reforms and agricultural reforms in Eastern Europe and the former Soviet Union (1998).

Notes

1. In making this argument, we want to be clear that we are not suggesting that all governments wanted to reform. They did not. Some were merely caught up in the wave that swept the Soviet Union and CEE in the period immediately after 1989. However, the tensions for reforms were faced by leaders—willing or not.
2. Most countries did execute in the first years of transition a reform package that included price reform, property rights reform and farm restructuring, and market liberalization. But, as we have explained in detail in Chapter 4, there is considerable variation among nations in CEE and the CIS states. Some, indeed, have moved gradually. For example, Belarus, Uzbekistan, and Turkmenistan did not move forward with a complete package of reforms, at least in the 1990s. Yet, these countries are the ones where political reforms have not made much progress. One could argue that the necessary political changes to make such economic reforms possible have not occurred there—we will discuss this issue in the last section of this chapter.
3. We ignore here exceptions such as in Albania, where the agricultural reforms were driven by grassroots initiatives, similar to East Asia (Cungu and Swinnen 1999).
4. Interestingly, there are several cases which suggest that where agriculture played a key role in the economy, e.g. as an important source of rents or government revenue, leaders were much more reluctant in liberalizing. Examples of this are grain sectors in Bulgaria and Ukraine. In Bulgaria, several ministers of agriculture had to resign in the mid-1990s when rumours emerged that wheat harvests

would fall short of domestic demand or when 'uncontrolled' exports had led to domestic price increases. The most extreme example is in the cotton sectors of Uzbekistan and Turkmenistan. In both countries cotton is an important economic sector, and an important source of government revenue. Both Uzbekistan and Turkmenistan claimed to model their reforms after China. However, the main similarity is slow market liberalization. Unlike China, leaders also decided to keep tight control on cotton production through a variety of measures (Lerman and Brooks 2001; Pomfret 2000). The underlying reason for this continued state control is that cotton is a major source of government revenue. The cotton sector accounted for 50% of total Uzbek export earnings. Calculations by Pomfret (2000) and Lerman and Brooks (2001) show that in both Uzbekistan and Turkmenistan state controls on cotton production and trade led to heavy taxation of cotton farms and rents extraction by the government. Farm gate prices for cotton tended to be half of the price cotton farmers could have earned for their output in neighbouring countries (Sadler 2004). Government rent extraction in the export cotton sector conflicted with market liberalizing and Chinese-type farm-level reforms. The absence of political reforms in these countries allowed this process to continue.

5. Also before 1989, there was some correlation between political and economic reforms. Although internal political changes in CEE and the Soviet Union were insufficient for radical reforms, in several countries some periods of political liberalization occurred in the 1950–89 period. Typically, such periods were also associated with moderate economic reforms.

9

The Political Economy of Property Rights Reform and Farm Restructuring

In Chapter 5, we explained the different impacts of the various approaches to land reform and farm restructuring. In this chapter we attempt to explain why different nations adopted different approaches. Given the wide variety of tenure forms in the transition nations and their changing nature over time, explaining all of the nuanced changes is infeasible. In addition, there also are many different determining factors and it is impossible to thoroughly explore them all. Instead, we focus on four questions that we believe match up important determinants with some of the key decisions that nations must make. First, we examine the decisions of nations to privatize or not and explore how their historical legacy in terms of past ownership affects their decision. Second, we study to whom the reformers give the privatized land. Conditional on the decision to privatize, nations also have to decide whether to practise restitution or not. The second part of the enquiry examines why it is some nations gave land back to their former owners and others gave land to the tiller. Third, we examine the land reform policies of those nations that did not restitute and seek to explain why some distributed land in kind to households and other distributed shares to groups of farmers.[1] Finally, we seek to understand why some governments imposed hard budget constraints on farms and others did not.

9.1. Classification of land rights types

While all transition countries have chosen to reform land property rights and restructure farms as part of their reform strategies, the procedures chosen and the implementation has differed strongly among transition countries and even within transition countries for different parts of the land. In implementing land reform, our discussion focuses on three main choices that nations face (see Figure 9.1). First, all nations in CEE privatized land, giving away land titles that bestowed on the holders complete control, income, and alienation rights (Figure 9.1, Choice no. 1).[2] Other nations, notably many CIS nations and China and Vietnam, did not opt for privatization, at least initially. Second, of those that privatized, countries also differed in to whom they gave titles (Choice no. 2). The Czech Republic, Slovakia, and Slovenia, for example, chose restitution, returning farmland back to the former owners who had lost their land during the collectivization process. Other nations in CEE (for example Albania) did not, and in the process of privatization gave land titles to the tiller. Third, for those nations that did not practise privatization, nations also differed in the way they managed land reform (Choice no. 3).[3] Some countries, such as China and Vietnam, gave control and income rights to individual farm households, while other countries, such as Russia and Kazakhstan, gave control and income rights to groups of farmers as shares.[4]

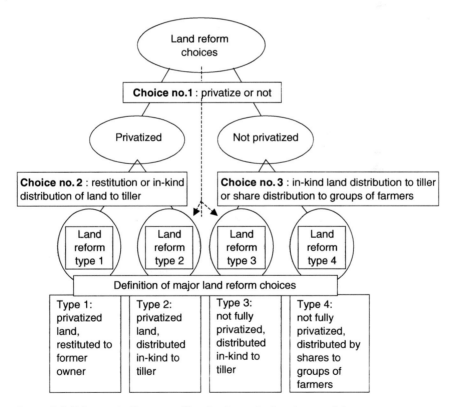

Figure 9.1 Schematic diagram of land reform choices in transition.

These choices resulted in four broad types of land property rights forms: *type 1*—land privatized by restitution; *type 2*—land privatized by distribution of land title to the tiller; *type 3*—non-privatized land in which control and income rights to the land were distributed by providing in-kind land to the tiller; and *type 4*—non-privatized land in which control and income rights were distributed to groups of farmer as shares.

In order to study the determinants of land property rights and farm restructuring, it is also useful to divide the land in several other dimensions.[5] First, land types 2 and 3 are similar in that land reformers created them by distributing in-kind land to the tiller. The only difference is that in one case (type 2) the farm household has alienation rights to the land and in the other (type 3) the household does not. Whether access to alienation rights is important depends on the nature of the tenancy contracts. If tenancy contracts provide control and income rights of sufficiently long time, are secure, and are transferable, they may provide much of the benefits of alienation rights. For example, in the case of Vietnam, farmers have been given control and income rights for fifty years; China's new contracting law gave farm household control and income rights for thirty years.[6] Households in both Vietnam and China have (at least in theory) unrestricted rights to transfer control and income rights during the duration of the contract and can also bequeath control and income rights to their children. Hence, in countries such as China and Vietnam, for all practical purposes (especially in Vietnam where land is formally titled and land can be used as collateral), there is little difference (especially in terms of production) between their form of tenure and private land. In the rest of this section, when we refer to *land to the tiller households*, we are referring to households that farm land types 2 and 3.

9.2. Historical legacy and privatization

One of the most fundamental decisions of those in charge of the reform of agriculture is whether or not to privatize land (Figure 9.1, Choice no. 1). When land is privatized, all property rights, control, income, and alienation rights, pass to the new title holder. The importance of the decision is clear. Land is an essential input into agriculture. It is an asset that is multifunctional, often providing non-market services such as insurance, collateral, and status. As such, it is particularly valuable in many economies. Being valuable, it is often a source of rents, a factor that makes it a source of contention between those who have the property rights and those that do not. Because of this, privatization has been a hotly debated and contested issue in many countries, but the actual choices differed (see Chapter 4).

When dealing with such a valuable asset, history of ownership may be particularly important in deciding why some nations privatized and others did not. In particular, all of the nations in CEE and those in the Baltics had a history of private landownership and family farms. In spite of this history, in the early 1950s, the cultivated land in most nations was collectivized or nationalized and run as cooperatively managed or state farms up to the late 1980s. The Transcaucasian countries, Moldova, western Ukraine, and western Belarus, also had a history of private landownership. In East Asia, although it is hard to generalize about such a big nation, most of the land in China historically was privately owned; however, in some areas that land had been heavily concentrated in the possession of absentee landlords, and tenancy was widely practised.

In contrast, there was less of a tradition of private family farming outside CEE and East Asia. In Russia, most of Ukraine, and most Central Asian countries, such as Kazakhstan, Uzbekistan, and Turkmenistan, when the Communist leaders nationalized the land, they did not take it from farm households that were farming individually, but the land was often transferred from large feudal estates to the state. In Eastern Slavic regions, such as eastern Ukraine, eastern Belarus, and most of Russia, a majority of the rural households were employed as serfs. Although some serfs had individual use rights on family plots, all land belonged to the feudal landlords and most farming consisted of feudal sharecropping. In many regions at the turn of the century, immediately before the rise of Communism, the basic unit of decision making, especially on the large plantations and in areas of land-extensive fields, was the communal village. Hence, in many parts of the region at the time of reform there was at most only a limited tradition of individual private farming.[7]

For some of the Central Asian countries, there was even less of a history of individual farming. Prior to the twentieth century, much of Central Asia and Mongolia was dominated by migratory or semi-migratory pastoralism. Much of the land in these countries was used and managed communally. Many of the original labourers on the Soviet-era collective farm in Central Asia consisted of the former nomads that the Russians forcibly settled. Therefore, these former nomads, and even more so the children of the former nomads, had little experience with family farming at the start of the transition era.

A historical legacy of privately held land in a country can have complex, but real effects on the decision of a leader to privatize or not. On the one hand, when a history of private property in farming is part of the past of a society and when it has been one of the major institutional forms for long periods of time before the Communist period it is likely that people in the country will demand private property in agriculture. At the same time, officials and commercial leaders may also be more familiar with the social, economic, and legal institutions that are needed to support a private property-based agricultural economy. For this reason, the historic legacy of private property may be an important determinant of the propensity of land reformers to choose to privatize land.

When examining the patterns of privatization, in fact, it is clear that the different historical legacies of landownership had an important impact. The still present memory of their history of private land rights provided a strong incentive for CEE reformers to choose to privatize land. While proximity to the EU and the familiarity of the local population with the land systems in Western Europe might also have reinforced this preference for private landownership, surveys confirm that households and individuals in regions in which there was a tradition of private farming before the period of Communist rule responded more favourably to reform policies based on privatization than those that lived in areas in which there was less private farming (Rizov et al. 2001).

In contrast, in Russia and Central Asia where no such tradition existed, research shows that the absence of a tradition of private farming cannot be understated in understanding why many of the former CIS states did not privatize land during the initial years of transition (Swinnen and Heinegg 2002). In many regions, there was a popular preference that land should not be privately owned. Traditional cultural, social relationships, and economic structures were organized around pre-Soviet communal institutions. At the time of collectivization, the communal farming villages were transformed into Soviet collectives. In these cases, if land reform forced individuals into private farming, it is possible that it would be forcing them into organizations that were more foreign to them than were collectives. If communal practices are deeply ingrained and/or embedded into the social and economic institutions that provide services for the rural population, the transition to individual farm organization may require a large, often difficult-to-carry-out modification of economic and social practices. Hence, it is easy to see why in some regions, reformers did not choose privatization.

An alternative hypothesis is that the differences in choice to privatize agricultural land are not so much due to the historical legacy of private property, but mostly to some factor associated with being part of the Soviet empire. Nations that had been part of the Soviet Union had gone through a certain set of experiences that might have convinced leaders to forgo privatization of agricultural land. However, the experience in some of regions of the former Soviet Union would suggest that the pre-collectivization experience with private farming is indeed a very important determinant and surpasses any experience-based factor. For example, although farms were collectivized in the Baltic countries by the Soviet Union after the Second World War, unlike many other regions in the Soviet Union most of the nations of the Baltics had a long history of private farming. For the next Forty years farmers in the Baltics worked in collective farms. However, soon after the commencement of transition, the leaders of the newly independent Baltics chose to privatize all agricultural land. Hence, this example of the Baltics suggests that it is not a nation's association with the Soviet Union, but rather the pre-Socialism experience with private farming, which played the key role.

The absence of a tradition in private farming may also be reinforced by the historic legacies of nations in another way: the length of time since the onset of collectivization. If it had been more than sixty years since collectivization, as was the case in many parts of the former Soviet Union, the absence of the skills and farming practices necessary for private farming could dissuade a nation from choosing privatization. Although collective workers may have had experience with household plots connected to collective farms, for the previous five to six decades none had ever run larger, independent farms. In contrast, in countries where individuals had more recently been farming on their own, privatization may be more palatable. Unfortunately, without rigorous statistical analysis available, there is little way to distinguish the importance of this lack of human capital since there is considerable overlap between those nations with little history of private household farming and those with a long history under Socialism.

The history of privatization, however, does not guarantee that a nation will choose privatization during its land reform. The two major exceptions are China and Vietnam. Unlike the nations in CEE, the private farming history in East Asia did not induce the leaders to privatize land. In both nations reformers distributed land in kind to households and provided (increasingly) well-defined control and income rights in thirty to fifty-year contracts. However, leaders did not transfer alienation rights to the land. In Vietnam, for example, land is almost de facto private. There are few differences between private property and the nature of land rights in Vietnam. In China, the situation is a bit more complicated. The collective (which is equivalent to the brigade or the team during the pre-HRS era) remains the legal owner of agricultural land.

While there are many reasons given in the ongoing debate in East Asia about why land should or should not be privatized, clearly, the continuation of the Communist regime and its ideology played an important role here. Most simply put, land is the most basic factor of production in agriculture (Brandt et al. 2002). As such, in a Communist country leaders will almost inevitably believe that the state, or its representative, the collective, should have control over land. Above all, it is important to have control since the collective is ultimately responsible for villagers, and land, in addition to being a household's means of production, can also serve as in-kind unemployment and social security policies (Burgess 1998). While there are different ways of interpreting it, in the cases of China and Vietnam ideology, or the historic legacy of political doctrine, not the historical legacy of private property, may be the key.

9.3. The determinants of restitution

Conditional on a nation's decisions to privatize, leaders have to make another decision (Figure 9.1, Choice no. 2). Should the nation choose restitution? Or, should it choose to distribute private land rights to the tiller independent of whether or not the tiller—or the tiller's family—owned the land prior to the Socialist era? In other words, we are trying to distinguish between the nations that choose between land types 1 and 2.

A historic legacy of another type, a nation's legal history, in this case played an important role in determining the decision to give the land to the former owner or to the tiller. The importance of the legal history of a nation is supported by the experience in a number of CEE nations. In fact, in many cases it carried more weight than economic arguments. Specifically, the proposal to restitute farmland to former owners, many of whom were no longer active in agriculture, was vehemently opposed by collective farm managers.[8] The argument was that those currently in farming should have access to the means of production. It was argued that the efficiency of farming would suffer due to a high incidence of tenancy and excessive fragmentation. Many economists and policy advisers were also opposed to restitution and frequently voiced their support for land-to-the-tiller privatization.

Despite the objections, land restitution became the most common process of land reform in Central and Eastern Europe, from the Baltics to the Balkans. When analysing the reason for the choice, one of the strongest determining factors appears to be the pre-reform legal ownership structure. In China in 1978, all cultivated land in the nation was either owned by the state or by the collective. Legal codes and national laws passed during the People's Republic period confirmed this. In China, until today the collective has retained legal ownership rights over cultivated land. In the Soviet Union all cultivated land also was owned by the state and there was almost no discussion of restitution.

However, in most CEE nations the legal status of land differed sharply. Through the entire period of Communism, individuals were still the legal owners of most of the farmland. Although control rights and income rights had been usurped by the collective farms after collectivization, the land titles had never been taken away from the original owners. In many cases the landowners had either never worked on the farm (they were absentee landlords) or had left the farm at some point between the 1950s and 1980s. Paradoxically, while these legal differences had little impact on the operation of the land in the countries in the pre-reform era, they had a much stronger effect on land reforms after liberalization. In short, the historic legal legacy in CEE made restitution the natural choice despite the counter economic arguments (Swinnen 1999).

Non-legal factors, however, also influenced the decision to restitute land to the original owners in some countries. For example, in the case of the Baltic nations, restitution was used as an expression of nationalism and a way to dissociate themselves from their former Soviet colonizers.[9] Although agricultural land was nationalized under the Soviet system, leaders boldly chose to restitute land to the former owners, despite the fact that there was no legal need to do so. Restitution permitted the transfer of landownership to native citizens and the exclusion of post-1945 Russian immigrants. It also introduced a radical break with the rural economic system imposed by the Soviet occupation.[10]

9.4. In-kind versus share distribution of land

In this section we seek to explain the third important dimension of property rights reform (Figure 9.1, Choice no. 3). There are two alternative ways to cast the question. First, we can study the property rights decisions of nations that chose not to privatize. More specifically, conditional on the decision not to privatize (that is, conditional on choosing to be either land reform type 3 or 4), we can try to explain why some nations decided to distribute control and income rights to individual households (land reform type 3), while other nations decided to (at least initially) distribute control and income rights to groups of farmers as shares (land reform type 4).

Alternatively, we can broaden the comparison groups, and (ignoring those that chose restitution—that is, setting aside those nations that chose land reform type 1) we can explain why some nations chose to give land in kind to rural households (or create land to the tiller households—land types 2 and 3) while others gave land rights only as shares to households. Since the only difference between land types 2 and 3 comes down to the alienation rights (that belong to type 2 but not type 3), there is little difference in our analysis regardless of the question that we are answering. Hence, we choose to answer the broader questions: why did some nations give land in specifically delineated plots to rural households and others decide to distribute land shares to groups of farmers?

Wealth, technology, and preferences for land distribution

Differences in wealth and technology (as we have defined these terms) played a key role in this choice. Undoubtedly, ideology and the personal preferences of politicians were important arguments in the political debates on the land reforms—see, for example, the various chapters in Swinnen (1997*a*) for detailed analyses of the positions of the political parties in the land reform debates in various CEEs. However, differences in wealth and technology are very important factors in explaining the differences across countries. These factors determine the efficiency and distributional effects of the land reform options (in-kind distribution—types 2 and 3—versus share distribution— type 4) in various countries, and thereby the preferences of the affected interest groups, and the pressure they put on the leaders and governments.

More specifically, the distribution of land in specific and clearly delineated plots to farm workers or rural households made it much easier for those households and individuals to use that land for themselves and leave the large-scale farm to start a farm on their own if they wished to do so. In contrast, the process of distributing land in the form of paper shares to farm workers could make it quite complicated for individuals to get access to land, in particular if they had to deal with managers of the large-scale farm who were hostile to the idea of farm workers leaving the farm and taking land and assets with them.

These differential effects had important implications for households and farm managers for two reasons, and the implications varied with technology and wealth. First, direct access to land was important for poor households to increase their food security, incomes, and assets. This effect was particularly important in the poorest countries. There, direct access to land played a primary role in increasing rural household incomes and enhancing their wealth. Poor households would therefore prefer in-kind distribution, ceteris paribus.

Second, the choice of land distribution had important implications for the restructuring of the farms. Some land reforms stimulated the process of farm individualization, others made it more complicated for farm workers who wanted to leave the collective or corporate farm. By making it more complicated for households to take their land and leave the collective or corporate farm, share distribution of land was more likely to stimulate the continuation of large farms and prevent fragmentation.

However, the relative costs and benefits of this process differ with the *technology*. As we explained in detail in Chapter 5, technology affects both the costs and benefits of the shift to individual farming. The greatest improvement in efficiency from farm individualization is attributable to rising effort from better incentives and will be relatively greater for systems in which labour plays a greater role. The efficiency losses (loss in scale economies and disruption costs) are also lower in labour-intensive systems. Hence, in areas in which the labour intensity is higher, the costs and benefits of farm restructuring reinforce each other in creating stronger incentives for the shift of large corporate and collective farming towards individual farming. Hence, in labour-intensive systems, households would be more inclined to take their land and start producing on their own. In those environments, rural households would also have strong preferences for in-kind distribution of land, since it would allow them to reap these efficiency, and thus income, gains.

In contrast, in land- and capital-intensive systems, households were less inclined to start farming on their own as they often lacked human capital, finance, and inputs to farm more efficiently, in the presence of market imperfections, and because the disruption costs would be relatively high (Rizov and Swinnen 2004).[11] In contrast, farm managers and employees with specific skills that were more valuable with the large farm organizations generally opposed any policies that undermined the survival of the collective, and later corporate, farms. Their status, income, and privileges were often directly related to the survival of the large farms. Farm managers therefore preferred share privatization over in-kind distribution. Moreover, share privatization offered additional benefits for farm managers and skilled employees. In several cases farm managers, often in collaboration with local officials, were able to exploit the share privatization system to accumulate shares for themselves in the reformed corporate farms, a process of personal wealth accumulation which was much more difficult with in-kind land distribution.[12]

However, in the poorest countries, such as China, the preferences of farm managers were also aligned with those of the rural households. In circumstances in which collective farms contributed to massive poverty and in-kind land distribution could have a dramatic effect on this, the preferences of farm managers may have been more likely to be closer to those of the rural households (Oi 1989).

Finally, wealth also affected the benefits of farm restructuring and, hence, the preferences of households. In rural areas, collective and state farms were often providers of services and non-agricultural employment for many rural households (Dudwick et al. 2003; Putterman 1992). Fragmentation of the farms could imply a loss of these services and non-agricultural employment. In general, these services were more important in richer countries, as in the poorest countries collective farms were mostly concentrated on agriculture and basic activities. Therefore, the loss of these services with fragmentation was less of a concern for households in the poorest countries, and more so in (relatively) richer countries.

In summary, because of these combined effects, there were important differences across countries in the preferences of rural households and farm managers. These differences were reflected in the social and political pressure put on leaders and governments. According to the logic presented here, we would expect reformers to give land in kind to households and stimulate the creation of relatively smaller farms in relatively poor and labour-intensive environments. In contrast, we would expect the choice of land distribution in shares in countries that have higher incomes and have relatively capital- and land-intensive farming systems that are integrated more into input supply chains and processing networks.

Empirical observations

Although data are difficult to obtain on the exact amount of land that was covered under different types of land reform programmes, using several key countries, we can illustrate that there is a strong empirical relationship between technology and the propensity to distribute land in kind to households. First, let us look at cross-country evidence. In poor nations with labour-intensive technologies (for example China, Vietnam, and Albania), almost all land was distributed in kind to rural households. The opposite case occurs in countries such as Russia, Ukraine, and Kazakhstan, nations that had a much lower man to land ratio at the start of reform. There all land was distributed as shares to groups of farmers. In between these extremes are countries such as Hungary and Romania. The man to land ratio is between that of Russia and China; part of their agricultural land was distributed to rural households, in addition to restitution.

Second, over time, we see that several of the most labour-intensive CIS countries, where the share distribution policy was initially introduced when they still followed orders from Moscow, changed their land reform policies later. This is the case in Armenia, Georgia, and Azerbaijan, all with labour–land ratios of 0.2 and more, where land shares were abolished at some point in the first half of the 1990s and land was distributed in kind to rural households.[13]

Third, there is clear evidence of much stronger grassroots pressure for inkind distribution of land to give households direct access to land and allow individual farming in poor, labour-intensive, rural economies. We have already documented the strong grassroots pressure in China and Vietnam. However, also in poor and labour-intensive European and Transcaucasian countries, such as Albania, parts of Romania, Armenia, and Georgia, there was a rapid shift to household-based farms, in several cases even before land reforms were formally implemented, when a collapse of the credibility of the ruling regime created a sufficient power vacuum for households to take their own initiatives, similar to the reforms in China. For example, widespread rural poverty in Albania, the poorest and most labour-intensive rural economy of Europe, induced many households to take a piece of land (effectively leading to in-kind land distribution) and whatever farm assets they could get and start farming on their own when stories of dramatic regime changes all over Eastern Europe further weakened whatever legacy remained of the Communist regime. This process of grassroots-driven land reform started already in 1990, and by October 1992, seven months after the first non-Communist government came to power, 87 per cent of the land had been transferred to households (Cungu and Swinnen 1999). Similar processes of so-called 'spontaneous privatization' took place in poor regions of Romania where households broke up collective farms (Gavrilescu and Sarris 1997). In Armenia and Georgia, household demand for land and individual farming was also stimulated by increased poverty in the wake of natural disasters and (civil) war in the early 1990s. In general, these spontaneous processes which effectively caused in-kind distribution of land in CEE and CIS countries reflected the grassroots initiatives for radical changes in China.[14] The regions where this occurred were typically poor with relatively recent experiences of family farming and with high labour intensity in agriculture.

Fourth, in contrast, in richer and more capital- or land-intensive regions, in which the disruption costs and scale economy losses would be much higher, there was less demand from farm workers for land and rules conducive to individual farming, and much stronger opposition by the farm managers and their allies. Farm managers pressured the governments for regulations and policies to maintain the large-scale farms. This contributed not only to government choices for share distribution of land, but also to additional government regulations favouring large corporate farms, such as rules governing farm debt, administrative requirements, and tax rules for starting family farms, etc. Mathijs and Swinnen (1998) calculate an 'exit cost index' for several CEECs in which they assess a package of government regulations which affect the costs of leaving large farms and starting an individual farm. They find that the governments of labour-intensive agricultures, such as Albania, made farm individualization easier than those of land- and capital-intensive farming systems, such as Slovakia.

9.5. Hard budget constraints and farm restructuring

One key policy variable in the farm restructuring process which has had an important impact on the change in management, and consequently efficiency, was the introduction of hard budget constraints. This, more than the size of the farms, distinguishes recovery and efficiency growth from continued decline (see Chapters 4 and 5). In this, transition nations of East Asia and CEE are more similar and differ from policies in Russia, Ukraine, and Kazakhstan.

In China and Vietnam, the move to household farming via the HRS reforms de facto meant the introduction of hard budget constraints. After reform, farm households were on their own to earn profits and the state was not involved directly in the process of farming after decollectivization. In other countries where workers started household farms, for example in Albania, Romania, and the Transcaucasian nations, the same happened.

Central European governments imposed hard budget constraints early on in the transition. The removal of budget support in many of these nations forced important changes in farm management. For example, in Central Europe the reforms basically gave control and income rights to the managers regardless of the exact organizational form of the farm. Moreover, many of the new farming enterprises no longer guaranteed employment to their shareholders. Farm managers also faced the threat of bankruptcy proceedings if they failed to pay back their loan in timely manner.

Unsurprisingly, when implemented faithfully in Central Europe, the imposition of hard budget constraints radically changed the organizational behaviour of farm enterprises. Many of the larger farms turned into market-driven corporations (Lerman, Csaki, and Feder 2004). Others began to make managerial decisions centred on improving the efficiency of the farms. The most pervasive effect was that corporate farms substantially reduced their labour use by laying off workers (Swinnen, Dries, and Macours 2005).

In contrast, leaders imposed far softer budget limitations on farms in Russia and several other CIS countries and as a result the restructuring of large farms was far less profound. For example, Csaki et al. (2002) argue that even after more than ten years of reform large farm decision making in Russia still has important features similar to those of the pre-reform collective farm structures. Farm leaders during the first ten years of transition were still committed to providing all members with jobs, regardless of cost-efficiency considerations. Farms were also obliged by tradition and sometimes by government pressure to maintain the social infrastructure of the village. In many cases, because of these other obligations, farms put little emphasis on profits. The continuation of many of these anachronistic practices is linked to the failure to eliminate soft budget constraints since managers could overspend and still get reimbursed, wages were paid regardless of farm profits, and banks continued to tolerate the non-payment of farm loans. Similarly, in some countries, such as Kazakhstan,

[i]nitial attempts at reform, which saw the state and collective farms converted first into collective farm entities and subsequently into producer cooperatives, involved little real change in patterns of ownership management and control [because] up to 1998 the former state and collective farms were never subjected to a hard budget constraint. . . . [W]ithout the sanction of the threat of bankruptcy there was little incentive for farm managers either to reduce their indebtedness or to reform their internal governance.[15] (Gray 2000: 1)

While it appears clear that the soft budget policy of a nation was linked to its progress in farm restructuring, this is clearly a proximate cause. Perhaps the more interesting political economy question is the one that seeks to get at the fundamental determinants: why is that countries such as Russia, Ukraine, and Kazakhstan were much slower in introducing hard budget constraints in farms than those in Central Europe? This question is of particular importance since it raises the issue of how and why certain governments could proceed (and others could not) with efficiency-enhancing policies despite obvious negative welfare effects for a significant part of the population, at least during a transition phase.

While difficult to measure, one factor many believe played an important role in determining the speed and extent of reform is the political and social consensus of a nation about its willingness to move toward a market economy. For a variety of political, geographical, and cultural factors, the consensus was much stronger in Central Europe and the Baltic countries. Simply put, after decades of Soviet domination these countries were strongly motivated to move towards 'the West'. In contrast, the absence of such a strong push made radical changes less compelling for Russia and many other CIS countries.

Second, wealth, in a number of forms, matters. The introduction of hard budget constraints, as seen, inevitably had negative consequences for a number of individuals, in particular those that got laid off. Besides losing their current income, loss of a job often meant the loss of the benefits associated with employment at the work unit. Therefore, to the extent that a nation could meet the needs of the laid-off worker, the magnitude of the loss could have been great or small. Two factors could greatly minimize the impact of a lay-off: fairly high prospects of finding a new job; and a nation-wide social security system that would be able to make unemployment or welfare payments and take care of health and other basic needs. In short, since access to social security, publicly provided insurance, and welfare systems is highly correlated with either relatively high growth or high wealth, the wealthier countries in Central Europe were the ones that moved most aggressively in hardening budget constraints and allowing lay-offs. They also were the nations in which farm restructuring proceeded the furthest during the first ten years of reform.

Interestingly, in the poorest countries, access to land for households also means that households could use land as a substitute for social insurance and income. In these countries, agriculture plays a 'buffer role' during transition, not only absorbing excess farm employment, but also employing additional workers when they return to rural areas after being laid off from their industrial jobs. In those countries pre-reform services were often limited and the growth of individual farming, with hard budget constraints, allowed households to cope with the situation.

In contrast, during the first ten years of reform the implementation of hard budget reforms was slower and less comprehensive in countries with relatively capital-intensive production systems but with social services linked to the farms and limited budgets for pensions and unemployment benefits. This was the case in countries such as Russia and Ukraine. The imposition of hard budget constraints was strongly opposed by local leaders and rural households because alternative income sources were limited and households were heavily dependent on farms not only for their current cash incomes, but also for a large set of social services. Rural households faced problems accessing basic social services if they became disconnected from the (reorganized) collective farms (Dudwick et al. 2003; O'Brien and Wegren 2002).

Some of the most important constraints on restructuring and labour adjustments in Russia and Ukraine took the form of the state's role in providing housing, education, and health care (Brooks et al. 1996). Mobility costs for workers were also high due to poorly developed housing markets. Access to health services outside the collective also affected the ability of individuals to shift their jobs. In part because of this system, at the end of the 1990s, in Russia most companies were paying at least part of their wage bill in kind and through fringe benefits rather than cash. Because most of the goods and services provided could not be converted into cash, this compounded the difficulty of workers being able to move to other jobs or regions (Friebel and Guriev 1999).

However, it should be acknowledged that the impact of this factor was mitigated by strongly reduced funding of rural services. Access to many of the social services formerly provided by the state and collective farms were already strongly reduced with dramatic cuts in budget allocations and subsidies in the early 1990s, independent of the farm restructuring process.

Notes

1. Because of the close association between tiller-cum-farmers that received in-kind distribution of land through privatization movements (that is, farmers received control, income, and alienation rights) and those that received control and income rights (but not alienation rights) through in-kind distributions (discussed more below), in fact, in addressing the third question it is difficult to distinguish between the two types of farms. Hence, in the analysis we are actually explaining the difference between these two types of farms and those that received shares as a group. After this analysis, however, we take a detour and ask the question why it is that some nations privatized land by giving land to the tiller and others distributed land in-kind rights to their farmers, giving them only control and income rights, and not alienation rights.

2. Privatization, in this chapter, is used in a specific way and includes land reform transactions that transfer full land control, income, and alienation rights to the new owner who becomes the bearer of the land title. According to this definition, privatization does not cover those groups of farmers that were allocated land shares.

3. When a nation did not opt for privatization, alienation rights to the land typically were held by either the state itself (as in many CIS nations), or the collective, or some local government or village (as in the case of China). Although it is possible that the exact landownership of land that was privatized matters in terms of how the land was ultimately managed, we do not attempt to explain the determinants of alienation rights for nations that did not privatize.

149

4. In addition, for those nations adopting the share approach, the process typically allowed shares to be identified with a particular piece of land in a second step, giving individuals ultimately control and income rights to specific plots, if individuals *chose* to exercise those rights. In practice, however, although income rights accompanied the shares, de facto control rights were often bestowed on the former farm manager or some other individual or committee chosen to manage the farm for the shareholders (see Chapter 4).

5. In working on the determinants of land rights and farm restructuring, it is important to recognize the difference between the property rights of the farm and its management. In particular, there is not necessarily a one-to-one mapping between farm operation and ownership, though in some cases there is. For example, in almost all cases, land that is distributed to the tiller households ends up being operated as a family farm. However, it is also possible that a family farm does not own the land it is farming, but is renting it from others. Corporate farms often rent most of their land from households.

6. Also in CIS countries, long-term lease contracts can be important if private land was not recognized. For example, in Kazakhstan, individuals could get individualized land plots if they converted their shares into actual plots. These plots were given under ninety-nine-year leases. (In 2003 these leases were converted into private ownership.)

7. Prior to the Revolution of 1917 a reform experiment was launched to break up the communal land into individual peasant farms—the so-called Stolypin reforms—see Macey (1990, 2003) for details.

8. This opposition continued during the implementation of the restitution process. To overcome the resistance of farm managers and local officials, reform-minded governments in some cases tried to explicitly exclude them from the reform implementation process (Swinnen 1997*a*). For example, in Bulgaria, when reformers came into government in the early 1990s they brought in outsiders to chair local committees implementing land reform and farm restructuring (the so-called 'Liquidation Councils'). This design of the implementing institutions was explicitly intended to break local resistance to reform implementation by former Communist officials and farm managers who had until then blocked implementation of the reforms by the local institutions responsible for doing thus (Swinnen 1997*b*). When the former Communists came back to power a year later, they 'liquidated the Liquidation Councils' and put the local managers and officials back in charge.

9. Another exception to the legal history argument is the restitution of state farm land in Slovenia. Here again, the historical legacy of this land was an important reason, as most of this land prior to the nationalization belonged to medium-sized farmers and not to religious institutions or large estates, as in many other CEECs (Bojnec and Swinnen 1997) and Swinnen (1999) for more details.

10. For example, in both Latvia and Lithuania the first privatization effort was still under FSU and the Communist Party (CP) regime, which gave land on a usufruct basis to rural workers. After anti-Communist coalitions overwhelmingly

defeated the CP in the 1990 elections, the new governments restituted land to former owners (all native Latvians and Lithuanians) as a strategy for securing their independence (putting landownership in the hands of native citizens). Interestingly, Latvia's emphasis on a radical and rapid agrarian reform is in stark contrast to its government's reluctance to privatize industry, where restitution to Latvians was impossible. Because most industry was built after 1945, any other privatization policy was likely to give an important share of the capital stock to the management and employees of the industrial enterprises, many of whom are Russians. Thus, while ethnic motivations induced a fast privatization in agriculture, they had the opposite effect in industry (Rabinowicz 1997).

11. A related factor is that in the Soviet Union and in most countries with large-scale collective and state farms, the process of collectivization after the Second World War included massive land consolidation programmes which wiped out entire villages and country roads and created large open fields, and moved farm households to new housing concentrated in farming towns. This 'socialization of the countryside' reduced the demand for decollectivization, and the costs of individualization.

12. In many CEE and CIS countries, after the fall of the Communist Party from power, former managers and officials tried first to block the reform implementation and later to predate on the system. Frye and Shleifer (1997) refer to this attitude as the 'grabbing hand' of Russian bureaucrats in the transition process, in contrast to the 'helping hand' in China where bureaucrats played a more constructive role. However, in CEE and CIS there were also important differences among bureaucratic attitudes. For example, officials in Poland played a much more neutral role than in Russia, where officials' rent seeking seriously harmed the reform process.

13. Land policies in Russia, Ukraine, and Kazakhstan also changed, but only much later, after 2000. In Kazakhstan, the demand for land in kind and individual farming differed strongly by region, reflecting large differences in technology, in particular between the north and the south.

14. In Albania, the government later implemented land legislation which was consistent with the de facto situation: it distributed land in kind to rural households. In Romania, where land was partially restituted due to historical legacy reasons, the government imposed tight maxima on the amount of land for restitution, and distributed the rest of the land in kind. Since many of the rural households also benefited from the constrained restitution process, the legislation was more or less consistent with the grassroots actions in most parts of Romania.

15. Also in Ukraine, Zorya (2003) argues that until 2000 the structure and behaviour of the large-scale farming enterprises did not differ significantly from the structure of Soviet agriculture, primarily because of the continuation of soft budget constraints and major constraints on individuals leaving the farms and enforcing their land rights.

Part III

Conclusions, Lessons, and New Developments

10

Conclusions

10.1. The economics of agricultural transition

In the first part of this book our primary goal was to understand the linkages between the shifts in pricing and subsidy policies, property rights reform and farm restructuring, and market liberalization and economic performance. Although striking differences have appeared in the nature of the reforms and their effects across the transition world, several strong empirical regularities linking reform strategies to performance have emerged.

First, pricing policy and shifts in relative prices between the pre-reform and post-reform eras have played an important role in output changes. In one sense these policies are what is in common in all transition countries. Virtually all nations experienced large shifts in relative prices due to pricing and subsidy policy changes. In most cases, the price shifts occurred in the initial year (or years) of reform. The objective of the policy—to bring agricultural output and input prices into conformance with those observed internationally—was also a common one.

Despite these commonalities, however, price and subsidy policies, more than any other factor, explain why agriculture output grew in East Asian transition economies in the immediate post-reform years and why it did not in CEE and the CIS nations. Virtually all reformers sought to bring their pricing structure more in line with international prices so they would better reflect the relative scarcities of resources and consumer demands. In the process of eliminating the distortions, however, relative prices moved in one direction in East Asia and the opposite elsewhere. During the planning era, China and Vietnam had tried to force industrialization in part by taxing agriculture with low prices in order to keep wages of industrial workers low. Their counterparts in most of CEE and the CIS nations, in contrast, had tried to stimulate food production by subsidizing inputs and providing high bonuses for marketed surplus. Hence, in the rationalization of prices, reformers in East Asia raised the prices of output, which strengthened the output-to-input price ratio. At the same time, their counterparts outside East Asia eliminated planning and many or all of the input subsidies and output premiums, which led to plummeting output to input price ratios. Since producers in all transition economies responded to price changes similarly (increasing output as output prices rose and decreasing output as input prices rose and vice versa), the direction of the price changes after reform helps explain why East Asia's output moved up in the initial post-reform era and those of CEE and the CIS nations trended down.

Beyond changes in relative prices, market liberalization policies reinforced the shifts caused by relative price changes and also help explain the sharp collapse in CEE and the CIS nations during early transition. When reformers took control they typically outright shut down the planning ministries in most CEE countries and curtailed their power in CIS countries. As a result, in most countries the systems through which the pre-reform producers had purchased their inputs and sold their output disappeared. Hence, it is easy to understand why production and productivity fell so dramatically in the first year or two after reform. In retrospect such a fall should have been expected since it is hard to conceive how completely new institutions of exchange could emerge in a matter of months. Perhaps more surprising is the speed with which institutions of exchange re-emerged in a number of CEE nations. Although deep markets characterized by the meeting of numerous buyers and sellers still had not materialized after several years of reform, the CEE experience shows how alternative institutions appeared to facilitate exchange. In those countries in which the institutions emerged, output and productivity began to recover by the mid-1990s and productivity growth has continued since. In those countries in which such institutions did not emerge, productivity continued to lag.

In East Asia reformers moved more gradually and in the initial years almost made no change to the state-dominated marketing channels that were set up during the planning era. So while market liberalization did not play much of a role in pushing up output and productivity of East Asian producers in the initial years after reform, it did not hold it back. In the longer run, however, policies in East Asia facilitated the entry of thousands of private traders, and the gradual rise of markets in the post-reform era has been linked with positive, albeit small, productivity increases.

Perhaps more than any other policy shifts, property rights reform and the farm restructuring that it facilitated are responsible for the rise of productivity in transition countries. It certainly was true in East Asia. In several Central European countries empirical studies almost all identify the strong positive links between property rights reform and productivity. It is probably safe to say that one of the necessary conditions of productivity rises during the first decade of transition was implementation of property rights reforms; it is hard to think of a single country that experienced positive productivity growth that did not have an aggressive and successful property rights reform programme.

But while the effects of land reform have been both positive and strong, the mechanism that has led to enhanced performance in East Asia and Central Europe has been quite different. In East Asia income and control rights were given to producers, creating millions of new family-run farms. Landownership remained with the state and privatization of land is still being debated today. The partial reforms, however, appear to have provided enough incentives and improved decision-making capacity to have ignited the rapid rise in output and productivity in Asia.

In contrast, privatization through restitution characterizes the main way that Central European reformers implemented the reforms. The reforms themselves, however, were not enough, since many of the new landowners had long since moved to the cities. Instead, the emergence of land leasing contracts allowed the growth of individual farms and the survival of large corporate farms (albeit with less labour which was systematically laid off by large reorganized farms in the most advanced Central European economies) (Vranken and Swinnen 2003, 2005). These institutional innovations have been essential ingredients of the rise in productivity in Central Europe.

While the picture in the literature on the CIS nations was fairly bleak in terms of property rights reform-induced productivity rises, it may be that the CIS nations are finally being affected by the reforms. During the early years after reform, the lack of clear rights that linked income to effort and inability to provide farmers with a way to restructure their farms held back any rights-generated output or productivity rises. Recent empirical work in Russia, Ukraine, and Kazakhstan (mostly on economic performance in the second decade of reform) may finally be showing that improvements in property rights and farm restructuring are affecting productivity. If so, it may be that the main difference between CEE and the CIS nations is the nature of the lag between reform and a turnaround in output and productivity.

10.2. The political economy of agricultural transition

In the second part of this book we explored the political economy of agricultural reform policies in transition countries. The approach we used was strongly empirical and positive. In other words, we looked at empirical evidence to explain why certain reforms have been chosen, or not. Our purpose was to try to explain which objectives, constraints, and incentives have induced leaders of different transition countries to choose different reform strategies.

Because the number of nations, the complexities of the policies and the timing of reforms differ so substantially, we necessarily limited the scope of our enquiry. In examining the determinants of the reform policies we limited ourselves to three broad questions. Why was the Communist government in China able to guide the reform process while it took a regime change in the Soviet Union (and in the CEE nations) to start the reforms? Why were many reform policies, in particular market liberalization and other reforms, implemented rapidly and simultaneously in some nations and only gradually, and with considerable time between them, in others? Why did the nature of property rights reform in land and farm restructuring differ so dramatically from nation to nation?

While we recognize that there are certainly other factors that influenced the decisions, we focused on four general categories of determinants: initial technological differences in farming practices and the environment within which farming occurs; differences in wealth and the structures of the economies; the ways the different governments are organized—especially focusing on the degree of decentralization; and the historical legacy of Socialism.

Why did the Communist Party reform in China, but not in the Soviet Union?

Radical reforms under the Communist regimes could only occur when there was simultaneously strong grassroots support for the reforms and support at the top of the Communist Party. If the support from both above and below is not there, it is likely that the policy efforts will succumb to inertia, foot dragging, and resistance from those that are not in favour of reform. For example, reform failed in China in the 1960s because there was no support by the leadership for radical decollectivization demanded by households at the grassroots level. Reform failed in Russia in the 1970s because there was neither grassroots nor leadership support for radical changes. Agricultural reform failed in the 1980s in Russia because the reform proposals from the top of the Communist leadership under Gorbachev were not supported at the farm level. Only in China at the end of the 1970s and the early 1980s was there a confluence of interests in favour of radical reforms at the top and at the grassroots, from both farm households and local officials.

One of the main points that we make in the book regarding the reform strategy of China is that decollectivization was not a fully top-down political decision. In fact, it should be seen in the perspective of a semi-continuous pressure by farm families to return to family-based production over the decades preceding the HRS reforms. The grassroots pressure was most intense at those times and regions where households suffered most from collective farming. The pressure to decollectivize was most strong in the aftermath of the famine created by the Great Leap Forward policy and in times of drought, when the problems of collective farming intensified. With such crises, the pressure to shift to household-based production systems was strong at the grassroots levels.

While pressure from below is an important part of the dynamic, it should also be noted that grassroots pressure by itself cannot explain why the reforms took place in the late 1970s. The same pressures existed in the 1960s, but then China failed to decollectivize. Earlier grassroots attempts to move to household-based production were resisted by the Communist regime under Mao. After Mao died in 1976, the balance of power changed and gradually support grew in upper-level governments and party cells for more fundamental reform in agriculture. In 1978 Deng Xiaoping had returned to assume important roles in the government and party, and support for HRS grew at the top.

It is this line of thinking then that underlies our observations of the need for both top- and lower-level support in order to have successful change under Communism.[1] The changes at the top—that is, the rise of the reformers—and the existence of grassroots support were mutually reinforcing in China at the late 1970s. While support in Beijing helped spread the HRS, the grassroots support also helped the pro-reform leadership win its case. Reform-minded Communist officials saw an opportunity to exploit the agricultural changes to oust the Maoists. The decision to reform was a delicate balance between pressure from the grassroots and preference to reform from a growing part of the top leadership. In the temporary leadership vacuum that existed after Mao's death, both reinforced each other in China's context. The success of the HRS reforms in increasing output, reducing poverty, and maintaining social stability in China's countryside reinforced the positions of the pro-reform groups in Beijing. Inversely, the enhanced position of the pro-reform groups created the policy space that was necessary for the grassroots initiatives to spread across rural China. By the time the leadership of the party formally announced its support of decollectivization, the HRS had already spread to most of China.

The situation was very different in the Soviet Union. There pressure for reforms came from the top. Mikhail Gorbachev, a strong proponent of agricultural reform, took charge of agriculture in the late 1970s and became the leader of the Soviet Union in the mid-1980s. He introduced several proposals to reform agriculture. Some of the proposals were similar to those forwarded by the Chinese leadership in the 1970s. However, the reforms generally failed to achieve the desired productivity changes. Instead of creating an economic miracle as in China, most of the old problems continued to affect farming and the impact of the reforms was disappointing.

In the Soviet Union reform was driven primarily by a Communist leadership that was unsatisfied with previous reform attempts. The central leadership in the Soviet Union, however, had little support from farmers or local officials or party leaders. Under the Gorbachev regime reforms were driven from the top and had to be supported by large-scale propaganda schemes. However, the proposals met with resistance and lethargy rather than enthusiasm at the farm level.

Causes of differences in grassroots support

Why were the attitudes towards decollectivization of farm workers and local officials in China and the Soviet Union so different? One factor sometimes suggested to explain the *difference in farmers' motivation* is the historical legacy of Socialism. Rural households in the Soviet Union had been working under the collective system for much longer than in China, and there was no memory of family farming. While this factor no doubt affected the attitudes of rural households, this is unsatisfactory as an explanation because it cannot explain why attitudes in many rural households in CEE countries were equally unenthusiastic about decollectivization.

A more convincing argument is the differences in standard of living offered by pre-reform collective agriculture between China and the Soviet Union. In China rural households had faced famine in the recent past and more than 30 per cent of households lived in utmost poverty. In contrast, farm workers in CEE and the Soviet Union benefited from large government subsidies, high wages, and were covered by social welfare benefits. Despite low farm productivity, workers in the Soviet Union's state farms and collectives had standards of living far higher than those in China's rural sector. In several countries rural incomes were actually higher than urban incomes.

With reforms, wages could fall, effort would have risen, and risk would have been higher. Moreover, with overemployment and soft budget constraints, agricultural reform would almost certainly have triggered significant lay-offs. Not surprisingly, many farm workers in the Soviet Union and CEE resisted agricultural reforms.

Technological differences reinforced these differences in attitudes. Farmers in China purchased few of their inputs. Supply channels were simple. They sold relatively little of their output into the market. Almost no farmers interfaced with processors. Most importantly, given the high labour factor share, the potential for efficiency-enhanced output would mean significantly higher incomes for farmers.

In contrast, farms in the Soviet Union and Eastern Europe were much more integrated into an industrialized production system and a complex network of relations with input suppliers and processors. Moreover, they were much more capital and land intensive. Under these conditions, farms were less likely to get a strong boost from incentive improvements, and more likely to face serious disruptions.

Because of the differences in the benefits from reform, there were differences in support from lower-level officials. For example, local officials generally supported the reforms in China. First, they were often closely aligned with the interests of farmers; being close relatives, friends, or acquaintances. Team and brigade leaders derived most of their income from their own farming activities, not from the salaries paid by the collective or government, especially in poorer areas. Hence, in the same way that farmers wanted decollectivization, local leaders supported this.

Second, local leaders could earn some rents from their position but, with the whole village mired in poverty, such rents were not large. The scope for rent collection would increase with the reforms as the level of wealth in the local economy grew. Empirical evidence shows that local cadres benefited more from the HRS reforms than the average farmers, but only moderately so.

Third, in the 1980s, the support of officials for reforms was sustained by reforms of the bureaucracy and by rural industrialization and fiscal reforms. Rural fiscal reforms and the creation of township and village enterprises were implemented from 1983 onwards. They were beneficial to local leaders and secured support for the overall reform agenda: they were instrumental in buying off local leaders and bringing their interests into alignment with those of the reformers. The economic reforms were further sustained by a massive mandatory retirement programme, effectively removing the old guard and moving up many younger and more pro-reform people in the bureaucracy. The bureaucracy changed dramatically in terms of its support for reforms and its competency. Another major change took place in the mid-1980s when bureaucrats were allowed to quit their government positions to join the business community. This 'bureaucratic revolution' had a positive impact on China's reform process in the second half of the 1980s and later, as it stimulated the interest of bureaucrats in local economic growth and new enterprises.

In the Soviet Union, local officials were also aligned with the farm managers' interests. They opposed reforms, partly for the same reason farm managers and many employees did. Breaking up the farms implied losses of scale economies and threatened their status and salaries, with few gains to expect. They benefited disproportionately from the subsidized farming system.

In addition, local officials were concerned about the wider effect of an aggressive reform policy on rural communities. The collective or state farm in the Soviet Union provided most rural social services. Reforms could result in declining social service provision and safety nets for many residents. Rent seeking aside, these were real concerns for local leaders since there were no alternative institutions available to provide local services and there were few off-farm jobs to which laid-off farm workers could have gone.

Possible disruptions and negative equity effects were also important *concerns for the central leadership* in China and the Soviet Union. The equality of benefits (or costs) of reforms was important to make the reforms socially and politically sustainable. Income distributional effects were as important as ideological arguments in the reform debate in the Chinese Communist Party on the HRS. Another concern was disruptions caused by the reforms. Disruptions could reduce the existing rents collected by Communist officials and/or they could have important negative social effects, like unemployment or income falls. As such they could also create strong political opposition and backlashes against the reforms.

The different nature of wealth, subsidies, and technology in the two systems of farming meant that these concerns were less problematic in China than in the Soviet Union.[2] In the labour-intensive Chinese farming systems, reform policies that changed incentives could increase incomes with little danger of disruptions to the rest of the economy. China's leaders also faced less of an equity trade-off. The distribution of land to all households allowed significant welfare gains. With few scale effects and better incentives, increased efficiency raised incomes substantially. In addition, because China's farmers were so poor, the reforms also helped improve equity. In China, because of the nature of the technology, it was win-win.

In contrast, in the Soviet Union, the subsidies and technology would have meant that there were inevitably going to be winners and losers from reforms, because they demanded restructuring, restitution, lay-offs, and other changes. Efficiency would have only come at the cost of equity. In a system like that in the Soviet Union, this would have caused tension among leaders who were willing to sacrifice efficiency for a relatively more fair distribution. This is another reason why leaders in China were more willing to push the agricultural reforms.

Experimentation and reforms

We find little support for the arguments that the organizational and hierarchical different structure of the central planning systems of China and Russia allowed for more reform experimentation by Communist leaders in China, and has therefore aided the initial agricultural reform process in China (i.e. the HRS in the late 1970s and early 1980s). First, the introduction of China's HRS reforms was regionally concentrated, not due to the design of planners, but because of grassroots initiatives. Second, the location of the start of the reforms was often determined by the relative absence of control of the planners. Third, the spread of the HRS system did not reflect the careful planning of experimental reflection.

In fact, experimenting with agricultural reform appears to have happened mostly in the Soviet Union. There was significant experimentation in the 1970s and 1980s in the former Soviet agricultural system, for example with brigade and team contracting and new forms of agricultural management. The decentralized nature of China played a more important role in the years afterwards, for example in market liberalization, in the implementation of the fiscal reforms, and in the emergence of TVEs.

Why were agricultural reforms implemented gradually in China, but simultaneously in many CEE and the CIS states?

Once China had successfully implemented property rights reform and restructured its farms (as well as adjusting prices to reduce the implicit tax on farmers), liberalizing markets became less imperative. The early pricing reforms and HRS helped the reformers to meet their initial objectives by increased agricultural productivity, higher farm incomes, and food output. The agricultural reforms fuelled China's first surge in economic growth and reduced the concerns about national food security. The leaders' legitimacy as a government that could raise the standard of living of its people was at least temporarily satisfied.

A new set of reforms would have exposed the leaders to new risks, in particular regarding the impact on the nation's food supply. Decollectivization had erased the worst inefficiencies. With the urgency for additional reforms dampened for both the top leaders (since their goals were met) and farmers (since their incomes and control over the means of production had both improved), there was less policy pressure from the top and the grassroots.

Hence, paradoxically and ironically, the radical economic reforms in the Chinese countryside did much to reinforce the Communist Party's hold on power; the complete opposite was true in the Soviet Union where the lack of significant reforms ultimately contributed to the fall of the Communist leadership. While radical agricultural reforms in the CEE and Soviet Union were only possible after major political reforms in CEE and CIS at the end of the 1980s, the radical reform actions in China, which looked like moves away from Socialism, probably did more to consolidate the rule of the Communist Party than any other measures taken during this period. Although it is well documented that the decisive change directly affected the incomes and livelihood of more than 70 per cent of the population, the agricultural reform also had a tremendous impact on the urban economy. The rise in food production and increases of food supplies to cities took a lot of pressure off the government. Urban wages, when raised, became real gains to income, since food became relatively cheaper. In addition, the rise of rural incomes created an immediate surge in the demand for non-food products. Many of the same dynamics occurred in Vietnam (Pingali and Xuan 1992).

Political changes in the Soviet Union and CEE states in the late 1980s caused reforms, not only in agriculture, but in the entire economy. The anti-Communist political forces that came to power were determined to get rid of the Communist system and to introduce democracy and a market economy. Reforms were launched despite resistance by farm managers, workers, and local officials. Reformers chose to push through as much of the economic reform agenda as possible at the time that they were (still) in charge. For political and economic reasons, radical reforms were introduced. Since the previous system had failed to result in efficiency improvements with marginal and slow reforms, a more radical and broad reform approach was inevitable in the view of the reformers.

The post-Communist reform programme needed to be sufficiently radical to have a significant impact on productivity of the entire food system.

This required a broad and encompassing reform strategy. First, the more industrialized nature of the Soviet agricultural production system and the inefficiencies embedded in the agro-food supply chain required an approach beyond the farm sector. The organizational inefficiencies in the supply chain would strongly limit the potential impact of farm-level reforms in the Soviet Union. They were a very important cause of low agricultural efficiency. Solving the problems of Soviet agriculture would require policy reforms beyond the farms.

Second, in terms of administrative feasibility, the more complicated technologies meant a more complex set of exchanges between a larger number and greater variety of firms. To design an optimal sequence of policy in a gradual reform strategy, policy makers would have been required to have access to extensive information on a vast number of processes.

Third, the importance of agriculture in the economy played a role as well. Unlike in China, where agriculture made up such a huge share of the economy at the outset of reforms, agriculture in the Soviet Union and the CEE was much less important in the economy. Reformers took several decisions which had a major impact on agriculture and on the sequencing of the agricultural reforms as part of a broader reform agenda.

Hence, for all of these reasons, the same factors that kept reform from occurring in the pre-reform era made it imperative that the reforms happened all at once when the decision to reform was taken. In this way, as in the case of China, there is an element of path dependency. The factors that put a country in a situation in which it was not able to reform during an earlier era pushed it to reform all at once when other events triggered the reforms.

Finally, it should be emphasized that in several CIS countries no leadership change occurred. The lack of political reform in several countries, in particular in the least reformed countries such as Belarus, Turkmenistan, and Uzbekistan, has been a major constraint on the progress of economic reforms in these CIS countries.

What are the causes for the differences in land and farm reform strategies?

First, the *choice to privatize land, or not,* was affected by historical and legal legacies of landownership. The still present memory of their history of private land rights provided a strong incentive for CEE reformers to choose to privatize land. Households and individuals in regions in which there was a tradition of private farming before the period of Communist rule responded more favourably to reform policies based on privatization than those who lived in areas in which there was less private farming. Proximity to the EU and the familiarity of the local population with the land systems in Western Europe might also have reinforced this preference for private landownership.

In contrast, in Russia and Central Asia where no such tradition existed, there was no privatization of land during the initial years of transition. In many regions, there was a popular preference that land should not be privately owned. There, the absence of a tradition in private farming was reinforced by the length of time since the onset of collectivization. After more than sixty years of collectivization, in many parts of the former Soviet Union, the absence of the skills and farming practices necessary for private farming could dissuade a nation from choosing privatization. Although collective workers may have had experience with household plots connected to collective farms, for the previous five to six decades none had ever run larger, independent farms.

In China and Vietnam, ideology still played an important role. Unlike the nations in CEE, the private farming history did not induce the leaders to privatize land. Clearly, the continuation of the Communist regime and its ideology played an important role here. With land the most basic factor of production in agriculture in a Communist country, leaders believe that the state, or its representative, the collective, should have control over land. Yet, in both nations reformers provided (increasingly) well-defined control and income rights, and the de facto difference with ownership of land is getting smaller.

Second, the *decision of land restitution* was strongly influenced by another historic legacy: a nation's legal history. Restitution of farmland to former owners, many of whom were no longer active in agriculture, was vehemently opposed by collective farm managers. It was argued that the efficiency of farming would suffer due to a high incidence of tenancy and excessive fragmentation. Many economists and policy advisers were also opposed to restitution.

Despite the objections, land restitution became the most common process of land reform in Central and Eastern Europe. The strongest determining factor appears to be the pre-reform legal ownership structure. In China and in the Soviet Union, in 1978, all cultivated land in the nation was either owned by the state or by the collective. However, in most CEE nations, through the entire period of Communism, individuals were still the legal owners of most of the farmland. Although control rights and income rights had been usurped by the collective farms after collectivization, the land titles had never been taken away from the original owners. The historic legacy in CEE made restitution the natural choice despite the counter economic arguments.

Third, among those nations that did not restitute land, why did some choose to give *land in specifically delineated plots* (*in kind*) to rural households while others decided to distribute *land in shares* to groups of farmers? There is a strong empirical relationship between wealth, technology, and the propensity to distribute land in kind to households. In poor nations with labour-intensive technologies (for example China, Vietnam, and Albania) almost all land was distributed in kind to rural households. In the richer and more capital-intensive farming countries, such as Russia, Ukraine, and Kazakhstan, all land was distributed as shares to groups of farmers. Also, in poor and labour-intensive European and Transcaucasian countries, such as Albania, parts of Romania, Armenia, and Georgia, there was a rapid shift to household-based farms. These processes included in-kind distribution of land. The regions where this occurred were typically very poor, with relatively recent experiences of family farming, and with high labour intensity in agriculture.

The distribution of land in specific and clearly delineated plots to farm workers or rural households made it easier for poor households and individuals to use that land for themselves and leave the large-scale farm to start a farm on their own if they wished to do so. Such direct access to land was particularly important for poor households to increase their food security, incomes, and assets. Poor households would therefore prefer in-kind distribution, ceteris paribus. These preferences were reinforced in labour-intensive farming systems—which are typical for the poorest countries. The benefits of farm individualization are higher and the costs lower with higher labour intensity. Hence, households would be more inclined to take their land and start producing on their own. Rural households would have strong preferences for in-kind distribution of land, since it would allow them to reap these gains.

Share distribution of land was more likely to stimulate the continuation of large farms and prevent fragmentation, as it made leaving the farms more difficult for households, in particular with farm managers hostile to the idea. In richer and more land- and capital-intensive systems, households were less inclined to start farming on their own, and to leave the large farms because the economic incentives were less, and because of the social benefits associated with the farms. Farm managers and employees with specific skills that were more valuable to the large farm organizations generally opposed any policies that undermined the survival of the collective, and later corporate, farms. Farm managers therefore preferred share privatization over in-kind distribution, as it also offered additional benefits to accumulate shares, and thus wealth, for themselves.

The empirical observations suggest that these different structural conditions have translated into different government choices. In the most extreme cases these differences have played out immediately (for example, in China and Albania), in other cases they have evolved gradually, with grassroots preferences and pressures gradually influencing new governments as they came to power (for example, in Azerbaijan).

Fourth, the last question we addressed is *why have some countries continued soft budget constraints?* Countries such as Russia, Ukraine, and Kazakhstan were much slower in introducing hard budget constraints in farms than those in Central Europe, although hard budget constraints were a key factor in inducing management change and efficiency growth in CEE. One factor is that in CEE there was a much stronger political and social consensus to move toward a market economy. For a variety of political, geographical, and cultural factors, the consensus was much stronger in Central Europe and the Baltic countries.

Another reason is that the richer Central European countries were better equipped to absorb the negative social effects of farm restructuring. The introduction of hard budget constraints had negative consequences for those that got laid off. Two factors minimize the impact of a lay-off: a new job or a nationwide social security system. Access to social security, publicly provided insurance, and welfare systems is correlated with high wealth, and the wealthier countries in Central Europe were the ones that moved most aggressively in hardening budget constraints and allowing lay-offs. Somewhat paradoxically, in the poorest countries, access to land for households also means that households could use land as proxy for social insurance and income. In these countries, agriculture played a 'buffer role' during transition, not only absorbing excess farm employment, but also employing additional workers when they returned to rural areas after being laid off from their industrial jobs.

In contrast, the implementation of hard budget reforms was slower and less comprehensive in countries with relatively capital-intensive production systems but with social services linked to the farms and limited budgets for pensions and unemployment benefits—and with few off-farm employment opportunities in rural areas. Rural households faced problems accessing basic social services if they became disconnected from the (reorganized) collective farms. Some of the most important constraints on restructuring and labour adjustments in Russia and Ukraine took the form of the state's role in providing housing, education, and health care.

Notes

1. This conclusion suggests an interesting analogy with major land reforms earlier in the 20th century in Europe. Significant changes in land regulations only followed a *combination* of both political changes increasing the representation of small peasants in parliament (changing the power balance at the top) and an agricultural crisis (inducing strong grassroots pressure for change) (see Swinnen 2002*a* for details).
2. Of course, ideology and politics also played a role in the timing and motivation of the leaders in both the Soviet Union and China.

11

Lessons of Agricultural Transition

So what lessons can readers take away from the analysis of success and failure of transition policies in agriculture and the choice of reform policies? We believe there are at least three sets of lessons that are helpful to the reader in understanding the main points of the book: (*a*) the importance of choosing the right indicator for measuring performance; (*b*) although there are a number of idiosyncratic reasons for differences among nations, structural differences in technology, history, and ideology can explain a lot of the similarities and differences in how countries have chosen different reform strategies; and (*c*) although there is lots of flexibility in how to put together a successful set of reforms, the work also tells us how some combinations have been more successful than others.

11.1. Getting the measure of success right

The first, and perhaps most basic, lesson is that we should be careful about which indicator we use to measure transition performance. If we use an indicator of efficiency or productivity instead of output, it is less clear that agricultural transition in CEE—especially that in Central Europe—was less successful than that in China and Vietnam. If prices need to reflect long-run scarcity values of outputs and inputs, then efficiency requires that leaders raise agricultural prices in East Asia, a move that naturally would lead to higher output. Likewise, when subsidies were removed, rational producers should use fewes inputs, actions which, as seen by the record in CEE and the CIS where the ratio of output to input prices fell sharply, led to falling output in these countries. In short, although leaders in many countries count increases in output as success, productivity shifts, not production trends, should be the primary metric for measuring success in transition agricultures.

11.2. Getting the institutional framework right

Assuming success is measured correctly, comparing the property rights and organizational reform processes across the transition world also yields several lessons about the determinants of reform success. First, the lesson regarding property rights reforms is nuanced. Good rights and the incentives they created certainly contributed to and will continue to affect performance positively. Poor ones undoubtedly account, in part, for the poor performance of some agricultural systems. This is well illustrated by the difference between China and Central Europe on the one hand and Russia, Ukraine, and Central Asia on the other hand. Despite being incomplete, East Asia's reforms allocated relatively strong property rights to individual land plots. In Central Europe, land was either restituted to former owners or distributed to farm workers in delineated boundaries and leased to new farms. Although the land reforms in these countries were complex and difficult to implement, they ended up with stronger and better-defined property rights for the new landowners than in Russia, Ukraine, and many other CIS countries. In the CIS countries, in contrast, land was distributed as paper shares to workers of the collectives and state farms. Individuals could not identify the piece of land that belonged to any given share, causing weak land rights for individuals and undermining their ability to withdraw land from the large farms and establish a private farm. As a result, family farming emerged only slowly and large farms have had fewer incentives to restructure. The empirical evidence in the literature, although fragmented, mostly supports these observations.

Despite the strong relationship between rights reform and performance, another important lesson is that full privatization of land is not needed to induce efficiency gains. In many countries the introduction of private ownership and sale of agricultural land encountered strong social and political opposition and kept reformers from providing a complete complement of rights to producers. For example, the top leadership in both China and Vietnam did not allow private ownership of agricultural land. Today, in China and Vietnam farmers still cannot buy or sell land. The strong positive effect of rights reform and restructuring on output and productivity demonstrates that allocating clear and well-identified land use and income rights can by themselves enhance efficiency, investment, and growth. In contrast, as seen from the cases of many CIS nations, if rights are too weak, there is little effect on performance.

Despite such progress, we do not want to suggest that a decade of agricultural transition has created a system of full and unencumbered property rights even in the best-performing countries; in fact, many major constraints remain. For example, China's leaders are still struggling to figure out a way to provide more secure tenure rights for farmers. Most pervasively, local leaders in many regions of the country continue to periodically expropriate land, shifting it among farmers for a variety of reasons (Brandt et al. 2002). Although the impact on the investment in land and other long-term farming assets is typically found to be relatively minor (Jacoby, Li, and Rozelle 2002), poor land tenure may be undermining the emergence of rental markets, keeping farm size from increasing, and precluding farmers from using land as an asset for collateral which could be constraining investment in non-farm activities (Benjamin and Brandt 2001; Deininger and Jin 2003). In CEE, observers of land reform are worried about excessive land fragmentation (for example in the Balkan countries) and monopolistic control of large corporate farms in an emerging land market (for example, in Slovakia).

Second, the lessons regarding the impact of farm restructuring are also nuanced. To start, it should be noted that except in labour-intensive agricultural economies, the individualization of farming should not be counted as an indicator of successful transition. Individualization has frequently been accompanied by a dramatic reduction in farm size, and in some cases, falling farm size leads to a loss of scale efficiencies. Smaller farmers in most CEE and CIS nations also experienced a sharp fall in their access to capital available for use in production (OECD 1999). While moves to small farms may make sense in some labour-abundant agricultural economies in the short run, in the longer run the transition to a modern state means that farm size must be sufficiently large and the intensity of capital use should remain fairly high.

We can see how natural resource availability and initial technology, which vary tremendously across the transition world, have played an important role in affecting the impact of farm restructuring (Swinnen and Heinegg 2002). For example, technology played a decisive role in creating the success of the break-up of collective farms. With labour-intensive technology, the cost of breaking up large collective farms in terms of losses of scale economies is smaller, and the gain from improved labour incentives from the shift to family farms is larger. As a result, since farms in China and Vietnam are much more labour intensive than the typical farm in the rest of the transition world, the reforms that provided farmers in East Asian nations with incentives and individualized their farms were able to create relatively large shifts up in productivity.

In contrast, many regions outside of East Asia were characterized by an entirely different farm technology which greatly affected the impact of farm restructuring. Large parts of Russia, Ukraine, and Central Asia are land abundant. Many of the richer parts of CEE also have much less labour-intensive production systems. The returns to breaking up the large-scale farms into individual farms in many of these countries are necessarily lower than the gains experienced in East Asia.

Strong benefits from farm individualization, however, were not completely absent from CEE and the CIS nations. In fact, several countries have gained, although the benefits were only enjoyed by the CEE and CIS countries with relatively high man/land ratios. The nations that benefited from farm individualization were those in the poor areas of the Balkan and Transcaucasian regions. Specifically, the four countries (Albania, Azerbaijan, Armenia, and Georgia) which have man/land ratios above 0.2 persons per hectare (ratios that are similar to those of East Asia) are the nations that have experienced the highest growth rates of TFP after land was distributed to households and large-scale individualization of farms followed.[1] Such high rates of productivity gain are similar to those experienced in Asia during the first reform years.

Even without individualization, corporate farm restructuring can lead to strong rises of productivity in transition agriculture. One of the main differences between Russia and Ukraine, where productivity fell, and some of the European countries, such as Hungary and the Czech Republic, where productivity increased, is not so much the scale of the farm operations, but rather the degree to which their management was restructured (Lerman, Csaki, and Feder 2004). In Central Europe, farm enterprise budgets were hardened and on-farm decision making became independent. Farm managers became primarily concerned with turning a profit and their increased managerial efforts induced sharp shifts in input use, management reforms, and efficiency increases. In contrast, large farm restructuring in Russia and in several other CIS countries was far less profound. For example, Csaki et al. (2002) argue that even in 2001 Russian large farm decision making still had important features similar to those of the traditional collective farm structures. Farm leaders are still committed to provide all members with jobs, regardless of cost-efficiency considerations. Farms are also obliged by tradition and sometimes by government pressure to maintain the social infrastructure of the village. In many cases, because of these other obligations, farms put little emphasis on profits.

The continuation of many of these anachronistic practices is almost certainly linked with the failure of restructuring. Above all, many nations failed to eliminate soft budget constraints and the government continued to tolerate non-payment of farm debts. Similarly, in some countries, such as Kazakhstan, former state and collective farms were never subjected to a hard budget constraint in the 1990s, leading to continued indebtedness and failed reforms of internal governance of the farms (Gray 2000). In addition, other researchers, such as Zorya (2003), argue that until 2000 the structure and behaviour of the large-scale farming enterprises in Ukraine did not differ significantly from the structure of Soviet agriculture, primarily because of the continuation of soft budget constraints and major constraints on individuals leaving the farms and enforcing their land rights.

Interestingly, in several transition countries 'hybrid' farm organizations have emerged that seem to address the need for institutions that allow both better incentives and labour governance and create organizations that can capture scale economies. For example, Sabates-Wheeler (2002) finds that in Romania the most efficient farm organizations for resource-constrained small farmers are 'family societies' in which farmers collectively share in the provision of mechanized services. Mathijs and Swinnen (2001) find that 'partnerships', small groups of farmers in East Germany that pooled their effort in certain production and marketing tasks, outperformed all other forms of farm organization between 1992 and 1997.[2] In Russia the most successful household farms refrain from registering as 'private farms', instead choosing to remain connected in some fashion to large farm enterprises. Such producers use their connections to gain access to inputs, marketing channels, and other services in an environment where traditional markets, if any, function poorly (O'Brien, Patsiorkovski, and Dershem 2000). Even in Turkmenistan, producers have begun to shift to family-based leasing within the nation's highly regulated environment in order to be able to access basic inputs, services, and output channels through the state marketing order system (Lerman and Brooks 2001).

Third, successful institutions of exchange—nascent markets, forms of contracting, etc.—also have many hybrid characteristics. In fact, some of the most successful transitions have not gone straight from planning to decentralized market-based exchange. Markets are emerging, but doing so quite slowly. China's experience demonstrates not only that, when politically feasible, partial reform by proceeding on a sector-by-sector basis (i.e. liberalize some products but not necessarily all) and by using a two-tier pricing system (i.e. a system of resource allocation that occurs half through planned transfers and half through the market) can end up creating markets that make the liberalization of the partially reformed sector successful. Such a reform strategy also has a longer-run effect of gradually creating a trading class that leads the push to expand the reforms and ultimately eliminate the need for planning.

In CEE the re-emergence of vertically integrated supply chains reflects the necessity of private contract enforcement mechanism for credit distribution and input supply in the absence of well-functioning public institutions. Other examples of non-traditional institutions in credit and input markets that appear successful in transition include a variety of financial instruments and enforcement institutions, such as leasing of equipment, warehouse receipt systems, bank loan guarantees provided by processors to farms, trade credit, etc. Variations in such instruments and institutions reflect differences in commodities, local institutions, and economic structure. To be successful these transition innovations have to be adapted and flexible to address transition and local characteristics.

Hence, whether considering institutions that create and maintain property rights or those that facilitate exchange, policies should accommodate institutions that are flexible. Flexibility is needed because transition is so uncertain and because there are many constraints that are still binding. Moreover, successful transition may trigger rapid growth which itself will require institutions to adapt quickly. For example, in land markets, the initial focus should be on stimulating short-term land leasing, an institution much more adapted to transition circumstances. Later on, long-term leases and land sales can develop. In general, non-traditional and flexible institutions have been more successful.

11.3. Packages of reforms

But the lessons go far beyond measuring success or failure of reform individually. More fundamentally, it appears from the evidence on the collective transition experiences that for any reform strategy to be successful it needs to include some essential ingredients. In other words, ultimately successful transition requires a complete package of reforms. All countries that are growing steadily a decade or more after their initial reforms have managed (*a*) to create macroeconomic stability; (*b*) to reform property rights; (*c*) to harden budget constraints; and (*d*) to create institutions that facilitate exchange and develop an environment within which contracts can be enforced and new firms can enter.

Our survey of the transition experiences in different countries clearly demonstrates the problems of not making progress in all areas. For example, when rights are not clear, as in Russia, producers have little incentive to farm efficiently or to invest, and restructuring is constrained. We see in other places that the creation of strong individual property rights is not sufficient. For example, in Poland in the initial years after reform, farmers had secure rights over their land. But their inability to access inputs or to sell output prevented them from reaping the gains of specialization and improved labour effort. Both output and productivity growth performed poorly. In general, in nations that created both rights and markets, productivity rose for most of the first decade of reform (at least after the initial transition); in those where either rights or markets or both were ignored, productivity declined or was stagnant.

That said, however, one of the most powerful lessons is that although all of the pieces of the reform package are needed, there is a lot of room for experimentation. Interestingly, if one chooses any two nations that had success, there was almost always variation in sequencing and in the form of the institutions that provided incentives and facilitated exchange. In other words, in our survey of the literature, we cannot find any single optimal transition path. The optimal transition strategy in any given country is one that contains the different parts of the package; the exact nature of the parts and the order in which they were implemented, however, has been different for each nation and takes into account the institutional and political characteristics of the country.

In terms of sequencing, while all of the ingredients are ultimately needed, this volume has also shown that reform policies do not need to come all at once. For example, in China and Vietnam, reform without collapse was possible by introducing property rights reform first and gradually implementing policies that liberalized markets and facilitate decentralized exchange. Such sequencing helped transition nations in East Asia grow rapidly in the initial years and steadily since. In CEE, however, after the initial politically led disruptions, the gradual emergence of well-defined property rights, markets, and other means of exchanging goods, services, and inputs has led to steady productivity growth.

The optimality of different sequences of policies (as well as the government's ability to implement them) almost certainly depends on the structure of the relationships between agriculture and the rest of the economy. There were important differences between East Asia versus CEE and CIS in this respect which reflect the different stages of development of the agro-food systems in each region of the transition world. While the relationships in the food systems of China and Vietnam were fairly basic, farms in the CEE and CIS needed to be integrated into a much more industrialized agro-food supply chain. Moreover, under the Soviet system, the tasks of providing inputs to farmers and managing their operations, storage, processing, transport, and road infrastructure were all allocated to different agencies. Farming was subordinate to as many as eight different ministries and local authorities had little control over any of these activities (Van Atta 1993). Warehouses and processing plants were hundreds of miles away. Hence, productivity improvements at the farm level would cause less impact unless simultaneous problems at processing and input supply industries were addressed (Brooks 1983; Johnson 1993). This required more of an encompassing and simultaneous reform approach beyond the farm sector, including the restructuring of food-processing companies, retailers, and agricultural input suppliers.[3] In terms of administrative feasibility, the much more industrialized nature of the agri-food supply chain (meaning a more complex set of exchanges between a variety of companies), and the fact that the various steps were functionally separated in the central planning system in CEE and CIS, were a severe constraint on optimal sequencing. A more gradual and orchestrated policy sequencing of a gradual reform strategy in the more developed economies in CEE (versus China and Vietnam) would have required more extensive information on the transformation process and the economy. In fact, most observers question the feasibility of plotting out any type of rational, systematically executed reform path ex ante. As McMillan (1997: 232) puts it: *'If it were possible to plan the transition it would have been possible to plan the economy.'*

11.4. Initial conditions and the impact of reforms

As we conclude this survey of reform policies and their impact on sector performance, it is important to reflect on a crucial and hotly debated issue.[4] Are the differences in performance between East Asia and the rest of the transition world due to the different reform strategies or to differences in initial conditions? In the previous paragraphs we have identified at least three sets of initial conditions that have affected the output and productivity changes in transition through their effects on reform impacts. Differences in initial price distortions affected the price reform effects; differences in technology affected the impact of rights reforms and farm restructuring; and differences in the structure of the agri-food chain affected the distortions in exchange relationships.[5] Each of these initial conditions favoured a more successful outcome in China compared to Russia. Or to put it in other words: implementing 'China's reforms' in Russia would not have yielded the same results. In summary, initial conditions were influential in determining the transition performance during the first ten years of transition.

As we have documented extensively in our political economy analysis, initial conditions have further affected agricultural transition and performance through their impact on the choice of the reforms. For example, initial legal and political constraints have affected the choice of governments in various areas, including land reforms, and technological biases under the Communist system have affected technology changes during transition.

Despite the importance of initial conditions, we also fully believe that they cannot wholly explain past performance and to an even greater degree will not determine the future of these economies. Initial price levels and technologies in some sense can be thought of as only establishing the boundaries within which the initial reforms take place. In almost all countries, there has been room for being bold or for being timid. Within regions with relatively similar initial conditions, countries have chosen different reform policies and with significant differences in growth and productivity effects. Moreover, the influence of initial conditions has declined over time. Hence, while the nature of the policies mattered in the past (over and above the effect of initial conditions), it will matter even more in the future.

Notes

1. See Table 2.5. In Azerbaijan this occurred only after 1996 when farm individualization and distribution of land rights started.
2. See also Gorton and Davidova (2004) for a review of efficiencies of CEE farm organizations.
3. Roland (2000) refers to this as the problem of 'sectoral gradualism' in the Soviet system.
4. See, for example, Balcerowicz (1994); Dewatripont and Roland (1992, 1995); Fischer (1994); Sachs and Woo (1994); Roland (2000); and Woo (1994).
5. For an interesting analysis of technological 'distortions' under the Communist system, see Pomfret (2002a).

12

The Second Decade of Transition

By design, our book has concentrated on the first decade of transition. To this point it has concentrated almost exclusively on tracking the changes to output and productivity during the first ten years after the start of the reforms, and on identifying key factors which have affected the choice of the governments during this period, and before. The analysis has considered the determinants of the changes that occurred during reform's first decade and measured some of the effects. As this book has demonstrated, much can be learned from studying the reforms, their causes, and their effects during this period.

However, institutional reform and economic change did not stop after ten years. Much has happened since. As in the first decade of transition, important variations exist among the regions. There are many common themes. For example, overall the picture in the second decade is generally more optimistic than that of the first decade. China and Vietnam have continued to grow at rapid rates for twenty years now and there is no end in sight. In Central Europe, productivity growth in agriculture has also continued. And, as before, there are still systemic differences among the CIS nations as some countries appear to be succeeding while others are continuing to struggle. For several countries in the CIS, the late 1990s are beginning to be recognized as a turning point. Russia's financial crisis in 1998 was in some ways at the same time the worst moment of transition and the start of recovery. Economic growth in countries such as Russia, Kazakhstan, and Ukraine has been strong since the crisis was resolved. Rural poverty has been falling strongly throughout the transition world since 1999 (World Bank 2005). Other nations, however, remain stagnant and are continuing to be plagued by corruption, inertia, and unrest.

There is something, however, fundamentally different about the second decade when comparing across nations. While economic fortunes are more similar in the second than in the first decade of transition, what certainly has differed has been the source of growth in agriculture. Economic transition, the realignment of prices, the emergence of property rights, and the appearance of institutions of exchange drove the rise in productivity (and explain the absence of productivity growth) in almost all of the transition nations during the first decade of reform. During the second decade, the main impetus of transition—in and of itself—is largely spent in several regions and the engines of growth, while still spinning, differ fundamentally from region to region. Despite this, we still believe that the analysis in this book remains valid for understanding several of the key changes that took place in the second decade.

12.1. East Asia

In China and Vietnam, although the effect of price realignments and property rights reforms had mostly been completed during the first decade, other forces have continued to produce strong growth in agriculture, in particular, and the rural economy, in general. In the agricultural sector, in the long run, the experience internationally is that technology is the most effective, and perhaps the only, factor that can underlie sustained productivity growth.

The story of China's agricultural sector during the second decade is mostly one of new technology. According to Jin et al. (2002), agricultural productivity growth in the 1990s has grown at 2 per cent annually. The growth has been enjoyed by all main crops—rice, wheat, maize, and soybeans. In a new paper on the expansion of the livestock sector (Rae et al. 2004), the total factor productivity of all major sectors—hogs, beef, poultry, and milk—has been positive and mostly strong. Most significantly, it has been shown that both the growth in cropping and livestock output and productivity have almost entirely been due to new technologies. Reports from Vietnam (Benjamin and Brandt 2001) show similar results.

The growth of technology, however, has not been free. It has only been generated by sustained investment by the governments of the East Asian countries. China has maintained an agricultural research system with more than 100,000 scientists. In the past decade, agricultural research expenditures have risen as a percentage of agricultural GDP (CCICED 2004). China has become the leader in the developing world in the area of plant biotechnology (Huang et al. 2002). According to a recent paper by Rozelle, Huang, and Otsuka (2005), China's agricultural productivity growth has not only risen in the past due to the access of its farmers to new technology, the stock of productive technology appears to be in place to sustain this growth in the future decades.

While new technologies have helped agriculture maintain its competitive position in the economy and lifted incomes, the real story of the second decade of the rural economy of China and Vietnam lies outside agriculture. In fact, most of the growth of rural incomes has come from the integration of the rural economy into China's rapidly expanding industrial economy. China's industrial growth was on average more than 15 per cent per year since the early 1980s; its industrial output increased more than five times (ZGTJNJ 2003). Along with this industrial growth the rise of jobs in the off-farm sector has induced one of the largest peacetime movements of a population in history. While in 1990, at the beginning of the second decade of transition, only about 20 per cent of the rural population worked off farm, by 2000 more than 45 per cent of rural labourers had an off-farm job, a rise of more than 100 million jobs (deBrauw et al. 2002). By 2000, more than 80 per cent of households had at least one member in the off-farm sector. Clearly China's rural economy—as it finally began its gravitation to urbanization and industrialization—was in the beginning stages of modernization. Vietnam was following a similar path.

12.2. Central and Eastern Europe

In Central and Eastern Europe, agricultural policies during the second decade have been strongly dominated by the EU accession process (Swinnen 2002b). Eight CEECs (the Czech Republic, Estonia, Hungary, Latvia, Lithuania, Poland, Slovakia, and Slovenia) joined the EU in 2004 and others (Bulgaria, Croatia, and Romania) are expected to join in the coming years. An extensive set of new regulations relating to the agricultural sector and the food industry, on land legislation, and many other measures were explicitly part of the EU accession conditions. Price and trade policies have also had to be brought into line with the EU's Common Agricultural Policy (CAP). In the meantime, the CEE countries also became members of WTO, further restricting the ways in which they manage their trade and subsidy policies.

While the impact of EU accession will be important in shaping the future of the sector, it should still be realized that many of the changes were already in process before accession negotiations began. Many of the basic land reform laws had been implemented already. While significant restructuring of the farms is continuing, none of the changes is as radical as the changes before 1998. Moreover, EU accession has also had a major effect on the land markets.

However, EU accession has brought some new phenomena. It used to be that there were widespread complaints of low prices—for both sales and rental—of agricultural land. All of that changed with EU accession. The prospect of large subsidies, often linked to the land, dramatically pushed land prices up. In some places the upward pressure on prices became so strong that in certain countries where rental is the most common, farm managers have begun to lobby governments to regulate rental prices.

The largest changes perhaps have been in the agribusiness and food industry, although these too are not entirely new. Since the early years of reform, large investments from the West have poured in. The new investments and the new ways of doing business have had a major impact on supply chains. Many of these changes have echoed through the farming sector. The prospects of EU accession have, if anything, accelerated the process. In the context of EU expansion, the agri-food industry of CEE often is seen as a source for lucrative investments. EU accession has further enhanced the attractiveness of investments in the CEE food industry and large shares of the CEE agri-food industry have been taken over by foreign investors. Through contracting and vertical integration, the foreign investments into the processing sector have resulted in improved access of farms to quality inputs, credit, modern technology, and higher-value output markets. Spillover effects of these investments on local agri-food companies and on the farm had strong effects on the productivity of the farm sector and the quality of farm produce.

The main new thrusts during the second decade can best be described by the continued penetration throughout the food sector. In the late 1990s foreign investment was extended to the food retail sector (Dries, Reardon, and Swinnen 2004). As the supermarketization of CEE has unfolded, the impact on the farm sector has begun to be felt.

12.3. CIS nations

While the sources of growth during the second decade in CEE are evolving, albeit still strong, even more fundamental changes are happening further east in the CIS nations. In fact, when assessing the strength of the effects on the agricultural sector over the entire time since the beginning of transition, some of the most fundamental changes have taken place in the second half of the 1990s and since 2000. Two new sources of change are, first, new and fundamental changes in land and farm reform policies following the disappointments of the earlier attempts to reform land policies, and, second, fundamental improvements in the terms of trade for several countries following the Russian financial crisis in 1998 that have greatly benefited the farming sector.

First, the disappointing results of the land shares policy caused several CIS governments to change land reform strategies, and move from the system of paper shares to one based on allocation rights on a plot-specific basis. The first to change were the poorest countries with the most labour-intensive agricultural systems.[1] In 1996, both Azerbaijan and Kyrgyz Republic began to replace ill-defined paper shares with the distribution of land in kind to rural households. A much more complete individualization of agriculture followed rapidly. In Azerbaijan, for example, individual land use increased from 14 per cent in 1996 to 93 per cent in 2000.

In the second decade this trend of land policy shift continued by spreading to other countries and taking deeper root. In 1998, a change in government in Moldova led to a similar change in land reform and farm policy.[2] Land was distributed in physical plots to individuals who had previously owned shares. This induced a large exit of individuals from corporate farms. By 2000 households were using almost 60 per cent of the land and more than 90 per cent of the livestock, producing 73 per cent of total output. In 1999, the Ukrainian government made a radical change in land policy by replacing the land shares by actual landownership titles and gave them to rural households. These policy implementation shifts made it easier for households to start their own farms. The new measures also increased the pressure on managers of corporate farms to manage their farm efficiently. In Kazakhstan important land policy changes also took place, albeit of a somewhat different nature. In 1998, a drought caused widespread crop failure. Many producers defaulted on their loans. Given the softness of the budget constraints that still dominated the relationship between farms and government, the drought-induced crisis nearly bankrupted the entire government. As a result, the government was forced to introduce for the first time bankruptcy proceedings. The impact of the new hard line was immediate and multi-dimensioned. In the most fertile parts of the northern region, large trading and processing companies purchased whole sets of bankrupt state and collective farms and established huge vertically integrated grain- and oilseed-growing companies. Many of the new farms owned hundreds of thousands of hectares of land. In other parts of the country the bankruptcy of farms reinforced the growth of individual farms. Whereas individual farming was once difficult and rare, after 2000 individual farms were producing more than 75 per cent of nation's total farm output. In 2003, a new land code replaced long-term leases with actual ownership titles.

Second, during the second decade shocks external to agriculture began to have major impacts—often positive ones—on the sector in many CIS countries. In the aftermath of the Asian financial crisis in 1997, a financial crisis in Russia in 1998 caused a large devaluation of the Russian currency. The same effect occurred, although to a somewhat lesser extent, to countries close to Russia, such as Ukraine, Belarus, and Kazakhstan. Around the same time, world oil and gas prices started rising.

These shifts in prices and currency values, as it turns out, had profound impacts on the agricultural economies even though the incidence of the shifts in resource prices had little to do with food. There were both direct and indirect impacts. The direct impact was a strong improvement in the competitive position of these countries' agri-food sector vis-à-vis the international market. Relative prices increased significantly. With higher prices there was suddenly a greater incentive to invest in the sector and seek out more effective ways to organize production. The most significant, positive indirect effect was that it improved the attractiveness of the food industry in these countries for capital investments. For the first time in years, there was interest by outside investors (both from outside the country and from other sectors inside the country) to bring injections of capital into the food economy. Furthermore, for those countries exporting oil or gas (for example, Russia, Kazakhstan, and Azerbaijan) the increase in oil and gas prices had a significant effect on government revenue and profits in other sectors of the economy. These in turn enhanced the availability of domestic capital in these countries.

In combination, these two factors—the rise of profitability of agriculture and the increased availability of capital—resulted in the inflow of considerable investments in the agri-food industry. Some of the new investments came via a system of vertical integration. Vertically integrated farms had access to inputs for their farms. Other investments were directly into the processing sector which made output markets more accessible. Both of these effects were the strongest in countries like Russia and Kazakhstan where the agri-food sector benefited both from improved competitiveness with the 1998 devaluation and from the effects induced by increased oil and gas prices.

Hence, although in the second decade we see the emergence of new sources of growth, the nature of the economic forces is actually similar to those that were underlying the changes to other regions (for example, East Asia and CEE) during the first decade. As the analysis in this book would predict, the combination of improved terms of trade and reform-induced property rights has led to significant growth in the farming sectors. For example, over the period 1999–2002, average growth of agricultural GDP was around 5 per cent in Kyrgyz Republic and Ukraine. Growth rose to around 9 per cent in Azerbaijan and Kazakhstan. Statistical sources report that agricultural growth exceeded 10 per cent in Russia and Tajikistan. In addition, some of the worst of the poverty in rural areas has begun to be mitigated in several of the CIS countries. For example, rural poverty declined strongly in Azerbaijan, Moldova, Russia, and Kazakhstan after 1999 (Macours and Swinnen 2005).

12.4. Implications and lessons

The discussion here shows that many of the insights in this book are important for understanding the changes that are taking place in the second decade of transition. Countries continue to vary in their transition paths, but basic reforms and external changes have important impacts on their performance, as can be predicted based on our analysis.

The recent changes, in particular those in the CIS, also confirm the importance of the interaction between structural economic pressures for change and political regime changes. While the inefficiencies of the land share distribution system contributed to the decline of the agricultural economies, policy changes have typically only been possible following either a change in regime or some large external shock. In Azerbaijan, Moldova, and Ukraine changes in the political alliances of those in charge of the government triggered the policy changes. In Kazakhstan and Russia extreme weather conditions and shocks in the macroeconomy played an important role in causing change to both policy and the way the producers and investors view the long-term prospects of agriculture.

With the turnaround of the economies in the CIS in the second decade, an important question that begs a more complete answer is whether the delayed turnaround in the former Soviet Union, compared to Central and Eastern Europe, reflects merely the larger institutional inertia in the countries which were further geographically and psychologically removed from 'the West' or which had been under Communist regime for much longer, or whether it merely reflects poor policy making in the countries further east. We will leave this to future research.

However, we can still draw some fundamental lessons. The observations on the second decade are consistent with our earlier conclusions that initial conditions matter but that there is not complete path dependency. Moreover, as time passes, the importance of initial conditions fades and the importance of policies grows. Hence, while the nature of the policies and other initiatives mattered in the past, it will matter even more in the future.

Regarding future policies, an important lesson that is clear from the case of China, Vietnam, and the other successful countries is that in order to sustain growth in agriculture, essential reform in land rights and farm structures needs to be complemented by other reforms, for example to remove constraints in rural credit and labour markets. Also, the importance of technology cannot be underestimated. In more mature economies, such as the USA and Western Europe, virtually all growth in agriculture in the long run is based on new technology. It is important to recognize that this is going to be true for all nations. The only basis for sustained agricultural productivity growth is fundamental technological change. In several of the now growing CIS agricultural economies, significant further reforms are needed to make the current growth sustainable.

Also, in the longer run, publicly orchestrated services, such as investments in public goods and infrastructure, are needed to continue productivity growth initiated by the reforms. Regardless of how successful the initial reforms are, once producers have good property rights and incentives, and once exchange is being facilitated by functioning institutions, sustained rises in productivity will depend on investments in other infrastructure projects, such as investments in water control and roads, that individual farmers will not be able to finance by themselves. In the long run, agricultural growth will suffer if such investments are ignored during transition. When nations reach the point when they are facing these longer-run problems, in fact, reform may be close to an end and transition problems may be evolving into more traditional development problems.

Notes

1. Pressures from war and natural disasters had induced the Armenian government already in the early 1990s to distribute land to rural households.
2. Recognizing that the debt overhang was a major constraint on the land reform and farm restructuring, the farm debt and land reform policies were addressed together. All existing agricultural enterprises were dissolved and their debts were written off.

References

Allen, Douglas W. and Dean Lueck. 1998. 'The Nature of the Farm.' *Journal of Law & Economics*, 41(2): 343–86.

Amelina, Maria. 2000. 'Why Russian Peasants Remain in Collective Farms: A Household Perspective on Agricultural Restructuring.' *Post-Soviet Geography and Economics*, 41(7): 483–511.

Balcerowicz, Leszek. 1994. 'Common Fallacies in the Debate on the Transition to a Market Economy.' *Economic Policy*, 9(19): 17–50.

Bardhan, Pranab and Christopher Udry (eds.). 1999. *Development Microeconomics*. Oxford: Oxford University Press.

Beckmann, Volker and Silke Boger. 2004. 'Courts and Contract Enforcement in Transition Agriculture: Theory and Evidence from Poland.' *Agricultural Economics*, 31(2–3): 251–63.

Benjamin, Dwayne and Loren Brandt. 2001. 'Agriculture and Income Distribution in Rural Vietnam under Economic Reforms: A Tale of Two Regions.' University of Toronto Working Paper, University of Toronto.

Bjornlund, Britta, Nancy Cochrane, Mildred Haley, Roger Hoskin, Olga Liefert, and Philip Paarlberg. 2002. *Livestock Sectors in the Economies of Eastern Europe and the Former Soviet Union: Transition from Plan to Market and the Road Ahead*, ERS Agricultural Economics Report No. 798. Washington, DC: USDA/ERS.

Blanchard, Oliver. 1997. *The Economics of Post-Communist Transition*. Oxford: Clarendon Press.

—— and Michael Kremer. 1997. 'Disorganization.' *Quarterly Journal of Economics*, 112(4): 1091–126.

Bojnec, Stefan and Johan F. M. Swinnen. 1997. 'Privatization of Slovenian Agriculture: Process and Politics.' In Johan F. M. Swinnen (ed.), *Political Economy of Agrarian Reform in Central and Eastern Europe*. Aldershot: Ashgate, 339–62.

Brada, Joseph C. and Arthur E. King. 1993. 'Is Private Farming More Efficient Than Socialized Agriculture?' *Economica*, 60(237): 41–56.

—— and Karl-Eugen Wädekin (eds.). 1988. *Socialist Agriculture in Transition: Organizational Response to Failing Performance*. Boulder, Colo.: Westview Press.

Brandt, Loren, Jikun Huang, Guo Li, and Scott Rozelle. 2002. 'Land Rights in China: Fact, Fiction, and Issues.' *China Journal*, 47: 67–97.

References

Brooks, Karen M. 1983. 'Productivity in Soviet Agriculture.' In D. Gale Johnson and Karen Brooks (eds.), *Prospects for Soviet Agriculture in the 1980s*. Bloomington: Indiana University Press.

—— 1990. 'Soviet Agricultural Policy and Pricing under Gorbachev.' In Kenneth R. Gray (ed.), *Soviet Agriculture: Comparative Perspectives*. Ames: Iowa State University Press, 116–29.

——and John Nash. 2002. 'The Rural Sector in Transition Economies.' In Bruce L. Gardner and Gordon C. Rausser (eds.), *Handbook of Agricultural Economics, iia: Agriculture and its Extesrnal Linkages*. Amsterdam: Elsevier Science Ltd.

—— Elmira Krylatykh, Zvi Lerman, Aleksandr Petrikov, and Vasily Uzun. 1996. 'Agricultural Reform in Russia: A View from the Farm Level.' World Bank Discussion Paper No. 327. Washington, DC: The World Bank.

Bruszt, Laszlo. 2000. 'Constituting Markets: The Case of Russia and the Czech Republic.' In Michel Dobry (ed.), *Democratic and Capitalist Transitions in Eastern Europe*. Dordrecht: Kluwer Academic Publishers.

Burgess, Robin. 1998. 'Market Incompleteness and Nutritional Status in Rural China.' Mimeo, London School of Economics.

CCICED [China Commission International Cooperation for the Environment and Development]. 2004. *China's Agricultural and Rural Development in the New Era: Challenges, Opportunities and Policy Options: An Executive Summary of Policy Report.* Beijing: China Commission International Cooperation for the Environment and Development, Agricultural and Rural Development Task Force.

Chan, Anita, Benedict Kerkvliet, and Jonathon Unger (eds.). 1999. *Transforming Asian Socialism: China and Vietnam Compared*. New York: Rowman and Littlefield.

Chen, Kang, Gary Jefferson, and Inderjit Singh. 1992. 'Lessons from China's Economic Reform.' *Journal of Comparative Economics*, 16: 201–25.

Cochrane, Nancy. 1990. 'Reforming Socialist Agriculture: Bulgarian and Hungarian Experience and Implications for the USSR.' In Karl-Eugen Wädekin (ed.), *Communist Agriculture: Farming in the Soviet Union and Eastern Europe*. London: Routledge, 233–50.

Conquest, Robert. 1986. *The Harvest of Sorrow: Soviet Collectivization and the Terror-Famine. Oxford: Oxford University Press.*

Cook, Edward C., William M. Liefert, and Robert B. Koopman. 1991. *Government Intervention in Soviet Agriculture: Estimates of Consumer and Producer Subsidy Equivalents*. Economic Research Service Staff Report AGES 9146. Washington, DC: USDA/ERS.

Csaki, Csaba. 1998. 'Agricultural Research in Transforming Central and Eastern Europe.' *European Review of Agricultural Economics*, 25(3): 289–306.

—— and John Nash. 1998. 'The Agrarian Economies of Central and Eastern Europe and the Commonwealth of Independent States: Situation and Perspectives, 1997.' World Bank Discussion Paper No. 387. Washington, DC: The World Bank.

—— and Laura Tuck. 2000. 'Rural Development Strategy: Eastern Europe and Central Asia.' World Bank Technical Paper No. 484. Washington, DC: The World Bank.

—— and Alan Zuschlag. 2003. 'The Agrarian Economies of Central-Eastern Europe and the Commonwealth of Independent States: An Update on Status and Progress in 2002.' ECSSD Environmentally and Socially Sustainable Development Working Paper No. 37. Washington, DC: The World Bank.

—— Zvi Lerman, and Sergey Sotnikov. 2001. 'Farm Debt in the CIS.' World Bank Discussion Paper No. 424. Washington, DC: The World Bank.

—— John Nash, Vera Matusevich, and Holger Kray. 2002. 'Food and Agricultural Policy in Russia: Progress to Date and the Road Forward.' World Bank Technical Paper No. 523. Washington, DC: The World Bank.

Cungu, Azeta and Johan F. M. Swinnen. 1999. 'Albania's Radical Agrarian Reform.' *Economic Development and Cultural Change*, 47(3): 605–19.

—— —— 2003. 'Investment and Contract Enforcement in Transition: Evidence from Hungary.' LICOS Discussion Paper 127/2003, LICOS—Centre for Transition Economics, Katholieke Universiteit Leuven, Belgium.

Davis, Junior R. and Angela Gaburici. 1999. 'Rural Finance and Private Farming in Romania.' *Europe-Asia Studies*, 51(5): 843–69.

deBrauw, Alan, Jikun Huang, and Scott Rozelle. 2000. 'Responsiveness, Flexibility and Market Liberalization in China's Agriculture.' *American Journal of Agricultural Economics*, 82(5): 1133–9.

—— —— —— 2004. 'The Sequencing of Reform Policies in China's Agricultural Transition.' *Economics of Transition*, 12(3): 427–65.

—— —— —— Linxiu Zhang, and Yigang Zhang. 2002. 'The Evolution of China's Rural Labor Markets during the Reforms.' *Journal of Comparative Economics*, 30(2): 329–53.

de Gorter, Harry and Johan F. M. Swinnen. 2002. 'Political Economy of Agricultural Policies.' In Bruce L. Gardner and Gordon C. Rausser (eds.), *Handbook of Agricultural Economics*, iib: *Agricultural and Food Policy*. Amsterdam: Elsevier Science Ltd, 2073–123.

Deininger, Klaus and Songqing Jin. 2003. 'Land Sales and Rental Markets in Transition: Evidence from Rural Vietnam.' Policy Research Working Paper No. 3013. Washington, DC: The World Bank.

de Melo, Martha and Alan Gelb. 1996. 'A Comparative Analysis of Twenty-Eight Transition Economies in Europe and Asia.' *Post-Soviet Geography and Economics*, 37(5): 265–85.

—— Cevdet Denizer, Alan Gelb, and Stoyan Tenev. 2001. 'Circumstance and Choice: The Role of Initial Conditions and Policies in Transition Economies.' *World Bank Economic Review*, 15: 1–31.

Desai, Padma. 1987. 'The Soviet Economy: Problems and Prospects.' Oxford: Basil Blackwell.

—— —— 1990. 'Perestroika in Perspective: The Design and Dilemmas of Soviet Reform.' Princeton: Princeton University Press.

Dewatripont, Mathias and Gérard Roland. 1992. 'The Virtues of Gradualism and Legitimacy in the Transition to a Market Economy.' *Economic Journal*, 102(411): 291–300.

—— —— 1995. 'The Design of Reform Packages under Uncertainty.' *American Economic Review*, 85(5): 1207–23.

189

References

Dries, Liesbeth and Johan F. M. Swinnen. 2002. 'Institutional Reform and Labor Reallocation during Transition: Theory Evidence from Polish Agriculture.' *World Development*, 30(3): 457–74.

Dries, Liesbeth and Johan F. M. Swinnen. 2004*a*. 'Foreign Direct Investment, Vertical Integration and Local Suppliers: Evidence from the Polish Dairy Sector.' *World Development*, 32(9): 1525–44.

—— —— 2004*b*. 'Finance, credit, and investments in Polish agriculture.' In David A. J. Macey, William Pyle, and Stephen K. Wegren (eds.), *Building Market Institutions in Post-Communist Agriculture: Land, Credit and Assistance*. Lanham, Md.: Lexington Books.

—— Thomas Reardon, and Johan F. M. Swinnen. 2004. 'The Rapid Rise of Supermarkets in Central and Eastern Europe: Implications for the Agrifood Sector and Rural Development.' *Development Policy Review*, 22(5): 525–56.

Dudwick, Nora, Elizabeth Gomart, Alexandre Marc, and Kathleen Kuehnast. 2003. *When Things Fall Apart: Qualitative Studies of Poverty in the Former Soviet Union*. Washington, DC: The World Bank.

Ellman, Michael. 1988. 'Contract Brigades and Normless Teams in Soviet Agriculture.' In Josef C. Brada and Karl-Eugen Wädekin (eds.), *Socialist Agriculture in Transition: Organizational Response to Failing Performance*. Boulder, Colo.: Westview Press, 23–33.

Epstein, Larry. 1981. 'Duality Theory and Functional Forms for Dynamic Factor Demands.' *Review of Economic Studies*, 48(1): 81–95.

European Bank for Reconstruction and Development (EBRD). 2002. *Transition Report 2002: Agriculture and Rural Transition*. London: EBRD.

Fan, Shenggen. 1991. 'Effects of Technological Change and Institutional Reform on Production Growth in Chinese Agriculture.' *American Journal of Agricultural Economics*, 73(2): 266–75.

—— 1997. 'Production and Productivity Growth in Chinese Agriculture: New Measurement and Evidence.' *Food Policy*, 22(3): 213–28.

—— 1999. 'Technological Change, Technical and Allocative Efficiency in Chinese Agriculture: The Case of Rice Production in China.' EPTD Discussion Paper No. 39, Environment and Production Technology Division, International Food Policy Research Institute, Washington, DC.

—— and Phil G. Pardey. 1997. 'Research, Productivity, and Output Growth in Chinese Agriculture.' *Journal of Development Economics*, 53(1): 115–37.

—— Linxiu Zhang, and Xiaobo Zhang. 2002. 'Growth and Poverty in Rural China: The Role of Public Investments.' EPTD Discussion Paper No. 66, Environment and Production Technology Division, International Food Policy Research Institute, Washington, DC.

Fidrmuc, Jan. 2000. 'Political Support for Reforms: Economics of Voting in Transition Countries.' *European Economic Review*, 44(8): 1491–513.

Fischer, Stanley. 1994. 'Structural Factors in the Economic Reforms of China, Eastern Europe, and the Former Soviet Union. Discussion.' *Economic Policy*, 9(1): 131–5.

Foster, Chris. 1999. 'The Impact of FDI in the Upstream and Downstream Sectors on Investment in Agriculture in the NIS.' In *Agricultural Finance and Credit Infrastructure in Transition Economies: Proceedings of OECD Expert Meeting, Moscow, February 1999*, Organization for Economic Co-operation and Development. Paris: OECD Publications.

Friebel, Guido and Sergei Guriev. 1999. 'Why Russian Workers Do Not Move: Attachment of Workers through In-Kind Payments.' RECEP Working Paper No. 5, Russian-European Center for Economic Policy, Moscow.

Frye, Timothy and Andrei Shleifer. 1997. 'The Invisible Hand and the Grabbing Hand.' *American Economics Review*, 87(2): 354–8.

Gavrilescu, Dino and Alexander Sarris. 1997. 'Restructuring of Farms and Agricultural Systems in Romania.' In Johan F. M. Swinnen, Allan E. Buckwell, and Erik Mathijs (eds.), *Agricultural Privatisation, Land Reform and Farm Restructuring in Central and Eastern Europe*. Ashgate: Aldershot, 189–228.

Gorton, Matthew and Sophia Davidova. 2004. 'Farm Productivity and Efficiency in the CEE Applicant Countries: A Synthesis of Results.' *Agricultural Economics*, 30(1): 1–16.

—— Allan Buckwell, and Sophia Davidova. 2000. 'Transfers and Distortions along CEEC Food Supply Chains.' In Stefan Tangermann and Martin Banse (eds.), *Central and Eastern European Agriculture in an Expanding European Union*. Wallingford: CABI Publishing.

Goskomstat, National Statistical Office of Russia. Various issues of Statistical Yearbook.

Gow, Hamish R. and Johan F. M. Swinnen. 1998. 'Up- and Downstream Restructuring, Foreign Direct Investment, and Hold-Up Problems in Agricultural Transition.' *European Review of Agricultural Economics*, 25(3): 331–50.

—— —— 2001. 'Private Enforcement Capital and Contract Enforcement in Transition Economies.' *American Journal of Agricultural Economics*, 83(3): 686–90.

—— Deborah H. Streeter, and Johan F. M. Swinnen. 2000. 'How Private Enforcement Mechanisms can Succeed where Public Institutions Fail: The Case of Juhocukor a.s.' *Agricultural Economics*, 23: 253–65.

Gray, John. 2000. 'Kazakhstan. A Review of Farm Restructuring.' World Bank Technical Paper No. 458. Washington, DC: The World Bank.

Gray, Kenneth R. (ed.). 1990. *Soviet Agriculture: Comparative Perspectives*. Ames: Iowa State University Press.

Green, David J. and Richard W. A. Vokes. 1998. 'Agriculture and the Transition to the Market in Asia.' *Journal of Comparative Economics*, 25(2): 250–80.

Hartell, Jason and Johan F. M. Swinnen. 1998. 'Trends in Agricultural Price and Trade Policy Instruments since 1990 in Central European Countries.' *World Economy*, 21(2): 261–79.

Hellman, Joel S. 1998. 'Winners Take All: The Politics of Partial Reforms in Postcommunist Transitions.' *World Politics*, 50(2): 203–34.

Hobbs, Jill E., Willam E. Kerr, and James D. Gaisford. 1997. *The Transformation of the Agri-Food System in Central and Eastern Europe and the New Independent States*. New York: CAB International.

References

Huang, Jikun and Chunlai Chen. 1999. 'Effect of Trade Liberalization on Agriculture in China: Institutional and Structural Aspects.' CGPRT Working Paper Series, Paper No. 42, May 1999. United Nations, ESCAP Centre for Research and Development of Coarse Grains, Pulses, Roots and Tuber Crops, Bogor, Indonesia.

Huang, Jikun, and Scott Rozelle. 1996. 'Technological Change: Rediscovering the Engine of Productivity Growth in China's Rural Economy.' *Journal of Development Economics*, 49(2): 337–69.

—— —— Carl Pray, and Qingfang Wang. 2002. 'Plant Biotechnology in China.' *Science*, 295(5555): 674–6.

Hughes, Gordon. 1994. 'Structural Factors in the Economic Reforms of China, Eastern Europe, and the Former Soviet Union. Discussion.' *Economic Policy*, 9(1): 135–9.

International Labour Organization (ILO). 1997–2002. *Yearbook on Labour Statistics*. Geneva: ILO Publications.

Jacoby, Hanan, Guo Li, and Scott Rozelle. 2002. 'Hazards of Expropriation: Tenure Insecurity and Investment in Rural China.' *American Economic Review*, 92(5): 1420–47.

Jin, Songqing, Jikun Huang, Ruifa Hu, and Scott Rozelle. 2002. 'The Creation and Spread of Technology and Total Factor Productivity in China's Agriculture.' *American Journal of Agricultural Economics*, 84(4): 916–30.

Johnson, D. Gale. 1993. 'Historical Experience of Eastern and Central European and Soviet Agriculture.' In Avishay Braverman, Karen M. Brooks, and Csaba Csaki (eds.), *The Agricultural Transition in Central and Eastern Europe and the Former USSR*. Washington, DC: The World Bank.

—— and Karen M. Brooks (eds.). 1983. *Prospects for Soviet Agriculture in the 1980s*. Bloomington: Indiana University Press.

Johnson, Simon, John McMillan, and Christopher Woodruff. 1999. 'Contract Enforcement in Transition.' EBRD Working Paper No. 45, European Bank for Reconstruction and Development, London.

Johnson, Stanley R., Aziz Bouzaher, Alicia Carriquiry, Helen H. Jensen, and P. G. Lakshminarayan. 1994. 'Production Efficiency and Agricultural Reform in Ukraine.' *American Journal of Agricultural Economics*, 76(3): 629–35.

Johnston, Bruce. 1970. 'Agriculture and Structural Transformation in Developing Countries: A Survey of Research.' *Journal of Economic Literature*, 8(2): 369–404.

Kandiyoti, Deniz. 2003. 'Pathways of Farm Restructuring in Uzbekistan: Pressures and Outcomes.' In Max Spoor (ed.), *Transition, Institutions and the Rural Sector*. Lanham, Md.: Lexington Books.

Klein, Benjamin and Kevin M. Murphy. 1997. 'Vertical Integration as a Self-Enforcing Contractual Arrangement.' *American Economic Review*, 87(2): 415–20.

Kornai, Janos. 2000. 'The Road to a Free Economy—Ten Years After.' *Transition*, 11(2): 3–5.

Kurkalova, Lyubov A. and Alicia Carriquiry. 2002. 'An Analysis of Grain Production Decline during the Early Transition in Ukraine: A Bayesian Inference.' *American Journal of Agricultural Economics*, 84(5): 1256–63.

—— and Helen H. Jensen. 2003. 'Impact of Human Capital on Technical Efficiency during Transition: An Analysis of Ukrainian Farm-Level Data.' Working paper, Iowa State University.

Kwiecinski, Andrzej and Natacha Pescatore. 2000. 'Sectoral Agricultural Policies and Estimates of PSEs for Russia in the Transition Period.' In Peter Wehrheim, Klaus Frohberg, Eugenia Serova, and Joachim von Braun (eds.), *Russia's Agro-Food Sector: Towards Truly Functioning Markets*. Boston: Kluwer Academic Publishers.

Lardy, Nicholas. 1983. *Agriculture in China's Modern Economic Development*. Cambridge: Cambridge University Press.

Lee, Hong Yung. 1991. *From Revolutionary Cadres to Party Technocrats in Socialist China*. Berkeley and Los Angeles: University of California Press.

Lerman, Zvi and Karen Brooks. 2001. 'Turkmenistan: An Assessment of Leasehold-Based Farm Restructuring.' World Bank Technical Paper No. 500. Washington, DC: The World Bank.

—— and Csaba Csaki. 1997. 'Land Reform in Ukraine: The First Five Years.' World Bank Discussion Paper No. 371. Washington, DC: The World Bank.

—— —— and Gershon Feder. 2004. *Agriculture in Transition: Land Policies and Evolving Farm Structures in Post-Soviet Countries*. Lanham, Md.: Lexington Books.

—— Yoav Kislev, Alon Kriss, and David Biton. 2003. 'Agricultural Output and Productivity in the Former Soviet Republics.' *Economic Development and Cultural Change*, 51(4): 999–1018.

—— Mark Lundell, Astghik Mirzakhanian, Paruir Asatrian, and Ashot Kakosian. 1999. 'Armenia's Private Agriculture: 1998 Survey of Family Farms.' ECSSD Environmentally and Socially Sustainable Development Working Paper No. 17. Washington, DC: The World Bank.

Li, David D. 1998. 'Changing Incentives of the Chinese Bureaucracy.' *American Economic Review*, 88(2): 393–7.

Liefert, William M., Bruce Gardner, and Eugenia Serova. 2003. 'Allocative Efficiency in Russian Agriculture: The Case of Fertilizer and Grain.' *American Journal of Agricultural Economics*, 85(5): 1228–33.

—— David J. Sedik, Robert B. Koopman, Eugenia Serova, and Olga Melyukhina. 1996. 'Producer Subsidy Equivalents for Russian Agriculture: Estimation and Interpretation.' *American Journal of Agricultural Economics*, 78(3): 792–8.

Lin, Justin Yifu. 1990. 'Collectivization and China's Agricultural Crisis in 1959–1961.' *Journal of Political Economy*, 98(6): 1228–52.

—— 1991. 'Prohibitions of Factor Market Exchanges and Technological Choice in Chinese Agriculture.' *Journal of Development Studies*, 27(4): 1–15.

—— 1992. 'Rural Reforms and Agricultural Growth in China.' *American Economic Review*, 82(1): 34–51.

—— Fang Cai, and Zhou Li. 1996. *The China Miracle: Development Strategy and Economic Reform*. Hong Kong: Chinese University Press.

Macey, David A. J. 1990. 'The Peasant Commune and the Stolypin Reforms: Peasant Attitudes, 1906–1914.' In Roger Bartlett (ed.), *Land Commune and Peasant*

Community in Russia: Communal Forms in Imperial and Early Soviet Society. New York: St Martin's Press, 219–36.

—— 2003. 'Demise of the Moral Imperative: Agricultural Reform in Russia Today.' Mimeo, Middlebury College.

McKinnon, Ronald. 1993. *The Order of Economic Liberalization: Financial Control in the Transition to a Market Economy.* Baltimore: Johns Hopkins University Press.

McMillan, John. 1997. 'Markets in Transition.' In David M. Kreps and Kenneth F. Wallis (eds.), *Advances in Economics and Econometrics: Theory and Applications,* vol. ii. Cambridge: Cambridge University Press.

—— 2002. *Reinventing the Bazaar. The Natural History of Markets.* New York: W. W. Norton & Company.

—— and Barry Naughton. 1992. 'How to Reform a Planned Economy: Lessons from China.' *Oxford Review of Economic Policy,* 8(1): 130–43.

—— and Christopher Woodruff. 1999. 'Interfirm Relationships and Informal Credit in Vietnam.' *Quarterly Journal of Economics,* 114(4): 1285–320.

—— John Whalley, and Lijing Zhu. 1989. 'The Impact of China's Economic Reforms on Agricultural Productivity Growth.' *Journal of Political Economy,* 97(4): 781–807.

Macours, Karen and Johan F. M. Swinnen. 2000a. 'Causes of Output Decline in Economic Transition: The Case of Central and Eastern European Agriculture.' *Journal of Comparative Economics,* 28(1): 172–206.

—— —— 2000b. 'Impact of Initial Conditions and Reform Policies on Agricultural Performance in Central and Eastern Europe, the Former Soviet Union, and East Asia.' *American Journal of Agricultural Economics,* 82(5): 1149–55.

—— —— 2002. 'Patterns of Agrarian Transition.' *Economic Development and Cultural Change,* 50(2): 365–94.

—— —— 2005. 'Rural Poverty in Transition Countries.' Unpublished working paper.

Mathijs, Erik and Johan F. M. Swinnen. 1998. 'The Economics of Agricultural Decollectivization in East Central Europe and the Former Soviet Union.' *Economic Development and Cultural Change,* 47(1): 1–26.

—— —— 2001. 'Production Organization and Efficiency during Transition: An Empirical Analysis of East German Agriculture.' *Review of Economics and Statistics,* 83(1): 100–7.

—— and Liesbet Vranken. Forthcoming. *Farm Structure and Agricultural Market Development in Hungary.* Lanham, Md.: Lexington Books.

Mead, Robert. 2000. 'China's Agricultural Reforms: The Importance of Private Plots.' *China Economic Review,* 11(1): 54–78.

Morduch, Jonathan and Terry Sicular. 2000. 'Politics, Growth and Inequality in Rural China: Does it Pay to Join the Party?' *Journal of Public Economics,* 77(3): 331–56.

Mueller, Dennis C. 2003. *Public Choice III.* Cambridge: Cambridge University Press.

Murova, Olga I., Michael A. Trueblood, and Keith H. Coble. 2004. 'Measurement and Explanation of Technical Efficiency Performance in Ukrainian Agriculture, 1991–1996.' *Journal of Agricultural and Applied Economics,* 36(1): 185–98.

Murphy, Kevin, Andrei Shleifer, and Robert Vishny. 1992. 'The Transition to a Market Economy: Pitfalls of Partial Reform.' *Quarterly Journal of Economics*, 107(3): 889–906.

Nyberg, Albert and Scott Rozelle. 1999. *Accelerating Development in Rural China*. World Bank Monograph Series, Rural Development Division. Washington, DC: The World Bank.

O'Brien, David J. and Stephen K. Wegren (eds.). 2002. *Rural Reform in Post-Soviet Russia*. Washington, DC: Woodrow Wilson Center Press and Johns Hopkins University Press.

—— Valeri V. Patsiorkovski, and Larry D. Dershem. 2000. *Household Capital and the Agrarian Problem in Russia*. Aldershot: Ashgate.

OECD. 1998. *Agricultural Policies in Non-member Countries*, Organization for Economic Co-operation and Development. Paris: OECD Publications.

—— 1999. *Agricultural Finance and Credit Infrastructure in Transition Economies: Proceedings of OECD Expert Meeting, Moscow, February 1999*, Organization for Economic Co-operation and Development. Paris: OECD Publications.

Oi, Jean. 1989. 'Market Reforms and Corruption in Rural China.' *Studies in Comparative Communism*, 22(2/3): 221–33.

—— 1999. *Rural China Takes Off: Institutional Foundations of Economic Reform*. Berkeley and Los Angeles: University of California Press.

Park, Albert, Hehui Jin, Scott Rozelle, and Jikun Huang. 2002. 'Market Emergence and Transition: Arbitrage, Transaction Costs, and Autarky in China's Grain Markets.' *American Journal of Agricultural Economics*, 84(1): 67–82.

Pederson, Glenn D., Karen M. Brooks, and Oleg Lekhtman. 1998. 'Russian Farm Enterprise Performance and Restructuring: A Debt Problem or a Profitability Problem?' Working Paper 98–5, Center for International Food and Agricultural Policy, University of Minnesota, St Paul.

Perkins, Dwight. 1988. 'Reforming China's Economic System.' *Journal of Economic Literature*, 26(2): 601–45.

—— 1994. 'Completing China's Move to the Market.' *Journal of Economic Perspectives*, 8(2): 23–46.

Persson, Torsten and Guido Tabellini. 2000. *Political Economics: Explaining Economic Policy*. Cambridge, Mass.: MIT Press.

Pingali, Prabhu L. and Nguyen Tri Khiem. 1995. 'Supply Responses of Rice and Three Food Crops in Vietnam.' In Glenn L. Denning and Vo-Tong Xuan (eds.), *Vietnam and IRRI: A Partnership in Rice Research*. Los Baños, Laguna, Philippines: IRRI.

—— and Vo-Tong Xuan. 1992. 'Vietnam: Decollectivization and Rice Productivity Growth.' *Economic Development and Cultural Change*, 40(4): 697–718.

Pollak, Robert A. 1985. 'A Transaction Cost Approach to Families and Households.' *Journal of Economic Literature*, 23(2): 581–608.

Pomfret, Richard. 2000. 'Agrarian Reform in Uzbekistan: Why has the Chinese Model Failed to Deliver?' *Economic Development and Cultural Change*, 48(2): 269–84.

—— 2002a. 'State-Directed Diffusion of Technology: The Mechanization of Cotton-Harvesting in Soviet Central Asia.' *Journal of Economic History*, 62(1): 170–88.

References

—— 2002*b*. 'Resource Abundance, Governance and Economic Performance in Turkmenistan and Uzbekistan,' paper prepared for the project 'Energy and Welfare in the Caspian Region,' September 2002, University of Adelaide.

Pospisil, Michal. 2001. 'Hidden Credits in the Agro-food System in the Czech Republic,' In *Agricultural Finance and Credit Infrastructure in Transition Economies. Focus on South Eastern Europe*, OECD Center for Co-operation with Non-Members. Paris: OECD Publications.

Prosterman, Roy and Tim Hanstad. 1999. 'Legal Impediments to Effective Rural Land Relations in Eastern Europe and Central Asia: A Comparative Perspective.' World Bank Technical Paper No. 436. Washington, DC: The World Bank.

Putterman, Louis. 1992. Dualism and Reform in China? *Economic Development and Cultural Change*, 40/3: 487–93.

Putterman, Louis. 1993. *Continuity and Change in China's Rural Development*. New York: Oxford University Press.

Qian, Yingyi and Barry R. Weingast. 1997. 'Federalism as a Commitment to Preserving Market Incentives.' *Journal of Economic Perspectives*, 11(4): 83–92.

—— and Chenggang Xu. 1993. 'Why China's Economic Reforms Differ: The M-Form Hierarchy and Entry/Expansion of the Non-State Sector.' *Economics of Transition*, 1(2): 135–70.

—— —— 1998. 'Innovation and Bureaucracy under Soft and Hard Budget Constraints.' *Review of Economic Studies*, 65(1): 151–64.

—— Gerard Roland, and Chenggang Xu. 1999. 'Why is China Different from Eastern Europe? Perspectives from Organization Theory.' *European Economic Review*, 43(4): 1085–94.

Rabinowicz, Ewa. 1997. 'Political Economy of Agricultural Privatization in the Baltic Countries.' In Johan F. M. Swinnen (ed.), *The Political Economy of Agrarian Reform in Central and Eastern Europe*. Ashgate: Aldershot.

Radvanyi, Jean. 1988. 'The Experiments in Georgia, 1974–1984: Quest for a New Organization in the Soviet Agricultural System.' In Josef C. Brada and Karl-Eugen Wädekin (eds.), *Socialist Agriculture in Transition: Organizational Response to Failing Performance*. Boulder, Colo.: Westview Press, 110–24.

Rae, Allan N., Hengyun Ma, Jikun Huang, and Scott Rozelle. 2004. 'Livestock in China: Commodity-Specific Total Factor Productivity Decomposition using New Panel Data.' Working Paper, Center for Chinese Agricultural Policy, Institute of Geographical Science and Natural Resource Research, Chinese Academy Science.

Rana, Pradumna B. and Naved Hamid (eds.). 1996. *From Centrally Planned to Market Economies: The Asian Approach*. Hong Kong: Oxford University Press and Manila: Asian Development Bank.

Republic of Azerbaijan. 2003. *Statistical Yearbook of Azerbaijan*. Azerbaijan: State Statistical Committee.

Rizov, Marian and Johan F. M. Swinnen. 2004. 'Human Capital, Market Imperfections and Labour Reallocation in Transition.' *Journal of Comparative Economics*, 32(4): 745–74.

—— Dinu Gavrilescu, Hamish R. Gow, Erik Mathijs, and Johan F. M. Swinnen. 2001. 'Transition and Enterprise Restructuring: The Development of Individual Farming in Romania.' *World Development*, 29(7): 1257–74.

Roland, Gérard. 2000. *Transition and Economics: Politics, Markets, and Firms.* Cambridge, Mass.: MIT Press.

—— 2002. 'The Political Economy of Transition.' *Journal of Economic Perspectives*, 16(1): 29–50.

—— and Thierry Verdier. 1999. 'Transition and the Output Fall.' *Economics of Transition*, 7(1): 1–28.

Rozelle, Scott. 1996. 'Gradual Reform and Institutional Development: The Keys to Success of China's Rural Reforms.' In John McMillan and Barry Naughton (eds.), *Reforming Asian Socialism: The Growth of Market Institutions.* Ann Arbor: University of Michigan Press.

—— and Johan F. M. Swinnen. 2004. 'Success and Failure of Reform: Insights from the Transition of Agriculture.' *Journal of Economic Literature*, 42(2): 404–56.

—— Jikun Huang, and Keijiro Otsuka. 2005. 'The Engines of a Viable Agriculture: Advances in Biotechnology, Market Accessibility and Land Rentals in Rural China.' *China Journal*, 53: 81–114.

—— Albert Park, Jikun Huang, and Hehui Jin. 2000. 'Bureaucrat to Entrepreneur: The Changing Role of the State in China's Grain Economy.' *Economic Development and Cultural Change*, 48(2): 227–52.

Rylko, Dmitri. 2002. 'New Agricultural Operators, Input Markets and Vertical Sector Coordination.' In Bruce L. Gardner, William Liefert, Zvi Lerman, Vasiliy Uzun, and Dmitri Rylko (eds.), *Factor Markets in Russia's Agri-Food Sector: Framework of Further Analysis.* Moscow: IET.

Sabates-Wheeler, Rachel. 2002. 'Farm Strategy, Self-Selection and Productivity: Can Small Farming Groups Offer Production Benefits to Farmers in Post-Socialist Romania?' *World Development*, 30(10): 1737–53.

Sachs, Jeffrey D. and Wing-Thye Woo. 1994. 'Structural Factors in the Economic Reforms of China, Eastern Europe and the Former Soviet Union.' *Economic Policy*, 9(1): 101–45.

Sadler, Marc. 2004. 'Vertical Coordination in the Cotton Supply Chains in Central Asia.' Unpublished Report prepared for the World Bank ECSSD project, *The Dynamics of Vertical Coordination in Agri-Food Supply Chains in ECA.* Washington, DC: The World Bank.

Sarris, Alexander H., Tomas Doucha, and Erik Mathijs. 1999. 'Agricultural Restructuring in Central and Eastern Europe: Implications for Competitiveness and Rural Development.' *European Review of Agricultural Economics*, 26(3): 305–29.

Schmitt, Gunther. 1991. 'Why is the Agriculture of Advanced Western Economies Still Organized by Family Farms? Will This Continue to Be So in the Future?' *European Review of Agricultural Economics*, 18(3): 443–58.

Sedik, David J. 1997. 'Status of Agricultural Reforms in the NIS/B Countries in 1997.' In *Newly Independent States and the Baltics, Situation and Outlook Series, International Agriculture and Trade Reports.* Washington, DC: USDA/ERS.

References

—— Michael A. Trueblood, and Carlos Arnade. 1999. 'Corporate Farm Performance in Russia, 1991–1995: An Efficiency Analysis.' *Journal of Comparative Economics*, 27(3): 514–33.

Shleifer, Andrei. 1997. 'Government in Transition.' *European Economic Review*, 41(3–5): 385–410.

Sicular, Terry. 1988a. 'Plan and Market in China's Agricultural Commerce.' *Journal of Political Economy*, 96(2): 283–307.

—— 1988b. 'Agricultural Planning and Pricing in the Post-Mao Period.' *China Quarterly*, 116: 670–705.

—— 1995. 'Redefining State, Plan, and Market: China's Reforms in Agricultural Commerce.' *China Quarterly*, 144: 1020–46.

Skinner, G. William. 1985. 'Rural Marketing in China: Repression and Revival.' *China Quarterly*, 103: 393–413.

Solinger, Dorothy J. 1984. *'Chinese Business under Socialism: The Politics of Domestic Commerce, 1949–1980.'* Berkeley and Los Angeles: University of California Press.

Sotnikov, Sergey. 1998. 'Evaluating the Effects of Price and Trade Liberalization on the Technical Efficiency of Agricultural Production in a Transition Economy: The Case of Russia.' *European Review of Agricultural Economics*, 25(3): 412–31.

Stiglitz, Joseph. 1999. 'Whither Reform? Ten Years of the Transition.' Paper presented at the Annual Bank Conference on Development Economics, April 1999. Washington, DC: The World Bank.

Stone, Bruce. 1988. 'Developments in Agricultural Technology.' *China Quarterly*, 116: 767–822.

Swinnen, Johan F. M. (ed.). 1997a. *The Political Economy of Agrarian Reform in Central and Eastern Europe*. Ashgate: Aldershot.

—— 1997b. 'On Liquidation Councils, Flying Troikas and Orsov Cooperatives: The Political Economy of Agricultural Reform in Bulgaria.' In Johan F. M. Swinnen (ed.), *The Political Economy of Agrarian Reform in Central and Eastern Europe*. Ashgate: Aldershot.

—— 1999. 'The Political Economy of Land Reform Choices in Central and Eastern Europe.' *Economics of Transition*, 7(3): 637–64.

—— 2002a. 'Political Reforms, Rural Crises, and Land Tenure in Western Europe.' *Food Policy*, 27(4): 371–94.

—— 2002b. 'Transition and Integration in Europe: Implications for Agricultural and Food Markets, Policy and Trade Agreements.' *World Economy*, 25(4): 481–501.

—— 2005. *When the Market Comes to You. Or Not: The Dynamics of Vertical Coordination in Agri-food Supply Chains in ECA*. Washington, DC: The World Bank.

—— and Ayo Heinegg. 2002. 'On the Political Economy of Land Reforms in the Former Soviet Union.' *Journal of International Development*, 14(7): 1019–31.

—— and Liesbet Vranken. 2004. 'Reforms and Efficiency: Survey Evidence from Transition Agriculture.' Working paper, LICOS—Centre for Transition Economics, Katholieke Universiteit Leuven, Belgium.

—— Liesbeth Dries, and Karen Macours. 2005. 'Transition and Agricultural Labour.' *Agricultural Economics*, 32(1): 15–34.

Szekelyhidi, Tamas. 2001 'Financing Agriculture through Vertical Integration: The Case of Hungary.' In *Agricultural Finance and Credit Infrastructure in Transition Economies. Focus on South Eastern Europe*, OECD Center for Co-operation with Non-Members. Paris: OECD Publications.

Tomich, Thomas P., Peter Kilby, and Bruce F. Johnston. 1995. *Transforming Agrarian Economies: Opportunities Seized, Opportunities Missed*. Ithaca, NY: Cornell University Press.

Tran, Thi Que. 1997. *Agricultural Reform in Vietnam*. Singapore: Institute of Southeast Asian Study.

Trueblood, Michael A. and Stefan Osborne. 2002. 'Has Russia's Agricultural Productivity Increased Since Reform?' Economic Research Service Unpublished Manuscript. Washington, DC: USDA/ERS.

Trzeciak-Duval, Alexandra. 1999. 'A Decade of Transition in Central and Eastern European Agriculture.' *European Review of Agricultural Economics*, 26(3): 283–304.

USDA. 1994. *Estimates of Producer and Consumer Subsidy Equivalents: Government Intervention in Agriculture 1982–1992*. ERS Economic Research Service Statistical Bulletin No. 913. Washington, DC: USDA/ERS.

Uzun, Vasily. 2000. 'Agrarian Reform in Russia in the 1990s: Objectives, Mechanisms and Problems.' In L. Alexander Norsworthy (ed.), *Russian Views of the Transition in the Rural Sector*. Washington, DC: The World Bank.

Van Atta, Don. 1990. 'Toward a Soviet "Responsibility System"? Recent Developments in the Agricultural Collective Contract.' In Kenneth R. Gray (ed.), *Soviet Agriculture: Comparative Perspectives*. Ames: Iowa State University Press, 130–54.

—— 1993. *The 'Farmer Threat': The Political Economy of Agrarian Reform in Post-Soviet Russia*. Boulder, Colo.: Westview Press.

Von Cramon-Taubadel, Stephan, Sergiy Zorya, and Ludwig Striewe (eds.). 2001. *Policies and Agricultural Development in Ukraine*. Aachen: Shaker Verlag.

Vranken, Liesbet and Johan F. M. Swinnen. 2003. 'Land Markets and Household Farms in Transition: Theory and Evidence from Hungary.' LICOS Discussion Paper 129/2003, LICOS—Centre for Transition Economics, Katholieke Universiteit Leuven, Belgium.

—— —— 2005. 'The Development of Rural Land Markets in Transition.' Working Paper, LICOS—Centre for Transition Economics, Katholieke Universiteit Leuven, Belgium.

Wädekin, Karl-Eugen. 1988. 'Agrarian Structures and Policies in the USSR, China, and Hungary: A Comparative View.' In Josef C. Brada and Karl-Eugen Wädekin (eds.), *Socialist Agriculture in Transition: Organizational Response to Failing Performance*. Boulder, Colo.: Westview Press, 55–76.

—— 1990. 'Determinants and Trends of Reform in Communist Agriculture: A Concluding Essay.' In Karl-Eugen Wädekin (ed.), *Communist Agriculture: Farming in the Soviet Union and Eastern Europe*. London: Routledge, 321–39.

References

Walder, Andrew G. 1995. 'Local Governments as Industrial Firms: An Organizational Analysis of China's Transitional Economy.' *American Journal of Sociology*, 101(2): 263–301.

Watson, Andrew, 1994, 'China's Agricultural Reforms: Experiences and Achievements of the Agricultural Sector in the Market Reform Process,' CERC Working Paper 94/4, Chinese Economies Research Centre, University of Adelaide, Australia.

Wegren, Stephen K. (ed.). 1998. *Land Reform in the Former Soviet Union and Eastern Europe*. London: Routledge.

Wehrheim, Peter, Klaus Frohberg, Eugenia V. Serova, and Joachim von Braun (eds.). 2000. *Russia's Agro-Food Sector: Towards Truly Functioning Markets*. Dordrecht: Kluwer Academic Press.

Weingast, Barry R. 1995. 'The Economic Role of Political Institutions: Market-Preserving Federalism and Economic Development.' *Journal of Law, Economics, and Organization*, 11: 1–31.

Wen, Guangzhong J. 1993. 'Total Factor Productivity Change in China's Farming Sector: 1952–1989.' *Economic Development and Cultural Change*, 42(1): 1–41.

Williamson, Oliver E. 1975. *Markets and Hierarchies*. New York: Free Press.

Wong, Christine P. W. (ed.). 1997. *Financing Local Government in the People's Republic of China*. Hong Kong: Oxford University Press (for Asian Development Bank).

Woo, Wing Thye. 1994. 'The Art of Reforming Centrally Planned Economies: Comparing China, Poland and Russia.' *Journal of Comparative Economics*, 18(3): 276–308.

World Bank. 1992. *China: Strategies for Reducing Poverty in the 1990s*. Washington, DC: The World Bank.

—— 1997. *At China's Table: Food Security Options*. Washington, DC: The World Bank.

—— 2000. *World Development Report 2000/2001: Attacking Poverty*. Washington, DC: The World Bank.

—— 2001. *World Development Report 2002: Building Institutions for Markets*. Washington, DC: The World Bank.

—— 2005. *Poverty in ECA 1998–2003*. Washington, DC: The World Bank. Forthcoming.

Wurfel, David. 1993. 'Doi Moi in Comparative Perspective.' In William S. Turley and Mark Selden (eds.), *Reinventing Vietnamese Socialism: Doi Moi in Comparative Perspective*. Boulder, Colo.: Westview Press.

Wyplosz, Charles. 2000. 'Ten Years of Transformation: Macroeconomic Lessons.' CEPR Discussion Paper No. 2254, Center for Economic Policy Research, London.

Wyzan, Michael L. 1990. 'The Bulgarian Experience with Centrally Planned Agriculture: Lessons for Soviet Reformers?' In Kenneth R. Gray (ed.), *Soviet Agriculture: Comparative Perspectives*. Ames: Iowa State University Press, 220–42.

Xie, Yaping. 2002. 'An Analysis of China's Grain Markets.' Unpub. M.Sc. thesis, Chinese Academy of Sciences, Centre for Chinese Agricultural Policy, Beijing.

Yang, Dali L. 1996. *Calamity and Reform in China: State, Rural Society, and Institutional Change since the Great Leap Famine*. Stanford, Calif.: Stanford University Press.

Ye, Qiaolun and Scott Rozelle. 1994. 'Fertilizer Demand in China's Reforming Economy.' *Canadian Journal of Agricultural Economics*, 42(2): 191–208.

ZGTJNJ. 2003. *China Statistical Yearbook, 2003.* Beijing: Chinese Statistical Press.

Zhou, Kate X. 1996. *How the Farmers Changed China: Power of the People.* Boulder, Colo.: Westview Press.

Zorya, Sergiy. 2003. *Interdependencies between Agriculture and Macroeconomics in Ukraine.* Doctoral dissertation, Georg-August-University of Göttingen, Göttingen.

Index

Index